MW00826830

Personalist Anthropology

A Philosophical Guide to Life

Juan Manuel Burgos

Translated by Benjamin Wilkinson, SEMV,
with James Beauregard

Series in Philosophy

www.vernonpress.com

In the Americas:
Vernon Press
1000 N West Street, Suite 1200
Wilmington, Delaware, 19801
United States

In the rest of the world:
Vernon Press
C/Sancti Espiritu 17,
Malaga, 29006
Spain

Series in Philosophy

Library of Congress Control Number: 2021950206

ISBN: 978-1-64889-351-3

Originally published as *Antropología: una guía para la existencia* (6th ed.), © Ediciones Palabra, S.A., 2017.

Cover design by Vernon Press using elements designed by LIMAT MD ARIF from Pixabay.

To Karol Wojtyła, philosopher

Table of Contents

Foreword to the English Edition

Personalism moves forward with determination in the 21st century, with new publications, Congresses and Associations, growing interest on the part of young researchers, and application in new fields such as psychology and education. However, there is still a long way to go, and a lot of work to be done, in order for it to become the philosophy of reference for those who are committed to the dignity of the human person.

This text wants to contribute to this path by providing a personalistic, integral and structured vision of the human being, placed within the intellectual framework of Integral Personalism (see *An Introduction to Personalism*). There are many personalistic essays on the person, the fruit of such brilliant minds as Marías, Mounier, Wojtyła, Guardini, Von Hildebrand and many others, but there are very few systematic presentations. This book offers one of those few presentations and, perhaps, one of the most accessible, pedagogical and structured, if we pay attention to its reception (six editions in Spanish).

Now is the time for its translation into English, an important moment for any text, given the global significance of that language. To this end, it has been completely revised and updated both in terms of content and bibliography. I harbor the hope that it will have a similar reception to that obtained in the Spanish language, since, according to the comments of readers and students, it seems that it contributes to improving the understanding of the human person and to forging minds capable of defending it with intelligence and open-mindedness.

Juan Manuel Burgos, May 2021

Introduction:
What is Philosophical Anthropology

1. The Genesis and Development of Philosophical Anthropology

The question regarding the human being is a universal constant. Every man, every woman, asks about him or herself, seeks to know what he or she is, or better, who he or she is, and seeks to respond to the fundamental questions about existence: What does it mean to be free? What are my feelings? Do I have a spiritual soul? What happens when someone dies? These questions form an inseparable part of life because we cannot live without answering these questions more or less explicitly. Not doing so would imply living in absurdity, in ignorance, or in irrationality, something evidently inhuman.

There exists, however, a special type of response to these questions: the philosophical response. A series of people throughout history have thought of going beyond the individual, quick answer, elaborating a field of knowledge that might respond with profundity, with precision, without improvisations, and with radicality. This field of knowledge is philosophy, and the field of knowledge that is focused on the study of the person is philosophical anthropology.

The perspective of philosophers in relation to the study of the human being has varied over time. Initially, the reflection was centered not so much on the human being as on the soul, due to the influence of the first work of systematic reflection on the human being, Aristotle's *De anima*, which marked the tendency of the following centuries until well into the 17th century. Thus, for example, Saint Augustine wrote treatises entitled *De inmortalitate animae*, *De quantitate animae* and *De anima et eius origine*; Ibn Rushd (Averroes) wrote a commentary on Aristotle's *De anima* and Thomas Aquinas, on this point, faithfully followed his venerated teacher by also commenting on *De anima* and studying human issues from this perspective. The last great work situated within these coordinates is, probably, Francisco Suárez's *De anima*, an important text in the history of philosophy, according to Heidegger.

The arrival of the Renaissance and the advent of modern philosophy by way of Descartes was an important change. The Renaissance, as is well known, emphasized the centrality of the human being, his or her importance as such and not just in relation to God, and this gave impulse to studies about the human being and not just about the soul. Descartes, for his part, insisted on the subjective and interior dimension of the person. This set of propositions allowed for a reconsideration of studies on the human being which, already in the context of the Enlightenment, were integrated into the name *rational Psychology*, popularized by Christian Wolf (1679-1754). The term "psychology" included the subjective aspects advocated by Descartes, and the term "rational" on one hand distinguished it from empirical or experimental psychology and, on the other, made reference to the zeal for the systematic and deductive, proper to rationalism.

The denomination *rational Psychology* was maintained for a long time, but at the beginning of the 20th century, it began to cede way to the term "anthropology". It seems that the origin of this term should be attributed to O. Casmann, who published in 1596 a work titled *Psychologia anthropologica*. Kant took a step forward with his four famous questions: What can I know? What should I do? What am I permitted to hope for? and, what is the human being? He comments that "to the first question, metaphysics responds; to the second, morality; to the third, religion; and to the fourth, anthropology. In the end, everything could be attributed to anthropology because the first three questions refer to the final one."[1] But Kant did not, properly speaking, elaborate an anthropology text and, in fact, the definitive consolidation of this term as we currently understand it only came at the beginning of the 20th century with Scheler's famous text, *Man's Place in Nature* (1928)[2]. There, Scheler proposed a unitary and integral philosophical vision of the person and his or her relations with the rest of reality, removing himself both from a fundamentally metaphysical analysis (*De anima*) and from an interior and subjective one (*Psychology*). From the time of these works onwards, the term philosophical anthropology imposes itself as a term corresponding to the systematic philosophical study about the human being.

It was not easy, however, for philosophical anthropology to take its place, because it was quickly put into question by an important group of philosophers in the second half of the 20th century (Foucault, Lévy-Strauss, etc.). Moreover, they posed the question in the most radical terms, because what was placed into doubt was not the terminology or content, but the very *possibility* of philosophical anthropology itself. It was argued, for example, that the current complexity, development and fragmentation of the sciences regarding the human being (ethnology, cultural anthropology, psychoanalysis, ethology, etc.) impeded a philosophical approach to the person with at least a

---

[1] Immanuel Kant, *Logik*, in *Kants Gesammelte Schriften*, vol. IX, 25.
[2] Max Scheler, *Man's Place in Nature* (New York: Noonday 1961). From the same year (1928) and also relevant for the consolidation of philosophical anthropology is H. Plessner's work *Levels of Organic Life and the Human: An Introduction to Philosophical Anthropology*.

minimum of precision, to the point that it would not be possible to even identify the "human object". There was also a question of whether philosophical anthropology was able to overcome its own presuppositions and perform a constructive development that was not a mere conclusion of what was already contained in the starting point.

These criticisms weighed greatly at the time, but today they have receded to a large degree because, although they have been accepted in part, it has also been noted that they do not have sufficient weight to invalidate the anthropological reflection. It is manifestly true, for example, that we all have cultural and philosophical presuppositions, but that in itself does not take away the validity of philosophical investigation or reflection on anthropology. It simply situates it within determined coordinates. In fact, today we are instead witnessing a revitalization of philosophical anthropology, and the reason, or at least one of them, is to be found precisely in the fragmentary and plural character of modern society, which previously appeared as an obstacle. The multiplication and specialization of the fields of knowledge is very beneficial from a technical and gnoseological point of view, but it requires, as compensation, an overall vision that may account for the human being as such. Otherwise, the person ends up being lost in the hyper-labyrinth of knowledge and information which shapes our society[3].

The present work is framed within this context, and its objective is to contribute a systematic and integral vision of the person from a precise philosophical perspective: personalism. Such a clearly defined position-taking calls for a more detailed explanation, but before we offer it, we will make a bit more explicit what we understand by philosophical anthropology.

2. Characteristics of Philosophical Anthropology

Philosophical anthropology[4] is nothing other than the philosophy of the human being, a much more common expression in the English-speaking world where the expression philosophical anthropology is not frequent. But, since philosophical perspectives can differ a lot, the ways of conceiving how to understand it also change. For this reason, we are going to indicate various characteristics which, in our opinion, a philosophical reflection on the human being should possess.

---

[3] Cfr. Juan Manuel Burgos, *La vía de la experiencia o la salida del laberinto* (Madrid: Rialp, 2018).

[4] Its etymology comes from the Greek *anthropos* (man) and *logos* (treatise or science).

- *Explicative:* Philosophical anthropology seeks to *explain and to understand*. From the standpoint of philosophical anthropology, it is not enough to describe what occurs or what one observes; rather, philosophical anthropology strives to comprehend, to relate and to reach the foundations of things. For example, it asks about the meaning of life, the significance of death, or what feelings are. In this, it differs from other sciences, which also study the human being, but which center more on the how and not on the why (sociology, psychology, etc.). Philosophical anthropology also differs from cultural anthropology, which basically intends to *describe* the different ways in which the human being confronts existence through culture but does not radically ask about the why of those customs or their meaning.[5]

- *Metaphysical or ontological:* many philosophical conceptions about the human being exist; the correct one understands the human being not as a flux of sensations or of phenomena that flows with time and does not have coherence (like Hume, for example), but as a subsistent being, permanent and rooted in being. Philosophical anthropology should adopt this metaphysical or ontological perspective.

- *Integral:* it should offer a vision of the human being which takes into account all its aspects and dimensions: psychological, biological, sociological, spiritual, etc. In this, philosophical anthropology is distinct from the *human sciences*, which only treat one concrete aspect, such as medicine, law or economics. Philosophy's mission is to consider the human being in a holistic way, something which is particularly important today given the fragmentation and multiplicity of knowledge. Without *synthesis* or *holistic visions*, the human being becomes lost in the ocean of information and knowledge.

---

[5] Logically, there is room for nuances. There are cultural anthropologists who pose questions about human topics in a deep way, but, in any case, the basic distinction is valid.

There are, however, philosophical anthropologies (that is, anthropologies that seek to comprehend) that adopt a *reductionistic* attitude because they center exclusively on one aspect of the person. For example, all the philosophies that dispense with the spiritual dimension, such as Marxism or scientistic materialism, are reductionistic. But it is also possible to fall into this error on the opposite extreme, dispensing with or undervaluing the corporeal and material character of the human being.

Due to its integral character, philosophical anthropology should take into account, as much as possible, the developments of the other sciences which contribute knowledge about the human being (law, ethics, psychiatry, etc.), because in this way its knowledge increases and is enriched and it avoids falling into errors that come from a reflection on experience which is too simple or not sufficiently the fruit of comparison and contrast.

- *Scientific:* Anthropology is a scientific field in the sense that it seeks to know with profundity, establishing connections and structuring knowledge in a systematic way. This does not mean that it is an experimental science like mathematics or physics. Until the beginning of the 20th century, the concept of science had been reduced and was erroneously identified with this type of sciences; but numerous subsequent studies (Kuhn, Popper, Polanyi) have allowed us to clearly comprehend that there are many different scientific fields of knowledge depending on the characteristics of the object to be studied.

- *Experimental:* philosophical anthropology arises from the analysis *of human experience* understood as integral experience (see chap. 5.2). It is not an abstract field of knowledge, deduced from theoretical and unreal premises, but rather a reflection on the human being and his or her life. Thus, whoever does philosophical anthropology should, as much as possible, have profound and rich contact with human existence. To this end, recourse to the experiences of others is of great usefulness, experiences which they transmit to us through literature, art, and film.

3. A Personalistic Philosophical Anthropology

The philosophical anthropology presented in this textbook is based on personalism, a philosophical current that began in France during the interbellum years of the 20th century and which later extended to other European countries: Italy, Spain, Germany, Poland, etc.[6]

Personalism is characterized by being, in a broad sense, a realist philosophy and thus is framed within what tends to be called classical philosophy, whose eminent representatives are Plato, Aristotle, Saint Augustine, and Saint Thomas, among others.[7] But within this wide framework, personalism develops some new elements which define it and distinguish it and which depend, in part, on modern philosophy. First of all, it is radically structured around the notion of person, which is the key to its conceptual architecture, and it elaborates specific philosophical categories to treat the person. And, on this basis, it develops a series of topics and perspectives in an original way: the radical importance both of affectivity and of relations, which leads to the importance conceded to interpersonal relationships; the primacy of moral and religious values in confrontation with a possible intellectualism; the insistence on the corporeal and sex-differentiated aspect of the person; the importance attributed to the social dimension of the person and to action as a manifestation and realization of the subject, etc.

A number of brilliant essays exist on many of these aspects, which have arisen from eminent personalists, like Maritain, Wojtyła, Guardini, von Hildebrand, Mounier, Marías, Marcel and Buber, to mention only some. But rarer are the visions of *synthesis* which bring together or systematize this thought, so rich and suggestive. This deficit is especially striking in the area of anthropology because, if personalism is some type of specific philosophy, it is evidently an anthropology. The objective of these pages is to fill this void, developing in a systematic way, with the format of a college textbook, the anthropological perspective which we consider proper to personalism.

A final nuance. There are different types of personalism which, within a common theoretical framework, possess relatively significant differences. In

---

[6] A detailed explanation of the essential characteristics of personalism and its principal representatives can be found in Juan Manuel Burgos, *An Introduction to Personalism* (Washington, DC: CUA Press, 2018). See also E. Mounier, *Personalism* (London: Routledge and Kegan Paul,1952); Th. R. Rourke y R. A. Chazarreta, *A Theory of personalism* (Lanham: Lexington Books, 2007); J. O. Bengtsson, *The worldview of personalism* (Oxford: Oxford University Press, 2006); J. N. Mortensen, *The Common Good. An introduction to personalism* (Wilmington: Vernon Press, 2017); B. Mondin, *Storia dell'Antropologia Filosofica, vol. 2* (Bologna: ESD, 2002): *Le antropologie personaliste,* 514-660.

[7] There is also an idealistic personalism whose main representative is Borden Parker Bowne. See, for example, Borden Parker Bowne, *Personalism* (Cambridge: The Riverside Press, 1908).

this text, we use as a basis the *Integral personalism* developed principally by Wojtyła and Burgos.[8]

The structure we have developed is the following one. Part I is an introduction to the notion of person and its key concepts. The second part (chapters 2-7) is an investigation into the structure of the personal being through three dimensions – corporeal or physical, psychological and spiritual – which traverses its most essential elements: the body, sensibility and inclinations, affectivity, intelligence, freedom and the personal self. Part III (chapters 8-10) is a reflection on personal action, both from a general point of view and in some of its modalities (language and work). Part IV (chapters 11-13) takes on interpersonal relationships on three levels: person to person, familial and social. Finally, in Part V (chapters 14-15), we have considered the ultimate questions which decide the holistic meaning of life: death, immortality and religion.

4. Methodological Novelties

This division in parts and chapters responds to a profound theoretical conception rooted in personalism and, more concretely, in Integral Personalism. Without burdening the reader with methodological questions, which are not to the point in this textbook, we will briefly indicate some of the most representative ones, so that the reason for the structure and configuration of this work, which is original, may be better understood.

    a)   The person as starting point. It has been frequent in anthropology treatises to begin with an ascent which leads from the mineral world to the vegetative-biological world, and from there to the human world. This perspective has its roots in a Greek type of vision according to which the human being would be a rational animal, that is, a very special animal, but, to a good degree, an animal. Personalism, on the contrary, without discarding the relevance of the somatic and biological aspects in the person, considers the person to be a unique reality, irreducible to the animal world and thus believes that anthropology should begin directly with the person, which is its topic of study; in addition, only in this way will it be able to develop authentic personalistic categories, that is, specific categories for the person, instead

---

[8] Cf. J. M. Burgos, *Wojtyła's Personalism as Integral Personalism. The future of an Intellectual Project*, Questionaes Disputatae, vol 9. N. 2 (2019) 91-111.

of using categories thought up for animals and modified to adapt them to the human being. This is the reason why this book begins, without any type of preambles, with the human being, that is, with the person.

b)   Integral experience. This book uses the philosophical method of integral experience (derived from a proposal by Karol Wojtyła), which consists of analyzing reality through our experience, conceived as a complex lived experience (*vivencia*) which has an objective and a subjective dimension and in which, from the gnoseological point of view, intelligence and the senses operate together. We experience reality in a unitary way thanks to our intelligence and our senses, and this rich (subjective and objective) reality is what we propose to analyze philosophically. Concretely, in philosophical anthropology we analyze the person's experience: our individual experience (to a great degree subjective) and the experience we possess of others (fundamentally objective).[9]

c)   Anthropological novelties. This text presents some very significant thematic novelties which it may be worth the while to make explicit: c.1) the tridimensional structure of the person. Amplifying the classical perspective which divides the person into body and soul, we divide the person into three dimensions: body, psyche, and spirit. In this way, the complexity of the human subject is better reflected and a *de facto* dualism is avoided; c.2) a great relevance is given to affectivity, which is understood as an original and founding reality of the person, with equal importance as the dynamic and the cognitive dimensions; c.3) attention is paid to the subjective dimension of knowledge and not just the objective dimension; c.4) freedom is understood not just as choice, but fundamentally as self-determination; c.5) action is not considered to be ontologically detached from the person, but

---

[9] Cf. Juan Manuel Burgos, *Integral experience: a new proposal on the beginning of knowledge*, in J. Beauregard, S. Smith (eds.), *In the Sphere of the personal. New perspectives in the philosophy of person* (Wilmington USA Vernon Press, 2016), 41-58. See also, Juan Manuel Burgos, *La experiencia integral. Un método para el personalismo* (Madrid: Palabra, 2015).

rather it is conceived as an active prolongation, that is, as the person in action. Action, moreover, is multiform, in such a way that it cannot be explained in a satisfactory manner by way of the simple tripartition of action proposed by Aristotle; c.6) An entire fourth part of the textbook is dedicated to studying interpersonal relationships (in addition to the references in the third part), due to its decisive role in the configuration and life of each human being; c.7) Finally, there is an insistence on the temporal character of the person due to the understanding that temporality forms part of his or her most basic configuration, in such a way that death and the hereafter pose a question which, in one way or another, should be answered by every human being.

d) The unity and diversity of the person. We strongly insist on the unity of the person. Thus, without radically putting into question the theory of the faculties, we have tried to develop an anthropology in which there is not a very strict differentiation between the subject and his or her faculties. In this way, the "personalization" of the faculties is avoided, a personalization which occurs when we forget that it is always a subject who performs the action, one of the results of which is the well-known short-circuits related to determining who has the final decision in human action: the intelligence or the will. Both potencies doubtless have a certain autonomy in the ensemble of the complex structure of the person, but in their deepest dimension, they are not autonomous entities, but dimensions of the subject. It is the *person* who is free, not just his or her action. And it is he or she who knows through the intelligence. Definitively: *I* want. *I* know. *I* love.

e) The diagram of the person (figure 0.1). Many of these features can be expressed pedagogically in a diagram, useful for understanding the fundamental structure of the human being, with the understanding that it is only a pedagogical instrument which facilitates an overall vision which allows one to perceive at first sight, for example, the tridimensional structure of the person, the importance of affectivity, the unifying role of the self, etc.

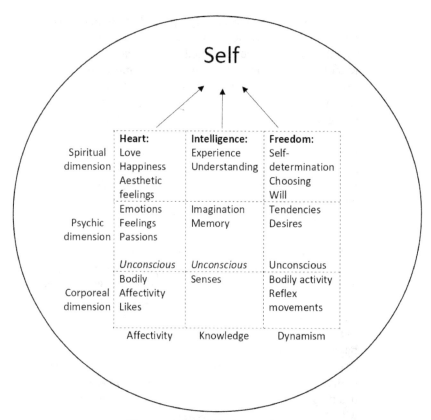

Figure 0.1: PERSON - *Burgos diagram.*

f) Priority of the person over the relationship. We grant great importance to the interpersonal relationship (and for that reason a large space is dedicated to it), but we have the understanding, in accord with the premises of Integral Personalism, that there is an ontological priority of the person over the relationship.[10] In the human realm (distinct from the divine), the relationship is founded on persons and depends on them, since without distinct persons there is no relationship.

---

[10] Cf. K. Wojtyła, *Persona y acción* (Madrid: Palabra, 2011). English version, *The Acting Person*. Translated by Anna-Teresa Tymieniecka. Annalecta Husserliana 10. (Dordrecht: D. Reidel Pub. Co, 1979).

Thus, this text speaks in the first place about the person and, later on, about interpersonal relationships, an order which evidently reflects an ontological and not a chronological priority: we are the fruit of a marvelous relationship, that of our parents.

5. A Word on the Bibliography

This text was originally written in Spanish and, therefore, an important part of the bibliography is in Spanish, which can pose a certain problem for the English-language reader. We have tried to solve this difficulty by eliminating non-relevant Spanish bibliography and looking for the English versions of the quoted books, a procedure that we have not always been able to carry out completely for different reasons: there was no English translation, we have not been able to locate it, we have located it but we did not have access to the content of the book so we must continue quoting by the Spanish version, etc. We apologize to the reader for these problems, even though, at the same time, we believe that we offer the reader a good opportunity to get to know philosophers (personalists or not) who write in Spanish and who, in our opinion, are philosophically valuable.

6. Acknowledgements

I want to thank all those who collaborated in one way or another to the six Spanish editions of this book: Alfonso López Quintás, Urbano Ferrer, Maribel Rodríguez, Carmen Ávila, Rafael Burgos, Rafael Serrano, Carlos Segade and Rigoberto Pérez. And, for this English version, I want to express my deep gratitude to the translator and friend Fr. Benjamin Wilkinson SEMV, to my friend James Beauregard, who has translated some chapters (3, 4, 13 and 15) and to John Martino, who has supported this project.

Part I. The Person: Man and Woman

Chapter 1

The Person: Dignity and Mystery

The men and women who populate the world and among whom we find ourselves are the ones who elicit in us questions and enigmas and thus open up the way to anthropology. We want to know more about them and about ourselves: how we are, how we relate to one another, and what our destiny is. Each one of these questions opens up an entire world of reflections, but the first step, the initial phase, cannot consist of anything other than a question regarding man and woman in general, that is, a question about the person.

This is the case for basically two reasons. First, because in any subject matter, one must begin with a definition, even if brief, of the object of study, since, otherwise, one runs the risk of falling into emptiness and generality. It is essential to know what one is going to talk about. But, in addition, in the case of anthropology, beginning with something different from the analysis of the person as such – for example, the dimensions of which the person is composed, the person's relations or the types of activity which the person may perform – can have an important negative consequence: the loss of unity. And the thing is that the fundamental fact before which philosophy finds itself and which it must account for is that there is a unitary and atypical, profound, multifaceted, paradoxical and marvelous being which is the concrete person, each man and each woman. Therefore, in the first place, a holistic and unitary consideration is necessary, after which, but only after which, must come an analysis in detail. Thus, we will avoid a danger in which some have fallen at times: missing the forest for the trees or, in other words, ceasing to see the person because we put an excessive emphasis on the analysis of its multiple facets and possibilities.

We have spoken of man and woman, and we have spoken of person and, although perhaps by habit we might think that we are before a common or popular word, such is not the case. The notion of person is a *concrete philosophical notion*, with a long history, which implies addressing anthropology from a determined perspective to which we have already referred: personalism. Thus, our first objective will consist of briefly describing the historical origin of this notion, which will also function as a more detailed introduction to the intellectual context of personalism.

1.1 The Notion of Person Throughout History

a) The Origins: Greece and Rome

The word person, from the etymological point of view, proceeds directly from the Latin *personare* and, in the second place, from the Greek *prosopon*. From the semantic point of view, it is influenced by two different cultural traditions[1].

The first of these traditions goes back to *Greek and Roman theater*. *Prósopon*, in Greek, literally means "what is placed before the eyes" and made reference to the mask which the actors used in ancient theater. The actors represented their character using a mask (the *prósopon*) which identified them before the audience as interpreters of a determined role. The Latin word *personare* means something different: "to sound through, to resonate", but it began to be applied to actors' masks as well, because their voice resonated through it. Little by little, this latter meaning (Cicero uses it with this meaning numerous times) became common and was generalized. Person, therefore, initially meant the mask with which the actor presented himself before the audience. Over time, this meaning was extended to the *role* the actor represented (king, soldier, slave) and, finally, it ended up as a denomination for the actor as such, the human being.

The second tradition is inserted into the framework of *Roman law* and comes from another possible meaning of the word "person," understood in this case as *per se sonans*, that is, as one who speaks for himself and has his own voice. This initial meaning was widened to mean he who has rights, status and social recognition and this is the notion that Roman law took up. To be a person, therefore, implied possessing rights and social dignity. But, as is known, in Rome not all persons were "persons." Slaves were considered to be animals or things, and neither barbarians (foreigners) nor those who were not noblemen, nor, obviously, women, had similar rights, but rather limited rights, as their social recognition was limited.

In conclusion, the Greek and Roman tradition presents us with the person as an interweaving of the human being and dignity.

b) Christianity: The Invention of the Person

Christianity used this basis to develop its own concept of person, the concept that has subsequently been received and made its own by Western

---

[1] See Maurice Nédoncelle, "Prosopon et persona dans l'antiquité classique. Essai de bilan linguistic." *Revue des Sciences Religieuses* 22, no. 3-4 (1948): 277-99

civilization. The Christian influence was basically exercised on two fronts. The principal and primary front was of a *social and human* order and consisted of a systematic rejection of any possible discrimination, which meant an authentic revolution in the ancient world, whose consequences were incalculable and would bear fruit through the centuries. The Christian doctrine on this point is clear and well defined and was presented with that same force in the Roman world. St. Paul explains, "for in Christ Jesus you are all children of God through faith. As many of you as were baptized into Christ have clothed yourselves with Christ. There is no longer Jew or Greek, there is no longer slave or free, there is no longer male and female; for all of you are one in Christ Jesus."[2]

This fundamental idea, with a religious origin, but with undoubtable social and anthropological transcendence, over time radically transformed ancient society: the elimination of slavery, equalization between man and woman, etc. But our interest here is to follow its influence on the elaboration of the *notion* of person which took place in the context of the Christological and trinitarian discussions of the first centuries.

One of the tasks which Christianity found itself in the obligation of performing, once it was solidly disseminated and had acquired a sufficient degree of stability, was to define its doctrine in a systematic way. A need for internal self-comprehension, that is, a need to know what it meant in-depth to be Christian, to express its doctrine systematically in order to improve the quality and depth of its dissemination, and also to confront the refutations of intellectuals formed in Greek philosophy impelled Christianity to take on this task. This process, long and complicated, had as essential steps the councils of Nicaea (325), Constantinople (381), Ephesus (431) and Chalcedon (451), and concluded with the formulation, through philosophical-theological categories, of the two principal mysteries of Christianity, Christ and the Trinity, in the following terms. God is simultaneously a trinitarian and a unitarian reality, which was expressed technically by saying that in God there are three persons (Father, Son and Holy Spirit) and just one substance or nature: the divine. On the contrary, in Christ, at once God and man, there are two natures (the divine and the human), but just one person, the person of the Word.

---

[2] St. Paul, *Letter to the Galatians*, 3: 26-28. See also, *Letter to the Colossians* 3:11. The originality of this position can be confirmed by comparing it with the affirmations of Aristotle – a very human philosopher in many aspects – about the similarity between slaves and beasts and the inferior nature of women (see especially Aristotle, *Politics*, I, 5 and 13).

Thus arose, for the first time in history, the *philosophical-theological notion of person*.[3] Said concept allowed for the description of the most elevated realities in existence (Christ and God) and did it by referring to what is peculiar, distinctive and singular in each being. Christ is just one person because he has just one identity, while in God it is possible to distinguish three persons because each one of them possesses features and personality proper to each one: the Father is not the Son, and the Son is not the Holy Spirit, although the three are God. The person, moreover, was also conceived as a substantial reality, that is, subsistent in himself because of the coherence of his being and not in reference to something else (as occurs with the Aristotelian accidents).

The notion of *nature*, on the contrary, was taken directly from Greek culture and was employed in this context to mean what is common or general. God the Father, God the Son and God the Holy Spirit have the same divine nature because the three are God; but in Christ, who is just one person, there are two natures: the human, which he shares with the rest of humanity, and the divine, which he shares with the other two persons of the Trinity.

The patristic reflection left us, therefore, with three fundamental notions. An original one, person[4], and two taken from the Greeks: substance and nature. Person is what is singular, proper and subsistent in itself and nature is what is common.

The conclusion of this itinerary can be emblematically placed in Boethius (c. 480-525). This Christian thinker applied these notions to the human being and coined his famous definition of person, which would be taken up by Scholasticism, including St. Thomas: *persona est naturae rationalis individua substantia* (the person is the individual substance of rational nature).[5] This definition, due to its precision and its value, would have a great influence throughout history, but it can also be considered the age of majority of the notion of person in the field of anthropology. The human being was a person, and to be a person meant to possess an individually subsistent rational nature.

---

[3] See St Augustine, *De Trinitate*. On the contribution of the Cappadocian fathers see John. D. Zizioulas. *Communion and otherness. Further studies in Personhood ant the Church* (T&T Clark International, 2009). An excellent study on the philosophical contributions of Christianity is proportioned by Étienne Gilson, *The spirit of mediaeval philosophy* (Notre Dame, Ind.: University of Notre Dame Press, 1991).

[4] Greek metaphysics "has a fundamental and very grave limitation, the complete absence of the concept and the very word person." Xavier Zubiri, *El hombre y Dios* (Madrid: Alianza, 1984), 323. English translation: *Man and God* (University Press of America, 2009).

[5] Boethius, *Liber de persona et duabus naturis contra Eutychen et Nestorium*, PL 64, 1343 D.

c) Scholasticism

Scholasticism took up and accepted Boethius' definition but did not develop it; rather, it centered on the concept of *substance*. The person is valued, and greatly so, but person is not employed as an original philosophical concept which determines and influences the other elements of anthropology; rather, it is understood as *a special type of substance*: the most perfect type in the world, if we are speaking of human beings, and the absolutely perfect substance if we are talking about God. Julián Marías has shown this clearly. "When, already in Scholasticism, the attempt has been made to think philosophically about the person, the notions which have been decisive are not those which proceed from these contexts, but the notions of 'propriety' or 'subsistence' (*hypóstasis*). Boethius' famous definition, so influential – *persona est rationalis naturae individua substantia* – had as its starting point the Aristotelian notion of *ousía* or *substantia*, thought up primarily for 'things,' always explained with the eternal examples of the statue and the bed, based on the old Greek ideal of what is 'independent' or sufficient, of what is 'separable' (*khoristón*). The fact that this substance or thing that we call 'person' is rational will doubtless be important, but not sufficiently so as to rework this character of the *ousía* and modify its mode of being, its way of reality. The person is a *hypóstasis* or *suppositum* like the rest, the only difference is that it is of a rational nature."[6]

This way of posing the question generated some important problems. The first was *an excessive dependence on Greek philosophy* which limited the philosophical development of philosophical categories *specific* to the human being. The person was not studied technically as a being essentially diverse from the rest, and thus in need of specific categories, but rather as a being of nature, although special.[7] And this means that, in order to describe this being philosophically, it was enough to use the general notions of the *ens* and apply them in a specific way to the case of the human being. We have already commented on how this approach developed in the case of the person and the substance: the person is a special type of substance; but the same thing happened with other anthropological notions like the good or the appetites. With regard to the good, for example, it did not occur to Scholasticism to

---

6 Julián Marías, *Antropología metafísica* (Madrid: Alianza, 1987), 41. English translation: *Metaphysical Anthropology: The Empirical Structure of Human Life* (University Park, Pa.: Pennsylvania State University Press, 1971).

7 This is not to say that Scholasticism (and above all late Scholasticism) was not conscious of the originality of the human being, but rather that the knowledge of this fact was not translated into an effort to elaborate original philosophical categories to explain it.

analyze directly what the good means in the life of the human being; rather, it first analyzed it in general: the good as a transcendental, that is, as a category which transcends a concrete area of reality, since it is present in all the *entes*, and only later, starting from this general notion, does it think about the good of the human being as a specific case. This position has, of course, very valid and interesting elements but, with respect to anthropology, it is not exempt from problems since it makes it difficult to have a deep understanding of what is specifically human. The general notion darkens, so to speak, the specific notion and makes it difficult to penetrate into what is proper to the person. In the case of the good, for example, this is especially clear. It is possible to speak analogically about the "good" in material beings, in animals and in human beings, but this has to do with profoundly distinct realities. The human good is governed by the *moral dimension* and by freedom and thus it has little to do with what one may call the "good" of an animal (that it be able to nourish itself, reproduce, etc.)

This is the second problem to which we referred: a certain *difficulty in capturing what is specifically human* which, in the long term, translated into the fact that the resulting anthropology, although correct, ended up being insufficient and poor in some aspects. Polo explains it clearly. From the starting point of classical metaphysics, one has access to a "correct anthropology, but one which falls short: it does not err, it is not wrong, but its thematic development is sparse."[8] In the concrete case of substance, the application of this method impedes seeing, for example, the *interior and subjective* dimension of the person.[9] Therefore, when, further on, modern philosophy discovered this dimension, it was not possible to establish a connection with Scholasticism. Modern philosophy was born with an anti-substantialistic trademark because it considered the concept of substance to be dark and impeded its access to the interiority of the human being. And, since in addition it progressively derived ever more toward idealism, it

---

[8] Leonardo Polo, *Antropología trascendental. I. La persona humana* (Pamplona: Eunsa, 1999), 31. Polo's specific proposal for overcoming this difficulty basically consists of reconsidering the relations between metaphysics and anthropology and of amplifying the transcendentals through the abandon of the mental limit. A general approach to this question in Juan Manuel Burgos, *Personalismo y metafísica. ¿Es el personalismo una filosofía primera?* (Madrid: Ediciones Universidad San Dámaso, 2021).

[9] In this sense, Wojtyła affirms that Thomistic ethics is sometimes too "objectivistic. It almost gives the impression that in it there is no place for the analysis of consciousness and self-consciousness as truly specific symptoms of the person-subject." (Karol Wojtyła, *El personalismo tomista* in *Mi visión del hombre. Hacia una nueva ética,* 2nd ed. [Madrid: Palabra, 1998], 311).

irreversibly distanced itself both from Scholasticism and from its later formulations.

d) Modernity's Names: Consciousness, Subject, Self

From this era on, with Descartes as the emblematic symbol of the birth of a new period, modern philosophy took control of the philosophical evolution, and the human being began to be identified with elements which that philosophy was discovering. With Descartes it would be *consciousness*, interior being, conscious of itself. Later on, it would also be *subject*: a being that places itself before the external world with an interiority, richness and specific capacity for action; later, *self*, understood as self-consciousness, etc.

These concepts constitute inestimable contributions to the philosophy of the human being, but they would have an important factory defect: modern philosophy would develop them from a fundamentally idealistic perspective.[10] Although the subject, for example, initially proceeds from the realist notion *subjectum*, that is, what lays beneath the accidents and generic determinations, it was transformed in a short time into Kant's transcendental subject which would continually distance itself from the concrete human being in order to transform itself into an abstract entity, over and above the individual. And, as an ulterior development of this process, the essential Hegelian self is situated very far from the specific self of each man or woman, being rather the self-consciousness of the absolute Spirit, of which the concrete selves are no more than manifestations or determinations.

In conclusion, modernity's philosophical itinerary discovered essential anthropological keys, but at the price of the disappearance of the *concrete person*, of the man and the woman who live their life in an autonomous and limited but real way. Thus, it progressively separated itself more and more from the philosophy of the realist tradition and, at the beginning of the 20th century, posed grave philosophical and social problems.

e) The Contemporary Notion of Person

At the beginning of the 20th century, therefore, we find the following situation. From the *philosophical* point of view there is an important dichotomy between realist philosophy, above all neo-Scholasticism, which defines the human being fundamentally as a substance, and the different modern philosophies, which describe the human being as a subject, self or

---

[10] This may be confirmed, for example, in Kant's main work, *Critique of pure reason*, or in Husserl's main work, *Ideas pertaining to a Pure Phenomenology* (Springer, 1983).

consciousness; that is, placing in relief, from different aspects, subjectivity and interiority, but generally from an idealistic perspective.

But, in addition, there is another more important problem: *the social situation.* The 20th century was the stage for a battle between two powerful ideologies: collectivism and individualism. The collectivisms (communism, Nazism, fascism) promoted the general values of society, but deprecated individuals.[11] The organicistic social vision on which they depended understood the human being as a part of the social whole, a whole for which he should sacrifice himself if necessary. What was essential was the organism (the society), while the part (the human being) was only important to the measure in which he served the organism. Individualism, on the contrary, adopted the opposing perspective: the exaltation of the individual lacking in solidarity who sought his own good and to that end used his economic means and intelligence, applying the "law of fittest". He who is able and powerful settles into the social texture; he who is weak is set aside (cf. Ch. 14.1).[12]

These two ideologies, as we know perfectly from history, did not remain in the terrain of theory but rather generated very powerful social and political movements which decided, in an at times very tragic way, the history of the 20th century. The two World Wars are linked to the totalitarianisms' intention to impose their vision of the world and augment their power and, with regard to individualism, it is unquestionable that it is one of the essential ideological elements of the savage capitalism of the end of the 19th century and the beginning of the 20th century.

This complex situation is the one which led to a recuperation of the *notion* and of the *reality* of the person.[13]

---

[11] A more detailed development of the causes which originate the birth of personalism may be found in Juan Manuel Burgos, *An Introduction to Personalism*, 7-50.

[12] At the time Maritain denounced and deeply and lucidly analyzed this question. Cf. Jacques Maritain, *Integral Humanism: Temporal and Spiritual Problems of a New Christendom*, in *The Collected Works of Jacques Maritain*, vol. 11, translated by Otto Bird, Joseph Evans, and Richard O'Sullivan. (Notre Dame, Ind.: University of Notre Dame Press, 1996), 141-345.

[13] "Life and thought find themselves before the same problem. Just as life easily believes that it has to choose between individualism and collectivism, so does thought also have the opinion, falsely, that it has to choose between an individualistic anthropology and a collectivistic sociology. The excluded 'genuine' alternative, once found, will show us the way." Martin Buber, *¿Qué es el hombre?* (Madrid: FCE, 1984), 146. English version: "What Is Man?" in *Between Man and Man* (New York: Routledge, 2002).

First of all, there was a *social* movement linked to the disasters of the war and of the ideologies, a movement that urgently demanded a new valorization of the human being. The human being could be neither a mere part of the whole nor an egotistical entity. The human being had to have value in himself; what is more, the human being was, doubtless, what is most valuable in the world. But this, in turn, could not mean that the human being had the right to behave egotistically and individualistically. The person should be at the service of others and live in generosity. The two World Wars were decisive in that change of perspective and, in this sense, the personal path of Gabriel Marcel is paradigmatic. This philosopher was initially an idealist, but he spent World War I working in the department of the missing in action, whose mission was to inform family members about the situation of soldiers whose whereabouts were unknown. In this situation, he acutely experienced the importance which *each concrete person* has and how the happiness of some people could depend on a few words: a yes or a no. It was then that his faith in the holistic and abstract idealistic systems definitively broke. The person is what is important, each concrete and individual person, and not abstractions. And if philosophy wanted to respond to reality and be useful, it had to articulate itself in relation to this essential value.

This type of experience or other similar ones was the path that led many philosophers to the *philosophical* recuperation and re-elaboration of the notion of person, which was performed in three basic ways.

The first and most important is the emergence of *personalism*, to which the current vision of the person is conceptually indebted. Personalism, which arose as a movement thanks to Emmanuel Mounier in interwar France[14], took the following as its basic presuppositions: the need to relaunch the concept of person as a philosophical remedy in the ideological fight between individualism and collectivism; the need for the new anthropology of the person to take up the contributions of modernity: consciousness, the subject, the self, freedom, dynamicity, etc.; the need for those contributions to be made in the framework of a realist philosophy, open to transcendence.

The result of these approaches was a really new vision of the person, to the point that it is possible to speak of a *reinvention of the notion of person*, which we can describe in summary as follows[15]. The person is a being who is worthy in himself but needs to give himself to others to achieve his perfection, he is

---

[14] Cf. N. Bombaci, *Una vita, una testimonianza: Emmanuel Mounier* (Armando siciliano Editore, 1999).

[15] Cf. Juan Manuel Burgos, *Person in personalism*, Conference "From *Logos* to Person", Instituto Polis of Jerusalem, John Hopkins University, Israel, 2021 (to be published).

dynamic and active, capable of transforming the world and reaching the truth, he is spiritual and bodily, possessing a freedom that allows him to determine himself and deciding in part not only his future but his way of being, he is rooted in the world of affectivity and is a bearer of and is destined for a transcendent end. This vision is the one which little by little has imposed itself as the definitive, modern concept of person, and not only in the academic world, but also on a social level, to the point that we can consider in to be accepted today to a great degree by Western civilization.

This cultural surge both of personalism and of the concept of person produced, in turn, the approach of other philosophical perspectives to this notion. On the one hand, *neo-Scholasticism and more classical realist philosophies* initiated a work of recuperation and development of the notion of person which, on the other hand, was not strange to them, since it belonged by right to their cultural patrimony.[16] And, although in this case without depending initially on French personalism, there was a passage of some sectors of modern philosophy to a realist refoundation of the notion of person. This basically corresponds to *phenomenology* and goes from Husserl and Scheler to Dietrich von Hildebrand and Edith Stein.

The perspective that we are going to use in this book is personalism as it has been formulated in the 20th century and, in particular, the personalist vision proposed by Integral Personalism that is based on the works of Karol Wojtyła and Juan Manuel Burgos[17].

1.2 What does It Mean to be a Person?

a) Is It Possible to Define the Person?

If, leaving aside historical questions, we begin by asking ourselves what it means to be a person, the easiest response would be to begin with a definition. The topic would thus be clear and expeditious, and the task would only be to develop it. The question, however, is not as simple, to the point that, as we will see, in reality it is not possible to define the person, and so we will have to make do with successive approximations.

---

[16] See E. Forment, *El personalismo medieval* (Valencia: Edicep, 2002).
[17] Cf. Juan Manuel Burgos, *Wojtyła's Personalism as Integral Personalism* and *¿Qué es el personalismo integral?*, "Quién. Revista de filosofía personalista", 10 (2020), 9-37.

a.1) Boethius' Definition and its Limits

Probably the best definition which exists of person is the one that Boethius gave and to which we have already referred: person is the individual substance of a rational nature.[18] This definition simultaneously places in relief many essential aspects of human beings:

- substantiality; that is, the fact that the person subsists through changes and has coherence. The person is a being who remains and has the ontic density of substances;

- individuality: the person is a unique and determinate reality; each person is distinct and different, and this aspect of Boethius' definition alludes to this;

- rational nature: within the wide world of substances, persons are a specific class, they are the substances which have intelligence, and thus are capable of understanding the world and possess spirituality.

Boethius' definition fulfills, in addition, *the rules of logic*, especially important in the Middle Ages, which require that every definition be constituted on the basis of a genus plus the specific difference. The genus in this case is substance and the specific difference, rationality. Thanks to its logical precision and the exactness of its contents, this definition became canonical and remained in force for centuries. However, little by little, some *limits and deficiencies* began to become apparent, and they widened to the point that it began to be accepted that it was a brilliant definition, ingenious for its time, correct, but insufficient.[19] The limits which this definition presents are basically of two types:

1) The characterization of the human being as a substance: we have already indicated the problems which this fact poses and we are not going to insist on it now, although we will treat it again later on (cf. Ch. 7.2);

---

[18] Boethius, *Liber de persona et duabus naturis contra Eutychen et Nestorium*, PL 64, 1343 D.
[19] The criticisms of Boethius' definition are very common. Here we only mention U. Ferrer, *¿Qué significa ser persona?* (Madrid: Palabra, 2002), 174-177, where references to other authors may be found: Seifert, Zubiri, Polo, Marías, etc.

2) The lack of an explicit mention of essential characteristics of
    the person such as freedom, consciousness, interpersonal
    relationships or the self. A person who is not free, who does not
    have self-consciousness, who does not enter into relationship,
    etc., is not a real person, and none of these elements, as it is
    easy to prove, appear in Boethius' definition.

Some have objected, in order to save the definition, that where it says
rational nature, one should, in reality, read spiritual nature, and it would
therefore implicitly include elements like freedom and consciousness. But
this argument, although it has a certain value, gives the impression of being
an emergency patch. On one hand, it leaves the problem of substantiality
unsolved, but in addition, it is not very convincing because Boethius'
definition is incomplete, not by accident, but for a precise reason: because the
tradition in which it was forged *had not developed the missing elements*. Those
elements were elaborated philosophically by modernity and thus they must
be incorporated "from the outside" and *a posteriori*. Finally, *precision*, above
all, is to be demanded of a definition, and if the elements that should
characterize what is defined are not found explicitly, but must be read
between the lines or added *ad casum* from outside, the definition ceases to
have value as such. In the end, as we commented, the valorization which
currently is made of Boethius' text is that it is a brilliant description of
personal being, but it does not have the value of a definition.

a.2) Personalism's Definition-Descriptions

If Boethius' definition is incomplete, we might wonder if today there is a more
precise one, which might have a higher degree of acceptance, but the answer
is negative. There is no definition which fulfills these characteristics; what is
more, in general the very possibility of a definition of the human being is
rejected. Personalism, in particular, has rejected that possibility for the
following reasons:

- a greater consciousness of the *complexity* of the person. The
  anthropological, psychological, and social discoveries, etc.,
  which have accumulated over the centuries mean that it
  continually appears more difficult to enclose *all the essential
  elements* within a definition;

- the insistence on the *personal* character of the human reality
  which would seem to be deformed if one enclosed it within the
  terms of a general definition. Mounier affirms, "Only the objects

exterior to the human being, capable of being placed before his gaze, are to be defined. Now, the person is not an object."[20];

- the relative *uselessness* of a definition in a complex society. Boethius' definition was very useful because the terms in which it was expressed (nature, substance, etc.) had a univocal meaning for the intellectual community in which he lived. Today, by contrast, this is not the case. If we say, for example, that the person is free, we must then explain what exactly we mean by freedom, since otherwise the definition will have little value. And this is the case with each one of the terms of the definition;

- the *attitude of rejection toward formal definition*. Following in the wake of Kierkegaard, the personalists rejected abstract Hegelian idealism which desired to enclose what exists within the nets of rationality. And this meant, for the topic which interests us, that the human being is not rationally explicable; not because the human being is irrational, but on the contrary, because the human being is much more than mere instrumental reason. Now, to attempt to enclose the human being within the margins of a definition is to fall into that which is being criticized. In addition, there is the possibility that a definition might limit the analysis of what is human. To define the human being could imply the danger that, if something does not appear in the definition, it might not be studied or sufficient attention might not be dedicated to it (as occurred in part with Boethius' definition) and, thus, there has been a preference to opt for open systems which do not exclude the possibility of additions or complements.

Now, admitting the impossibility of a strict definition does not mean that we renounce any definition or description of the person. This would not make much sense in a philosophy founded precisely on that notion. For this reason, personalism has opted for *an intermediate path* which has the following characteristics:

---

[20] E. Mounier, *El personalismo* (Madrid: PPC, 2004) 10.

- it seeks to describe the essential elements which characterize the personal being,

- it does not have a pretension of exhaustivity,

- it does not seek formal rigor,

- it is conscious of the fact that the description only finds full meaning in the context of a philosophy in which each one of the terms which compose it is developed with precision.

From this approach, basically *two* types of text have arisen. In the first, which we may call *definition-descriptions* and may be more or less explicit, the personalists have attempted to reflect essential elements of the person. Thus, for example, Mounier affirms: "a person is a spiritual being constituted as such by his form of subsistence and of independence in his being."[21] Lacroix, laconically as well, indicates: "the person is master of himself and gift of himself."[22] And Maritain, in a clearer example of what he has called description-definition, affirms: "When we say that a human being is a person, we do not only mean that he is an individual like an atom, a grain of wheat, a fly or an elephant are. The human being is an individual who directs himself with intelligence and with will; he does not exist only in a physical way, but also super-exists spiritually in knowledge and in love, in such a way that, in some sense, he is a universe in himself, a microcosmos in which the whole, great universe can be comprehended with knowledge, and with love he can give himself entirely to beings which are before him as other selves, a relationship of which it is impossible to find an equivalent in the physical world. The human person possesses these characteristics because, in the end, the human being, this flesh and these bones, both perishable, which a divine fire makes to live and work, exists 'from the uterus to the tomb,' by work of the very existence of his soul which dominates time and death. The spirit is the root of the personality."[23]

To which we could add our own version. The person is a being worthy in himself but needs to give himself to others to achieve his perfection, he is

---

[21] E. Mounier, *Manifiesto al servicio del personalismo* (Madrid: Taurus, 1967), 75-76. English Version: *A Personalist Manifesto,* edited by Joseph T. Delos et al. (New York: Longman, Green, 1938).

[22] J. Lacroix, *Le personnalisme* (Lyon, 1982), 27.

[23] J. Maritain, *Principes d'une politique humaniste,* Oeuvres Complètes, vol. VIII, 188.

dynamic and active, capable of transforming the world and reaching the truth, he is spiritual and bodily, possessing a freedom that allows him to determine himself and deciding in part not only his future but his way of being, is rooted in the world of affectivity and is a bearer of and is destined for a transcendent end.

The second type of text that personalism has produced is a more detailed description of the characteristics of the personal being, obtained through phenomenological or experiential analysis, and which it is customary to make explicit indicating and developing a series of *features* which characterize the personal being.

b) Main Features of the Person

The main features which characterize the person are the following:[24]

b.1) Substantiality-Subsistence

With this feature, of an Aristotelian-Thomistic root, the intention is to indicate that the person is a being with an existential density that is so strong that the person remains in himself through all the changes. The person is always himself, although the world around the person changes and the very person changes. Similar to Theseus' ship, in which each one of the pieces that composed it was eventually substituted along the journey, but which continued to be the same ship, the human person, while he changes interiorly and exteriorly, even organically, continues to be *the same person*. In addition, that "being oneself" is something profound and decisive, because the person is not a mere flux of experiences, nor a temporary grouping together of phenomena which time dissolves and transforms, but a being with coherence which resists the passage of years and days, and while it is more difficult for philosophy to confirm it, possesses an eternal dimension. This reality is called the subsistence of the personal being.

b.2) Interiority-Subjectivity

That which remains through the changes in the person is not a "thing," but a "who," a "someone," a very profound reality with a great interior richness which manifests itself and exercises itself through specific qualities:

---

[24] There are quite a few descriptions of this type. We use as a basis, although with some modifications: R. Yepes, *Fundamentos de antropología. Un ideal de la excelencia humana* (Pamplona: Eunsa, 1996) ch. 3 and L. Pareyson, *Esistenza e persona* (Genoa: Il Melangolo, 1985), 173-205.

sensibility, affection, feelings, consciousness of self. All these characteristics form subjectivity: what is proper and specific to each person, his interior, intimate world, different from any other man or woman. This world, in part, can be manifested outwardly through feeling and actions, but in part it is inexpressible because it constitutes the identity of the person, which is non-transferable. Thus did the classical philosophers say that in the person there is something incommunicable.

In addition, the person is conceived as an autonomous being, conscious of self and independent, that is, as a someone, a subject, a self, capable of deciding about himself and placing himself before the world. Person, as Karol Wojtyła says, is someone who "possesses himself".[25]

b.3) A Corporeal, Spatial and Temporal Being

The person possesses a material and corporeal dimension; the person is subjectivity and interiority, but in a concrete, physical and determinate body; the person is "someone corporeal", as Julián Marías says.[26] This has numerous consequences, but one of the principal ones is that the person is not a purely spiritual being, but is localized, and wounded by time.

Space: the person moves in a physical, geographical and human space, which is necessary in order to live and which conditions the person: house, city, country, etc.

Time: the person is not a static being, but in constant evolution; the person has a lifetime that flows and makes the person essentially dynamic and projective. The person is always situated facing the time he disposes of, in a constant and paradoxical struggle. On one hand, the person seeks to detain time, keeping memory of the past and eternalizing the present which is pleasurable or happy. And, simultaneously, the person seeks to anticipate the future in order to be able to decide his destiny and exercise that self-dominion which characterizes the person. But it is always, at least at first sight, a lost battle. Death always comes and time always conquers, although the longing for immortality, present in every human being, demands an answer.

b.4) Openness and Definition

Although the person has his own personal and non-transferable life, the person is not a being closed within himself, but rather *open*, a being who

---

[25] K. Wojtyła, *Persona y acción*, 168 (*The Acting Person*).
[26] J. Marías, *Persona* (Madrid: Alianza, 1997), 135.

needs to *transcend* himself and go out of himself to develop himself fully.[27] All human beings need to go out of themselves and make of themselves a gift to others if they want to fulfill themselves; and they do so, fundamentally through their most elevated, spiritual capabilities and faculties: affectivity, intelligence and freedom.

The human being relates to reality on three fundamental levels: things, interpersonal relationships and God; and those relations are established, in turn, in two directions: receptivity and influence. The human being is affected by the world which surrounds him, but in turn, through his action, the human being can modify that world and transform it according to his desires and needs.

That openness, moreover, is not the modification of an undifferentiated being, but rather the perfection of a definite being with a precise nature. Thus, as Pareyson indicates, the person is "at the same time open and closed. The person is closed due to the immanence of his past in his present, due to the condensation of his entire history in the present instant, due to a general valorization which, taking stock of his conquests and achievements, establishes the validity of what the person has been able to make of himself. And the person is open because his present opens to the future, because an impulse runs through the person which places him before himself, because the imperative that moves the person obliges him to new decisions and to a continually greater dedication to the task in which the person recognizes himself."[28]

b.5) Man and Woman

Until now we have shown valid traits for every human being, for every person. But a glance at reality makes us see that the person doesn't present itself in an abstract and undifferentiated way, but in two different modalities: man and woman. This is not a theoretical statement but a mere experiential verification consistent with the fact that anthropology must be based on reality. And indeed, a look around us, at the world and at history shows us the human being, in an overwhelming way, as a man and as a woman. The theory or interpretation appears only in a second moment, when we ask ourselves how to understand this *fascinating reality, namely masculinity and femininity.* The

---

[27] Polo is one of the recent authors who has most insisted on the person as gift. Cf. L. Polo, *Antropología trascendental*, 217-228, and *Tener y dar*, in *Estudios sobre la Laborem excercens* (Madrid: BAC, 1987).

[28] L. Pareyson, *Esistenza e persona*, 181.

answer of personalism and, in particular, of integral personalism, is that this essential anthropological fact is explained by the existence of two different ways of being a person, the masculine person and the feminine person, and is justified by the simultaneous affirmation of equality and the difference[29]. Man and woman are essentially equal as persons, which means, in the context of this text, that the diagram of the person (see, Introduction, 4, e) is identical for both and, consequently, they have exactly the same structures, powers, spiritual centers, unifying self, etc. But, at the same time, these structures have peculiar features that distinguish them[30]: male intelligence is different from female intelligence[31], as are sociability, affectivity, the relationship with corporeality, or even the self. Different, of course, does not mean better or worse as it was sometimes mistakenly considered in the past, but just different, diverse.

Masculinity and femininity are affected by culture, like any essential human aspect. They are not immovable and static biological structures, but they undergo temporal and social changes. Gender theory, developed from the works of John Money, was the first to notice this fact clearly, generating a remarkable advance in the study and understanding of human sexuality. However, some later thinkers radicalized this position by stating that sexual identity can be completely constructed and decided by each individual person or, in other words, that masculinity and femininity are not shaping elements of human identity, but just one more constructive possibility among many others[32]. However, it seems that this position cannot be considered more than a theory that contradicts what experience shows: masculinity and femininity as a fundamental human fact, which is subject, like all human reality, to cultural variations.

Finally, it should be noted that there is still no theory that satisfactorily explains in a complete way the ontological level at which the male-female differentiation occurs and how this would be combined with unity. But this difficulty, in a way, is not surprising. No matter how much we advance in the

---

[29] Cf. K. Wojtyla, *Man and Woman He Created Them: A Theology of the Body.* Trans. by Michael Waldstein. (Boston: Pauline Books & Media, 2006); B. Castilla, *Persona masculina, persona femenina* (Madrid: Rialp, 1996; Di Nicola, G. P., *Uguaglianza e differenza. La reciprocità uomo donna* (Rome: Città Nuova, 1989).

[30] Cf. A. Danese-G. P. Di Nicola, *Lei & Lui. Comunicazione e reciprocità* (Turin: Effatà, 2001).

[31] Cf. L. Brizendine, *The Female Brain* (Harmony, 2007); *The Male Brain: A Breakthrough Understanding of How Men and Boys Think* (Harmony, 2011).

[32] J. Butler, *Gender Trouble: Feminism and the Subversion of Identity* (Abingdon: Routledge, 2006).

knowledge of the human person, he or she is always a mystery impossible to fully unravel.

1.3 The Dignity of the Person

The main features of the person point in a precise direction: men and women are very special beings due to the intrinsic perfection which they possess and which places them above the rest of the beings in nature, on another level. *Persona significant id quod est perfectissimum in tota natura*[33], St. Thomas affirmed, and in our time, that perfection has a specific name: dignity. The person is the being with dignity *par excellence*, above the cosmos, matter, plants and animals. Despite the intrinsic perfection of the universe and of natural organisms, which science shows us in an ever more fascinating way, the human person goes radically beyond them because the human person is situated on a different and superior plane: that of personality and spirit. That is why the person has dignity in a radical sense.

Let us now see some developments of this concept.

- *The dignity of the person is an intrinsic and constitutive perfection*, that is, it depends on the existence and essential characteristics of the person's being, not on the possession or ability to exercise determined qualities. Each person has dignity due to the very fact of being a person, even though he may lack or deficiently possess one or the other of the specific characteristics of what is human (physical or psychological disabilities, undeveloped aspects, etc.). In other words, a being is or is not a person in a radical way; a being cannot be more or less a person. Consequently, approaches like abortion or euthanasia which limit the condition of personhood and the corresponding dignity to the effective possession of some physical or psychological qualities (self-consciousness, satisfactory quality of life, etc.) are incorrect.[34]

- *The dignity of the person makes the person a value in himself, so that the person cannot be instrumentalized.* The intrinsic

---

[33] Thomas Aquinas, *S. Th.*, I, q. 29, a. 3; in a. 4, Thomas even speaks of the possible relational character of the notion of person.

[34] Cf. Robert Spaemann, *Persons. The difference between "someone" and "something"* (Oxford: Oxford University Press, 2006).

perfection of the person has as a consequence that the person
has value in and of himself, due to the simple fact of being a
person or of existing. For this reason, there is a positive
obligation to seek the good of the person and the negative
obligation to not utilize the person as a mere instrument for
other ends, because it would go against the person's dignity.
No one (not even God) may instrumentalize the person, that
is, use the person *only* as a means for his interests, because
that would mean that the person would be identified with a
thing and one would be denying his personal character.

As is known, the first explicit formulation of this idea is due to Kant. "The
human being," he affirms, "and in general every rational being, exists as an
end in itself, *not merely as a means* for the capricious use of this or that will;
rather, it should be considered *at the same time as an end* in all actions, both
those directed toward oneself and toward another rational being (...). The
beings whose existence does not depend on our will, but on nature, have only
a relative value when it is a matter of irrational beings, and therefore they are
called *things*; but rational beings are denominated *persons*, because their
nature already signals them as ends in themselves, that is, as something which
cannot be used as a means."[35]

- *The value of the person is absolute.* The person is a value in
  himself, but it is important to specify that it is an absolute
  value. This means, on one hand, that it is superior to any
  other value we could find in our environment: nature,
  animals, material or spiritual goods. But, still more radically, it
  means that it is a value which is not interchangeable, which

---

[35] I. Kant, *Fundamentación de la metafísica de las costumbres* (Madrid: Santillana, 1996),
50-51 *(Foundations of the Metaphysics of Morals)* K. Wojtyła has proposed an interesting
reformulation of this principle through the *personalist norm* which attempts to go
further and bring the principle closer to the "commandment of love". "This norm, in its
negative content, determines that the person is a good which is not in accord with
utilization, since the person cannot be treated as an object of pleasure and, therefore, as
a means. In a parallel way, its positive content is also revealed: the person is a good in
such a way that only love can dictate the appropriate and valid attitude with respect to
the person. This is what the command of love exposes." (K. Wojtyła, *Amor y
responsabilidad* (Madrid: Palabra, 2008), 51; English version: *Love and Responsibility*
[Pauline Books & Media, 2013]).

cannot be manipulated or substituted by anything.[36] One may not infringe upon the dignity of the person. On the contrary, the adequate attitude in relation to the person is that of respect, recognition and promotion.

- *The dignity of the person is the foundation of human rights.* The absolute value and intrinsic dignity of the person translate, at the juridical-social level, into the existence of *human rights or fundamental rights* which the person possesses due to the mere fact of being a person; these have two dimensions. From the subjective point of view, human rights are understood to be the areas of social liberty which are at the person's disposition and in which the State may not and should not intrude (religious freedom, freedom of expression, right to privacy, etc.). These rights *are not concessions* which the State makes, but interior demands which emanate from the personal being and which the State, if it acts correctly, cannot but recognize. It corresponds to the State also to promote the adequate conditions so that the person may exercise his rights in an effective way, without obstacles (right to education, to a living place, etc.); in this second sense, we speak of objective rights.

- *The dignity of the person makes each man and each woman unrepeatable and unsubstitutable[37].* The particular characteristics of the human person permit us to comprehend that each person is unique and has an unrepeatable value, independent of his conditions (physical, intellectual, etc.). No one can be substituted in the strict sense, something which becomes manifest in the family and in relationships in which love intervenes (cf. Ch. 12).

The recognition of this fact has made necessary a *re-elaboration of the notions of individual and species for human beings.* In the animal kingdom,

---

[36] God is the absolute value *par excellence* (metaphysical absolute), but the person, in his or her ambit, is also an absolute value. In this sense, in order to differentiate, one could speak of the human person a "relative absolute". Cf. X. Zubiri, *El hombre y Dios,* 376 (*Man and God*)

[37] See J. F. Crosby, *The Selfhood of the Human Person* (Washington, DC: The Catholic University of America Press, 1996).

what principally counts is the species; the individual is at the species' service and should sacrifice itself for the species if necessary. In addition, an individual of an animal species – except perhaps in superior animals – is practically equivalent to another individual. Ants have no name. But this approach cannot be applied as such to the human being. The person is not at the service of the human species nor are human beings interchangeable. In this sense Spaemann affirms that "the person is not a synonym of the concept of species, but rather that mode of being with which the individuals of the 'human' species exist. They *are* in such a way that each one of those who exist in that community of persons which we call 'humanity' occupies a unique place which is not reproduceable and not susceptible to substitution."[38] Along these same lines, but going still further, Pareyson affirms that, "in the human being, every individual is, in a certain sense, unique in his species."[39]

- *The affirmation of the dignity of the person is historically linked to Christianity.* We have already seen that the notion of person arose from Christianity and something similar can be said about the concept of dignity. The intrinsic dignity of each person, independently of his sex, culture, value, wealth, etc., has only been implemented effectively thanks to Christianity, although subsequently it has been generalized as a civil value which has been accepted (at least theoretically) by other societies and cultures. We know that this was not the prevailing practice in antiquity (slavery, limitation of civil rights according to social condition and sex, etc.) and it was the Church that insisted on the dignity of each person. Today, the situation is in part different and in part similar. While there is a general recognition of the dignity of every born and normal person[40], there is, however, a tendency to restrict that condition in the situations in which the person is weakest: the

---

[38] R. Spaemann, *Persons*, 22. "In the human genus, the situation, due to Christianity, is inverted and the individual is higher than the genus." Søren Kierkegaard, *Diario*, 1854, XI (Madrid: Planeta, 1993), 485.

[39] L. Pareyson, *Esistenza e persona*, 176. Cf. J. M. Burgos (ed.), *El giro personalista; del qué al quién* (Salamanca: Mounier, 2011).

[40] The leader of the thinkers opposed to this position is Peter Singer, who, based on the premise that "a week-old baby is not a rational and self-conscious being," concludes that "the life of a newborn baby is of less value than that of a pig, a dog or a chimpanzee." P. Singer, *Practical Ethics* (Cambridge: Cambridge University Press, 1973, 122-123.

phases previous to birth (abortion) and the moment of death (euthanasia). And now as well, the Church continues its task of defense of the dignity of *every* person.

We just saw that the person is unique and unrepeatable, and that the person does not form part of the human species in the way that animals form part of their species. But, while this is true, it is also true that, in the end, all human beings are human beings; that is, they possess common features which permit us to identify them as persons and not as lions, rocks or monkeys. The notion that reflects this similarity most adequately is the notion of nature.

1.4 Human Nature

a) The Notion of Human Nature

a.1) Definition and Historical Origin

The notion of nature comes from the Thomistic-Aristotelian tradition. Aristotle, in the framework of his teleological doctrine, indicates that all beings have a determined mode of being, which is called essence. This essence or mode of being is not static, but rather it has an internal dynamism that drives it to act in order to reach the end (*telos*), which is adequate to the characteristics of the essence. That internal dynamism or, in other words, *the essence inasmuch as it is a principle of operations, is what is called nature.*

Natural beings work spontaneously in accord with their nature and in this way reach their proper fullness and that which suits them. A horse, for example, has a determined mode of being and, therefore, a nature. And that nature is what drives it to perform actions proper to the horse: run, galop, nourish itself in a determined way, reproduce in a characteristic way, etc. In this way, it is able to develop correctly and reach the fullness which is permitted to it or to which it can aspire due to its mode of being.

The same thing occurs in the human being. Persons also have an essence and a nature and, therefore, have to act in a determined way in order to achieve what their perfection demands. But, in this case, there is a fundamental difference: *freedom.* A flower, a dolphin or a rhinoceros cannot choose their mode of behavior and act (which greater or lesser efficacy, this is another question) following their own determined and specific patterns of activity. But in the case of the human being the same thing does not occur. The human being is free, which means, among other things, that he can invent new forms of behavior, go against what he thinks he should do or perform because he wants to, that is, freely. And this implies that human action is governed by morality. If the human being freely follows what suits his nature, the human being will act morally well and, in addition, will achieve happiness. If the human being does not do it, then he will act badly from a moral point of view, and in addition, will be wretched because he will go against himself and his own good.

a.2) Cultural Applications

The notion of human nature is a response, therefore, to an experiential fact: the existence of common elements which allow one to affirm and prove that we are human beings. And for this reason, this notion has important ethical and cultural applications:

- it allows for the founding of the *essential equality of all human beings*. Since everyone possesses the same nature, we are all essentially equal. There may be, and in fact there are, significant differences between persons, but deep down, our nature does not change, and it is identical in all;

- it allows for the founding of a *universal ethics*, that is, an ethics which is valid for all human beings for the simple reason that, if we have our nature in common, ethical principles must also be in common;

- it allows for the founding of the existence of *absolute moral imperatives*; that is, actions which may never be committed, since those actions which gravely oppose human nature can never be good[41];

- it allows, finally, for the *transcendent founding of the person* since, although the human being is free, he does not create his own nature but rather receives it. Nature is something given, which the human being encounters at the beginning of his existence, and this characteristic of being given necessarily remits to a giver, that is, to God as the final transcendent foundation of human nature and, therefore, of the person.

---

[41] Cf. John Paul II, Encyclical *Fides et ratio*, n. 68.

b) Criticisms of the Notion of Human Nature

The notion of human nature, despite its potential, has suffered different criticisms, so it is necessary to analyze these objections, although in summary, in order to evaluate their substance[42]. A first type of criticism comes from *those who consider that the human being does not have a nature*, and that it is rather freedom that radically makes the human being human (Sartre); the human being would, therefore, be a being in continuous evolution. This position, however, is in contrast with experience. If we leave aside the ancient archeological remains that show us fragments of a remote world that we cannot adequately reconstruct and we limit ourselves to the civilizations of which we have a documented record, we can verify that, although we have changed profoundly, we continue to be human beings and we can identify with the aspirations, desires and problems of our ancestors in remote cultures. Egyptians, Incas, Indians and Greeks are, without a doubt, human beings like us, and it would never even occur to us to think that they belong to another species of beings. What is more, the differences among human beings from different eras and cultures are meaningful for us precisely because they stand out against a backdrop of equality.

A second type of criticism is that which, affirming the essentiality and permanence of the human phenomenon, questions, however, the *validity of the notion of nature*. Part of this group of critics is nourished by a certain *terminological ambiguity of the concept of nature* since, contrary to what one might think, this concept is not as precise as it may seem at first sight and it may be used with several meanings and levels of profundity.[43] In current language, for example, "natural" or "nature" is habitually understood to mean what comes from the physical and biological world and which, therefore, is not free but necessary. In this way, if the exact philosophical meaning of this term is unknown, it may seem startling or even erroneous to use it for the human being. To say that the human being has a nature would be equivalent to saying that he is not free.

A second group of objections comes from a *philosophically deficient conception of the concept of nature*. In general, and even though the criticisms vary according to the conceptual scheme of the philosopher who makes

---

[42] An in-depth review of the notion of human nature in J. M. Burgos, *Repensar la naturaleza humana* (2ª ed.) (Ciudad de México: Siglo XXI, 2017).

[43] "Hundreds of definitions of the term 'nature' have been given and, in addition, in different areas." (Cf. J. Ferrater Mora, *Diccionario de Filosofía*, entry: "Naturaleza" [Barcelona: Ariel, 2004]).

them, the basic mechanism is very similar: the starting point is a definition of nature which lacks essential elements of the person (freedom in the case of Kant, for example) and consequently it is concluded that it is an inadequate notion for understanding the human being. The solution to these difficulties consists in avoiding those incorrect reductionisms. Finally, the criticism which has the greatest weight, in our opinion, is the one that rejects the *rationalistic vision* of the concept of nature.[44] This objection is based on the fact that there are two possible conceptions of the term nature: 1) a common generic nucleus of qualities and characteristics common to all human beings; 2) an abstract, impersonal and perfectly defined nucleus that supposedly exists in the human being and which would not be altered at all either with time, or with cultures, or with persons.[45] The first posture responds to the nucleus of what constitutes the notion of nature. The second does as well, but it insists so much on the aspect of immutability that it ends up posing some important problems. It poses, in the first place, a *conflict between nature and culture*. How does one reconcile, to give one example, the notion of human nature formulated in this way with the important modifications which different cultures impose on the life and conceptions of human beings?[46] And it also poses a *conflict between nature and freedom*, because it leaves aside the fact that the nature of the human being is to a certain degree indeterminate, since, in contrast to animals, which always behave identically, the human being partially modifies his way of being and decides on his own destiny. The human *telos* is in part *indefinite* because the human being, to a certain extent, establishes his own ends, and the notion of nature should be capable of taking this in.

The problems we just mentioned can become substantial if we take the positions to the extreme, but they can be resolved if one understands, authentically and without rigidity, the nucleus of the concept of nature, making it harmonizable with other essential concepts like culture and freedom. In this sense, Isaiah Berlin's commentary seems very enlightening to us: "moral categories – and the categories of values in general – are not as firm and ineradicable as those which correspond, for example, to the perception of the material world, but nor are they so relative and fluid as some writers tend

---

[44] See, in this sense, R. Yepes, *Fundamentos de antropología*, 95-96.

[45] This is the characteristic posture of the rationalists of the 17th and 18th centuries. Cf. J. Maritain, *La loi naturelle ou loi non écrite* (Fribourg, Switzerland: Édition Universitaires, 1986).

[46] Some of these problems are indicated in J. M. Burgos, *La inteligencia ética. La propuesta de Jacques Maritain* (Bern: Peter Lang, 1995), 127-175.

too easily to suppose in their reaction against the dogmatism of the classical objectivists. A minimum of common moral background, of categories and concepts related to one another, is intrinsic to human communication."[47]

c) The Notions of Person and Nature

The reflections we have just made clearly indicate that the notions of nature and person need one another in order to integrally reflect the human being. The notion of person principally refers to the concrete, unrepeatable and existent individual, the man or woman who, with a proper and unique name, is differentiated profoundly from the rest of men and women. The notion of nature, on the contrary, refers to what is common, to the fact that that man (or that woman), different from any other man (or woman) who has populated our planet, is, in spite of it all, essentially equal to them, is a human being. Each man, each woman, is in this way a unique and unrepeatable being (person), but also a human being essentially equal to others (nature).

Now, curiously, and precisely due to this complementarity, it is not always easy to harmonize both concepts from a technical point of view, since one of them places personal individuality in relief and the other what is common and, for that very reason, impersonal. Hannah Arendt has acutely summarized this paradox, affirming: "nothing gives us the right to assume that the human being has a nature or essence in the same sense as other things do. In other words: if we have a nature or essence, only a god can know it and define it, and the first requisite would be that it speaks about a 'who' as if it were a 'what.'"[48] Now, the problem consists precisely in the fact that in the human being the "what" and the "who" are simultaneously given. We are human beings, essentially equal to other human beings, but each one has his own proper name, which differentiates us from the rest of humanity.

There is, however, a way to harmonize both notions or, better, to solve the underlying problem. To use, almost exclusively, the notion of person, which is what we will do in this book. The notion of person, in effect, can be thought of as what is peculiar and specific to the human being as opposed to the notion of nature which would show what is common. But it can also be thought of as *the complete, entire human being*. That is, we can use the term person to refer to individual subjects, Peter and Mary, and we can use the term person to

---

[47] I. Berlin, *Cuatro ensayos sobre la libertad* (Madrid: Alianza, 1998), 37-38. English version: *Four essays of Liberty* (Gryffon Editions, 1996)

[48] Hannah Arendt, *La condición humana* (Barcelona: Paidós, 2001), 24. English version: *The human condition* (Chicago: University of Chicago Press, 2018).

refer *also* to the common, since Peter, Mary and John, are persons. That is, if the notion of person is considered in its maximum amplitude, it can absorb the notion of nature since it can be used both to indicate what is singular and what is common in the human being. And this is how we will use it habitually in this book, as *the term that expresses what is individual and what is common simultaneously.*

Part II.
The Structure of The Person

Having been introduced into the reality of the world of the person, we will now go on to analyze the different aspects which constitute the person. In this second part, we will treat the internal structure of the person. Later on, we will treat action (Part III), the relationship with other persons (Part IV), and the person's fate (Part V).

Our first objective will consist of describing the dimensions or structures which define the personal being, something which, in anatomical terms, we could compare with the attempt to achieve a description of the human body: determine and characterize the bones and the muscles, establish which ligaments permit them to move and how, etc. There is, however, an important difference. The muscles and bones are physical entities, perfectly distinguishable and separable, but this does not occur with the structures of the person. I am free and intelligent, but freedom is not separated from the intellect, nor can I localize and delimit freedom in the same way that I indicate a bone in my body. Freedom is not *there*; rather, it is a quality or capacity of mine which does not reside in any concrete place. In addition, and this is the second aspect, these structures are not completely autonomous and independent entities. We cannot speak of a feeling, a freedom and a self which, gathered together and put in relation to one another, end up forming a man or a woman; rather, on the contrary, what exists is a person in whom we can distinguish a feeling, a freedom and a self. That does not mean – such would imply committing the opposite error – that these elements do not have a relative autonomy and their own physiognomy. Certainly they do: the body, for example, is not the self, nor can it be identified with feelings. But that autonomy is never complete, since it never exists separately. In conclusion, the person cannot be identified with the sum of the elements which make up the person; and those elements, on the other hand, are not perfectly isolatable or separable from each other. They are always dimensions of the personal being, which is the one who really exists and in whom they cohabit, intimately intermixed.[1]

The dimensions of the person we are going to consider in this second Part are the following: the body (Ch. 2); sensibility and inclinations (Ch. 3); affectivity (Ch. 4); the intellect (Ch. 5); freedom (Ch. 6); and the self (Ch. 7). It is a classical structure in which, however, one may identify some new perspectives: the importance given to corporeality, affectivity and freedom, and the inclusion of a specific chapter for the self. Freedom is a topic of undisputable relevance in our time, and thus it requires special attention. The same occurs with affectivity which, moreover, has frequently been the "Cinderella" of some philosophy textbooks. In opposition to such an approach, in this work we will vindicate its importance as an autonomous dimension of the person which, on the other hand, opens up the way toward a consideration of the heart from a philosophical point of view. Finally, the inclusion of the self has seemed to us to be necessary in order to treat the deepest nucleus of the person, without which the person would be reduced to a patchwork of faculties or dimensions. In every human being and in every person there is a final nucleus which unifies our being and it seemed necessary to mention it.

These elements, in turn, can be framed into a horizontal structure in which there are *three levels of perfection*: body, psyche and spirit, instead of the classical division in body and soul. The body or somatic dimension cannot be identified with matter because it has a personal character. In addition, we can find in it affective, cognitive and dynamic traits. The psyche comprehends sensibility, tendencies and a second level of affectivity. And the spiritual part comprehends spiritual affectivity, intellectual knowledge and freedom. All of this, finally, is linked and controlled, at least in some way, by the individual and unique Self. And the complete whole of these traits and others that will not be dealt with make the whole and real person.

All this, as we said in the introduction, can be represented pedagogically through the following diagram (figure II.1):

---

[1] We are somewhat insistent on this point because it seems to us to be important to establish the adequate perspective capable of balancing what must be admitted regarding the unity of the person and what must be admitted regarding the autonomy of the person's faculties and dimensions.

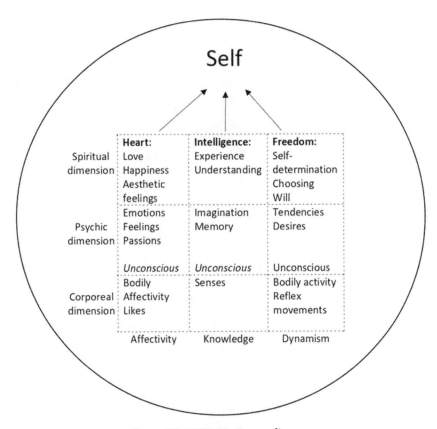

Figure II.I: PERSON - *Burgos diagram.*

Chapter 2

The Body

2.1 The Person: Someone Corporeal

The body is the first manifestation of the person. I see a figure which approaches, I distinguish a known profile and I say: it is John. John is everything, the entire person in all his dimensions, but what first appears before me, which makes the person manifest and present to me is his body. The human person is totally unthinkable without the body, to the point that some philosophers, like Marías, have described the person as "someone corporeal".[1] But, we may wonder, what is the body? The body is above all the physical, organic or material dimension of the person. My hands, my feet, my heart have a volume, a profile and a size. If I cut myself, I bleed, and if I bump into something, the rough contact with matter hurts. The body is my material dimension and when I die, it will disappear. The organic dimension of the body is evident and therefore there is no reason to insist on it. What is interesting to stress is another aspect, at first less manifest and which may even surprise us: the human body, while organic and material, is not a "physical object or a thing, but rather the psychophysical or psychoworldly mediation. It is the surface of contact of subjectivity with the cosmos"[2] or, more radically, it is a *dimension of the person* and, thus, it possesses a subjective and personal component.

We may obtain a first approach to this idea from a *negative* point of view, the *impossibility of separating the body from the person*. When a part of the body is separated from the person, it ceases to exist as something corporeal. A hand cut off is not a hand and a dead body is not a human body; it was one, but no longer is one and for that reason it decomposes. Here we already find indications of that personal character of the body.

From a *positive* point of view, we can express this idea by saying that the human being *is a bodily being*, that is, that human existence is not comprehensible or thinkable without the body. In any human action (external or internal) corporeality is involved. A way of expressing this fact is to affirm:

---

[1] J. Marías, *Persona*, 135.

[2] J. Vicente y J. Choza, *Filosofía del hombre. Una antropología de la intimidad*, 4th ed. (Madrid: Rialp, 1995), 134.

"I am body," but it seems more precise and less ambiguous to say, "I am bodily." That is, I, a person, a spiritual subject with self-consciousness, I am, at the same time and inseparably, a bodily reality. The body forms part of my being, it is not external matter which I use or an instrument which I employ for ends which interest me. The body is me, my hands are me, my brain is me, although I am more than my hands, my brain or my muscles. The body is my organic-material dimension, but for that very reason, it has a subjective and spiritual dimension.

"The human body," Ferrer explains, "simultaneously participates in the subjective condition and in worldly objectivity. Through it, the subject is inserted into the world and subjected to its laws and external conditioning."[3] Mounier has explained it in a particularly beautiful way. "I cannot think without being, nor be without my body; I am exposed by my body to myself, to the world, to others; through it I escape the solitude of a thought which would not be more than thought of my thought. By impeding me from being totally transparent to myself, it casts me ceaselessly out of myself into the problematics of the world and the struggles of the human being. Through the solicitations of the senses it launches me into space, through its aging it teaches me duration, through its death it confronts me with eternity. It makes me feel the weight of slavery, but at the same time it is at the root of all consciousness and of all spiritual life. It is the omnipresent mediator of the life of the spirit".[4]

The permanent presence of corporeality, on the other hand, has the effect that the human being is *neither self-transparent nor completely opaque* to himself. In other words, our self-consciousness is real and powerful, but dim. The reason is that the human being cannot objectify his body as something totally external to his consciousness, because the human being becomes conscious of himself precisely through the body; that is why there will always be shadowy corners in our self-gaze, since we cannot enter entirely into our own interiority. Now, this is not a limitation which the body imposes on the person, but rather one of the modes in which the person is constituted because, since the human being is conscious of himself through the body, if the latter were lacking, the human being would be self-transparent, that is, he would not exist.

---

[3] U. Ferrer, *¿Qué significa ser persona?*, cit., 138. Ferrer also indicates that one must avoid an instrumental vision of the body, as if it were external to the self. The human being does not simply have or possess a body, but rather, he is bodily. Marías, Wojtyła, Mounier, Ingarden and many others express the matter in a similar way.
[4] E. Mounier, *El personalismo*, 22.

The radical integration between body and person is not only activated in the adult human being, but in all stages of life. In this sense, the evolution of children is particularly interesting, because it allows us to see clearly how *personal and bodily development are intrinsically linked.* The child who is able to stand up and start to walk begins a new relation with the world and amplifies his field of living enormously; and, when he does not just walk, but is able to control and dominate his body, the possibility of interacting with the world and persons in a controlled way opens up before him. This means, in other words, that the child starts to be free, because, as Wojtyła indicates, "the ability to objectify the body and employ it in action is an important element of personal freedom (...). The human being as person possesses himself in the somatic aspect to the extent in which he possesses his own body, and the human being dominates himself in dominating his own body."[5]

In summary, the body is the material-organic dimension of the person, his first manifestation and his most external facet, but which also has a subjective, psychological and even spiritual character. The body is neither a thing, nor an instrument in the Platonic sense; it is the human being in his external appearance, the person's physical border, the horizon between the material world and the mystery of the personal self.[6] Thus, respect is due to it, since it is the epiphany of the person. By touching a body, we touch the person; by caressing a body, we caress the person; by disdaining the body, we disdain the man or the woman who is that very body.

2.2 Other Visions

The relation between body and person which we just described is relatively recent and implies a vindication of corporeality with respect to a certain disdain which has been common throughout history. Personalism has intended to emphasize the value of the body without damaging the unity of the person, but that unity has not always been maintained philosophically. The relation between the body and the person, or between the soul and matter, has been subject to many interpretations throughout history and not all have been correct or balanced. In some cases, the spiritual aspect has been excessively prioritized over the bodily aspect; in other cases, like Marxism, the contrary has occurred; and in still others, both aspects have been prioritized, but the unity has been hampered. Let us now see some of the more important positions.

---

[5] K. Wojtyła, *Persona y acción*, 300.
[6] Cf. R. Guardini, *The World and the Person*. Translated by Stella Lange (Chicago: Henry Regnery, 1965).

a) Dualisms

The dualist positions have explained the human being through the division of the latter into two separate realities: matter and spirit. It is, certainly, an incorrect doctrine, but it may be said that it has a good "justification," because it is really surprising that in the human being two realities, spirit and matter, which are so antithetical that they have permitted Ortega, with a beautiful expression, to define the human being as "an ontological centaur"[7] may live together harmoniously.

Many modalities of dualism exist. A paradigmatic example of *spiritualistic* dualism is proportioned by Plato. "We, too," he affirms in *Gorgias*, "are in reality perhaps dead. I, too, have heard the wise say that we, now, are dead, and that the body is for us a tomb."[8] For Plato, what is essential in the human being is the spirit, the soul, to the point that he considers that souls exist before bodies, in some place, and only later are they enclosed within a body and sent to the earth. This enclosure is an evil, a punishment from which the soul should free itself through purification in order to return to its perfect initial situation.

Platonic philosophy impressed the *first Christian theologians* quite a lot, because it clearly affirmed the spirituality and immortality of the soul and because its vision of the liberation of the soul from the body coincided in part with some ascetical practices. Thus, corrected from its non-Christian element – the preexistence of souls – it was assimilated and sustained by a good portion of the Church Fathers. In this way, an high-quality instrument was found for the theological elaboration of the Christian message, but a certain spiritualism and a negative view of the body was furtively introduced and took a long time to disappear. This perspective, however, is opposed to Christianity, which is a religion of the *Incarnation*, of a God made flesh. Thus, the assumption of Aristotelianism, with its biological and realist aspects, which St. Thomas audaciously performed in the 13th century, was providential for correcting the course.

Another characteristic example of dualism is proportioned by the philosophy of Descartes. His search for a mathematical certainty like that of the experimental sciences led him through universal doubt to the "*cogito*" (I think, therefore I exist) as the starting point of his philosophy. But, once this

---

[7] J. Ortega y Gasset, *Meditación sobre la técnica* (Madrid: Santillana, 1997), 34. A current *status quaestionis* may be found in J. J. Sanguineti, *Filosofía de la mente* (Madrid: Palabra, 2007), 11-44.

[8] Plato, *Gorgias*, 439a.

principle was set in place, he was not able to reconnect that spiritual center with the material and external world, which had previously been radically put into question. In consequence, the human being ended up being divided into two "substances": the "res cogitans" (spirit) and the "res extensa" (matter) connected to each other only in an external way through the pineal gland situated in the brain. Along similar lines, although from their own different perspectives, are Leibniz and Malebranche. For Leibniz, the body and the soul are two distinct substances but, contrary to what occurred in Descartes, they do not interact with each other, but follow separate and independent processes, although these are parallel, in accord with his theory about the preestablished harmony. Malebranche, for his part, in line with his occasionalism, considers that the body and the mind evolve in a separate and independent way, but they relate to one another through the mediation of a divine being which intervenes in those occasions in which the mind influences the body.

b) Monisms

Another historical way of resolving the problem of the soul-body relation has been to annul one of the members of the equation. It is evident that eliminating or reducing to a minimum either corporeality or spirituality resolves the problem of human complexity and, for that very reason, the problem of explaining the unity disappears. Depending on which element is eliminated, this option leads to monisms of a spiritualistic or a materialistic type.

In the last few centuries monisms of a materialistic type have prevailed, favored by the spectacular advance of the experimental sciences and technology, which led to an over-valuation of the physical-material world.[9] The experimental sciences were imposed as the model of science *par excellence*, and the scientific method was imposed, in turn, as the only valid method of knowledge. Consequently, the fields of knowledge that could not adapt to that method, and the realities to which that method could not be applied – the humanistic fields in general – lost interest and importance and, in extreme cases, their validity was doubted or their very existence was rejected. A paradigmatic example of this posture is offered by behaviorism, a reductionist vision of psychology which attempts to limit itself as much as possible to the quantifiable and measurable aspects of human behavior, denying and rejecting any explanation which implies an interior and transcendent dimension.

---

[9] It is not, however, an entirely new phenomenon. It is enough to remember the Greek atomists.

Together with behaviorism could also be situated the biologism of Monod (the human being is biology), other types of scientism, or Marxism. In any case, it is a matter of different types of reductionisms which, blinded by a material aspect of the person, lose sight of the complexity and transcendence. The irruption of post-modernity, which has highlighted the complexity of the human being and the incapacity of reason to encompass the richness of reality, has allowed for the overcoming of modernity's scientistic rationalism and has placed many theoretical materialisms in crisis. Today, however, favored by the comforts of the welfare society, a practical materialism, understood as a life behavior in which the spiritual dimension is weakened or absent, is very widespread.

2.3 What is the human body like?

a) Human Body and Animal Body

A first way to deepen the comprehension of the human body is to establish a comparison between the body of human beings and that of the animals, because this comparison is very illuminating. That the two are very different can be confirmed, for example, by the treatment which human beings and animals give to cadavers. A television documentary, harsh but real, once reflected how some lion cubs literally ate a member of their own litter with which they had been playing moments before, but which had been killed by a male adult lion. This, evidently, is unthinkable among human beings because, among another reasons, as we have seen, the body manifests the person. But the differences between the body of the human being and of the animal are not only limited to this aspect, but are manifested in the *bodily structure* itself. Although we share with animals relevant biological aspects, the somatic structures are very different.

Probably the principal characteristic which differentiates the human body from the body of animals in non-specialization. All animals have bodies that are perfectly prepared to perform determined tasks. It is enough to think, for example, of an anteater, a shark, a giraffe or a cheetah. Each one of these animals completely exceeds the human being in some specific activity. The human being, however, thanks to his lack of specificity, has a flexibility which, placed at the service of intelligence and freedom, and through the use of adequate instruments, allows the human being to perform the same tasks better than animals: swimming, rapid movement, reaching elevated objects, submerging to unsuspected depths or even flying. Thus, it may be said that the non-specialization of the human body is in a certain sense like bodily freedom or the *bodily basis of freedom*. If the human being had a highly defined body, he could only perform determined tasks and his freedom would be seriously thwarted. We can think, although it is absurd, of a human being with the body of a mole or an ant. As powerful as his intelligence or freedom might be, his abilities would never be developed. And this is what occurs to a great measure when, due to an accident or other causes, the body suffers serious injuries, as in the case of people who are quadriplegic. The conflict between what they would like to do and what they can in fact do becomes a constant frustration, very difficult to overcome.

The human being is also different from animals with respect to the time he takes to reach adult age, an aspect which is related to non-specialization. The bodies of animals are very well defined, in such a way that all that they can and cannot do is already genetically determined. Their development basically consists of activating their instincts. Superior animals require a period of learning, but in the human being that time is maximal, because it implies very complex processes of coordination of motor, perceptive and cognitive abilities.

In any case, non-specialization is related to the existence of *special bodily structures* which only occur in the human being and which make him an atypical animal. Some of them are bipedalism, the particular field of vision due to the disposition of the eyes, the localization of the sexual organs which implies a face-to-face sexual relation, unique in the animal kingdom, the functional asymmetry of the brain, etc. One of the most important bodily structures which is exclusive to the human being are *the hands*, which in a certain sense, can be defined as the specific manifestation of non-specificity, because they are not structured to accomplish anything in particular, but due to their very peculiar structure, they are able to do anything. It is thus that they have received special attention on the part of philosophers, who have referred to them as the "instrument of instruments" or also as an "unspecified instrument." One may also make reference to the *vocal structure*, which is *unique and sophisticated* (lips, teeth, vocal cords, etc.) and allows the human being to emit sounds and words and to create languages.

This set of qualities allows us to conclude that the human body is different from the animal body and, if we would like to place in relief the central element of all these characteristics, we could affirm, following Yepes, that from the structural point of view, the human body is different from the animal body in the fact that it "*is configured to accomplish non-organic functions*"[10], that is, to allow the person to express and develop his psychological and spiritual possibilities through corporeality.

---

[10] R. Yepes, *Fundamentos de antropología*, 32.

b) Bodily Activity and Its Relation with the Self

Another important aspect of the human body is its activity. The body is not something inert or merely exterior, it is a living reality, with a certain autonomy and its own laws. The detailed study of the functioning of the body corresponds, in any case, to medicine and other sciences. From the philosophical perspective, what interests us is to take note of a series of questions by way of summary.

The first and fundamental question is that there are different levels of biological and bodily activity on which the self, through the will, has a different influence:

- at some levels, that intervention is minimal (some types of reflexes, the circulation of the blood, digestion, hormonal processes, instinctive reactions to stimuli, etc.). In these cases, the body, under the control of the autonomous nervous system, responds to stimuli independently of the will;

- at other intermediate levels, the body-mind relation is greater. There are processes which are partially controlled by the person, such as breathing, and there are others which depend entirely on the subject, like motor activity, the external part of nourishment, etc.

It is also important to emphasize that *merely bodily or merely spiritual processes never occur*. Both need each other and influence one another in very different ways. The more inferior processes – biologically speaking – need the person to be alive in order to occur, since, when the person dies, they cease quickly, which means that they are not completely autonomous. And, vice versa, the psychological and spiritual processes always need a bodily base. In order to think, the brain must function correctly. It is dramatic to note the terrible consequences that a stroke can have. In a few minutes we have before us "another person": with difficulties in speaking, moving, with an altered affectivity, with difficulties in reasoning, etc. Similarly, we need the eyes to function correctly in order to see and there are merely biological or chemical problems which can alter behavior (a lack of serotonin, for example, produces depression).

The relation between body and self, moreover, is not limited to the mere reciprocal need; it is something mysterious and profound which is born from multiple and hidden relations which exist between human subjectivity and the different levels of corporeality.[11] The needs, joys and ills of one of the elements are hiddenly but decisively transmitted to the expectations and possibilities of the other. Being healthy, being able to unfold the possibilities of the body in a controlled and efficacious way, feeling the pleasure of bodily wellbeing is a situation which we all desire and which contributes efficaciously to the overall wellbeing of the person and his attitude on life: the *mens sana in corpore sano* of which the classics spoke. Illness, on the contrary, is a heavy burden to carry and it impairs all of our activity: we feel old, tired, defensive before the world which exceeds us.

But it is not only the body which influences the soul, the contrary also occurs. The influence of mental illnesses on some aspects of bodily activity is something well known[12], but there are even more hidden but real paths. We all know or have heard of, for example, people who "have renounced" living, because the loved ones and friends who surrounded them have died and they consider that they no longer have anything to do on earth. The organism of some of these people would live on longer, even years longer, but, influenced mysteriously by the subject's decision, it is quickly consumed and is extinguished.

c) The Anthropological Dimension of the Body

Finally, we are going to consider what we have called the anthropological dimension of the body and which we have defined as *the relation which we establish with our body and with the bodies of others*. It is an essential aspect of life that has a multitude of facets. We will now note some of the most important ones.

The *face*: in the faces of others we discover their intimacy, their attitude toward us, their mood. It is "the center of organization of all corporeality,"[13] Marías affirms, like the summary of the person. The face is the mirror of the soul, as a proverb correctly says, and it is also common to affirm that, starting at a certain age, the human being is responsible for his face because in the face is imprinted his irritation or joy, lightheartedness or tenseness, tiredness with life,

---

[11] See J. Mouroux, *The Meaning of Man* (London: Sheed & Ward, 1948).

[12] The connection between the mind and the body has been greatly deepened thanks to the neurosciences, although they frequently adopt a reductionist vision. For a personalist approach see James Beauregard, *Philosophical Neuroethics: A Personalist Approach*. Volume 1 - Foundations (Wilmington: Vernon Press, 2019).

[13] J. Marías, *Antropología metafísica*, 132.

despair or hope.[14] Therefore, in the face and especially in the eyes we find the person. From there comes the transcendence of the *look* or *gaze*. Aggressive or hateful looks, looks of fascination or surprise, of apprehension or indifference. We can disdain someone with our look or, even more so, by not looking at someone, as if he did not exist or as if we wanted to reduce that person to nothingness, while two people who are in love, on the contrary, cannot but look at each other intently because they seek to penetrate the soul of the other through their eyes. For that very reason, a direct look by a stranger puts us on guard, since the person seems to seek an intimacy to which he does not have a right, and we avoid such a look when we are circumstantially obliged to share are limited space (an elevator, a table), because we do not wish to nor do we know how to share an intimacy which the look would seem to suggest.

Beauty (masculine and feminine) is another of the essential dimensions of the body. Fascinating and seizing, it has inspired artists of all times and can mark the life of people and even influence the destiny of history, as Helen of Troy or Cleopatra teach us. Normally beauty is a good thing, but not necessarily, if one does not know how to integrate it harmoniously into the totality of life. A beautiful person always creates a special space around him: such a person attracts, arouses passion or admiration, causes contradictory feelings. That person has the world in his favor, but can also be turned into a mere object of admiration or desire and succumb under the weight of his beauty. Marilyn Monroe is not the only case. And the contrary occurs with ugliness, especially in the case of women. It can be a constant hindrance which, without any other profound motive beyond the merely physical, makes social relationships difficult and burdens life.[15] *Physical abilities* can also influence life in a way similar to beauty, perhaps in this case especially in men. Having reflexes, strength, abilities, standing out in sports, opens or closes fields of existence, shapes assured or aggressive attitudes or, on the

---

[14] Levinas has especially developed the analysis of the human face, insisting on its ethical dimension: "The face is what cannot be killed, or at least that whose *meaning* consists of saying, 'You shall not kill.'" (E. Lévinas, *Ética e infinito* [Madrid: A. Machado Libros, 2000], 72. English version, *Ethics and Infinity: Conversations with Philippe Nemo* [Pittsburgh, Pa.: Duquesne University Press]). See also E. Levinas, *Totalidad e infinito. Ensayo sobre la exterioridad* (Salamanca: Sígueme, 1995), especially 207-233. English version: *Totality and Infinity: An Essay on Exteriority* (Pittsburgh, Pa.: Duquesne University Press, 1969).

[15] On the special relation of women with beauty, both from a historical point of view and in our society, cf. G. Lipovetsky, *La tercera mujer* (Madrid: Anagrama, 1999), 93-180, and J. Marías, *La mujer y su sombra* (Madrid: Alianza, 1987), 95-105.

contrary, weak and shy ones, and on occasion (in sports stars, for example) projects the person on unique and privileged paths.

Clothing is another phenomenon – specifically human in this case – related to the body. We clothe ourselves to protect ourselves from the environment, but also for other reasons: to hide our bodily intimacy because we do not want our body, especially the sexual organs, to be visually available to anyone: it is the reality of modesty which has been lived out in all cultures.[16] And we also clothe ourselves to show who we are, to decorate ourselves and highlight determined aspects of our body, to seduce or to attract attention.[17]

Bodily contact, which is sought (not the uncontrolled bump), is very important because it places one in an especially direct and profound relation with persons: a caress, a kiss, cannot be substituted by any other type of relation. And despite being "physical" or "bodily" they are particularly profound because they allow us to mysteriously access the intimacy of the subject. One caresses a loved one and also those who have a living need for tenderness: children, affective and fragile, innocent and trusting. In addition, each part of the body has its own meaning. It does not have the same meaning to kiss on the lips as it does to kiss the forehead or the cheek; in turn, there are different ways to kiss: affectionately, delicately, passionately, with indifference or with betrayal, like Judas. The importance of bodily contact can also painfully be seen when it is not desired but imposed. The drama of a beating, of a rape, affects not just the body but the soul.

All of these aspects, and others which could be added, have their reflection in what is called *body language*. Through the body we communicate an infinity of non-verbal messages: disquiet, unease, rejection or attraction. It is a type of message sometimes surer than words, since, in certain circumstances, it is more difficult for the body to lie than for the mind. We have all had the experience of seeing a person who lies blush or another person who says he is calm, but who nervously moves their hands or legs. An especially beautiful manifestation of body language is dance (*danza*), in which the beauty of the body and its ability to communicate are unfolded in artistic unification. Dancing (*baile*) is more the result of an expressive need and is united to music: the joy of moving, of feeling alive, dynamic and free, of experiencing one's own body and being able to dominate it, to attract a man or a woman through bodily movements, are some of the elements which dancing puts in play in a singular way.

---

[16] On the interpretation of shame, cf. K. Wojtyła, *Amor y responsabilidad*, 213-235.
[17] Cf. the suggestive essay by Marañón on the cultural function of clothing in G. Marañón, *Vocación y ética y otros ensayos* (Madrid: Espasa-Calpe, 1981).

Finally, a very important aspect in the anthropology of the body is the *differentiation between the man's body and the woman's body*.

1) The man's body and the woman's body *are profoundly different*, not just superficially. We are different, not just in size, strength or sexual organs, but in bone structure, hormonal activity, the characteristics of the hair, motor coordination ability and the localization of the center of gravity. Therefore, bodily dimensions and actions – beauty, sexuality, physical ability, the meaning of determined gestures or actions – do not have the same value nor do they mean the same in a man or in a woman.[18]

2) But there is still more. Not only do the body and determined bodily actions and dimensions differ in the case of man and woman, but *the overall relation with one's own body is different*. Man's relation with his body is more *instrumental*: he usually employs his body to do things, he wants it to work well, to be in condition, to not fail, but he is not very concerned about it nor does he observe it at length nor does he analyze it in detail. He dedicates to it the energy necessary for its good functioning and an adequate presentation.

Woman, however, *identifies more with her body*. There is a physical basis linked to sexuality that imposes this inevitably. Menstruation, with its corresponding hormonal activity and the consequences that it unleashes, affects and alters woman's body each month; pregnancy modifies her corporeally in an essential way, both externally and internally. But it is not just a hormonal issue; rather, it is an anthropological one: woman, so to speak, is her body to a greater extent and thus dedicates so much attention and care to each and every one of its parts, since it is dedication to herself, something which, if a man did it, would be seen as a waste of time or as extravagance. And perhaps, in conclusion, the most illustrative example of all is the relative importance of beauty in man and in woman. In both it is important, but in the case of woman it is more decisive and relevant both for her personal self-esteem and for her possibilities for social relations.

---

[18] Cf. J. Marías, *Antropología metafísica*, Ch. XIX y XX.

Chapter 3

Sensibility and Tendencies

Sensibility and tendencies are the next personal structures that we will analyze. The main mission of these two structures is to establish the basic interactions of persons and their environment. Sensibility permits a first cognitive type of access to the world and affects a primary elaboration of these perceptual acquisitions in the interior of the person. Sensation, perception, memory and imagination are their basic components. Tendencies are our most basic reaction to the world that sensibility reveals to us. Explaining both of these capacities is the objective of this chapter.

3.1 Sensation and Perception[1]

a) Sensation

a.1) The Concept and Characterization of the Senses

Sensation is the primary element in our grasping the world, as the atom of knowledge; to see a color, to hear a sound, to feel the hardness of a rock. The act of sensing is not something purely physical, but subjective, because what does the sensing is the subject, but sensing depends directly and totally on the material or physical reality. It does not exist without it. The sensations are associated with the senses, the faculties with which we grasp sensations. As is well known, there are five senses: touch, taste, olfaction, hearing and sight. Each one of these permits us to grasp essential and unitary dimensions of the physical world: colors, sound, the texture of objects, etc. They are, then, our first element of connection with reality.[2]

Many classifications of the senses have been made in relation to their importance, their utility, their ontological status, etc. One of these divides them into two classes: the "objective" senses, that is, vision and hearing, and

---

[1] Regarding this entire question, both from a psychological and from a philosophical point of view, see J. L. Pinillos, *Principios de psicología* (18th ed.) (Madrid: Alianza, 1994), 107-217. From a strictly psychological point of view, a useful text is J. Beltrán, *Para comprender la psicología* (6th ed.) (Estella: Verbo Divino, 2000), 75-100.

[2] All human beings possess all the senses (except in cases of abnormality or illness, as in the blind and deaf), but their perfection or sensibility can vary enormously.

which are so named because the object toward which they are directed is physically *separate* from the subject, and because there is a greater independence between the two; and the "objective-subjective" senses, touch, taste and olfaction, which have to be in *direct contact* with the object in order to be stimulated. In order to caress a person, for example, I have to physically touch them, which implies a certain modification in my own body, something that does not happen, or at least not in so substantive a manner, in vision and hearing. It is for this reason that the sensations associated with the objective-subjective senses have a much stronger emotional charge.[3]

Julián Marías, for his part, considers that the *importance of the senses changes with the evolution of human beings and the individual development of the person.* In pre-civilized times it is quite probable that hearing and olfaction were much more important than they are now, and in the early phase of each human being it is clear that the most important sense is taste. The child divides things into those which can be sucked and those which cannot (because they are rough, coarse, hurting, etc.). With regard to adults, the fundamental classification of the senses is divided into two large groups: those which are essential in our lives: touch, sight and hearing; and the two remaining senses, also important, but much less essential: taste and olfaction.

With respect to touch, Marías explains that this is an essential sense because "it shows us the 'effectiveness of things'. As soon as the distinction between 'appearance' and 'reality,' between 'to seem' and 'to be' is introduced into the mind – and into lived experience – touch becomes the decisive element: what is real is what can be touched, in contradistinction to every illusory form or spectral presence. Everything that cannot in fact be touched, to the extent to which it is effective, is imagined as capable of being touched, as 'tangible'. Touch is, therefore, the organ of possession, from appropriation with the hands to sexual 'possession,' or that other possession which is eating, and which implies, beyond mere 'taste,' the tactile taking hold of the food, which is grasped, torn, chewed, swallowed, and assimilated."[4] *Vision*, on the other hand, is what provides us with the context and organization of the world. Thanks to vision we know where we are, the world that surrounds us, how it is structured and also have a perspective that indicates to us the dimensions of things and their importance. What is important is situated in the center of our attention, what is less so is further from the center and less in focus, because

---

[3] From a physiological point of view, this is due to the fact that they have more interconnections at the brain level, and in consequence they activate more circuits and produce more stimuli at many levels.

[4] Julián Marías, *Antropología metafísica*, 107.

it is dispensable. Lastly, *hearing* "is the ambient sense par excellence. Sounds surround us, are perceived simultaneously or successively, are straightforward or confused, proceed from different directions and variable distances, but from no precise point." And, Marías concludes, "the vital dimension of audition is the human voice."[5]

a.2) The Psychological Process of Sensation

The process through which our senses are activated has been studied principally in psychology and can be essentially summarized in the following phases. Initially, the physical environment in which the person finds him or herself produces a physical stimulus of an electromagnetic, chemical or mechanical type that impacts and alters sense organs.[6] But not every stimulus possesses this capacity. In order to affect a sense organ it must exceed a barrier that is called a *threshold*. There are three types of thresholds: lower, upper and differential. If the stimulus is below the lower threshold or above the upper threshold the subject senses nothing. For example, in the case of the ear, the person never senses a sound with a frequency below 16 cycles per second or above 20,000 cycles per second. At the same time, the differential threshold indicates a minimal variation that a stimulus must have in order for the person to grasp the difference. If this variation is extremely small, the person will be unable to notice it.

A stimulus affects the sense organs through what are called receptors.[7] There is no commonly accepted classification for the receptors, but we can follow the commonly accepted criteria of Sherrington, who distinguished the following types: "the five classical senses form what are called exteroceptors, or senses open to analysis of the sensation exterior to the organism, but also some sensations from our own body. The group of proprioceptors is comprised of a disparate set of receptors situated in the muscles, joints and the inner ear, that tell the subject about muscle tone, bodily movement and equilibrium or postural relationship in relation to the ground, through appropriate kinesthesias. Finally, sensory terminals rooted in the viscera form

---

[5] Julián Marías, *Antropología metafísica*, 110.

[6] In reality, with greater precision one may distinguish between stimulus and object-stimulus. For example, the book we are reading is the object-stimulus and the electromagnetic waves which penetrate the book and, later on, our retina, are what properly constitutes the physical stimulus.

[7] This concept was introduced by Sherrington (1906) and, in a certain sense, what it does is amplify and modernize the classical Aristotelian division of the five senses, allowing for the incorporation of other sensations.

the class of interreceptors, responsible for synesthesias, or diffuse visceral sensations."[8]

These are the steps that the process of the psychology of sensation follow, but it should be noted, in keeping with what I indicated in the introduction to this second part, that this is in a certain way an abstraction, the result of isolating and separating an element of a process that is much more complex. In practice, there are few instances in which we are given a purely isolated perception: to see a color only, for example. Usually what occurs are complex perceptions, of which sensation constitutes only one element. We perceive a rose as a unitary and multiple entity simultaneously, and we perceive the smell of its fragrance, we distinguish its form and appreciate its diversity of color and shape. Sensation is there but it forms part of a cognitive process that is much more complex which – if we limit ourselves to the sensible part – is usually denominated perception.

b) Perception

Perception, as just indicated, *is the cognitive process by which we grasp as a unitary, integrated and stable form the physical and sensible elements which are provided to our senses.*[9] Although we may not in practice realize it, perception is very complex since it involves phenomena such as the identification of objects, the grasping of forms, the determination of movement associated with objects, etc.

Just as in the case of the senses, the perceptive capacity of persons is essentially similar but can vary in an important way. Someone may be entranced by the combination of shapes and colors of a sunset, of a forest in autumn or of a piece of music, while others can remain indifferent to them or not perceive their beauty with the same level of intensity. A more developed perception is a gift because it permits a person to grasp aspects of reality that are inaccessible to other persons.

As I have said, the mission of perception is to integrate, coordinate and stabilize the elemental data that the senses provide in order to have a unitary

---

[8] J. L. Pinillos, *Principios de psicología*, 133-134.

[9] We use here the term perception in this restricted sense, although in common language it is also used in a much wider sense which encompasses knowledge in which intelligence intervenes explicitly. Pinillos gives the following definition: "perception is, above all, the psychophysical process by which the stimulating energy is manifested to us as world" (*Principios de psicología*, 170).

and structured vision of the world. Some of the *laws* that govern this activity are as follows[10]:

- the spatial or temporal *proximity* of an element is a favorable condition for perceiving it as a part of a unitary whole;

- stimuli that share some similarity tend to cluster in perceptual structures;

- perception tends to give *continuity* to objects that may not possess it intrinsically;

- *common destiny*: stimuli that change together in one direction tend to be organized together. An example is the lights of an airplane against a background of stars at night. The collective movement of those lights allows us to distinguish them from the starry background as a different object;

- *the law of closure*: this is the tendency to close the spaces or distances of information as we can do, for example, in an incomplete drawing;

- *the law of figure-background*: this law is the most important one of all and indicates that we tend to organize perception by establishing a common foundation and to superimpose it on specific figures. The most illustrative example of this law is a drawing or "optical illusion" that consists of faces or a vase according to one background or the other. The drawing makes manifest that we can determine which is the background and highlight over it the complementary figure, but we can never see the two figures or the two backgrounds at the same time.

---

[10] These laws were discovered and formulated by Gestalt, a term used as the self-denomination of a group of German psychologists from the beginning of the 20th century which centered on the perception of the form, considered as something different from the mere addition of individual elements. See Juan Manuel Burgos, *Historia de la psicología* (Madrid: Palabra, 2017) 213-231.

These are some of the laws through which sensory data are structured and as a result, our image of the world is much more perfect and complete. Perception permits us, for example:

- to establish the constancy of size of objects. We know that a person maintains her size, even though as she moves away she appears increasingly small;

- to establish the constancy of the form of an object even when we see it distinctly due to the position it takes or for other reasons;

- to perceive space and depth, information that is not directly provided to any of our senses;

- to perceive movement;

- to perceive time through factors such as succession, the nature of a situation in which we find ourselves or the tasks we do;

Finally, considering now the perceptual process in general, we encounter something different from sensation. Sensations are, fundamentally, passive, while perception is not, and manifests a *constructive* characteristic of the human mind. The world is there but, as Piaget and others[11] have shown, human beings need to elaborate internal structures in order to grasp the world, and these mechanisms always involve some mediation that can later be strengthened through learning, the formation of habits, and intellectual activity.

A clear example in this sense is the phenomenon of *attention* by which perception selects the stimuli that respond to the interests of the subject and ignores others that are not interesting. Someone who likes music, for example, can quickly detect a song from among other ambient sounds while someone who is not interested in it may not even be aware that a song is playing.[12]

c) Some Reflections

Now that we have described the process of perception, it is time to deal with two questions of a more philosophical character that present us with some

---

[11] See, for example, J. Piaget, *The psychogenesis of knowledge and its epistemological significance*, in M. Piatelli-Palmarini (ed.), *Language and learning* (Cambridge, MA: Harvard University Press, 1980).

[12] Regarding attention, cf. J. Beltrán, *Para comprender la psicología*, 121-137.

difficulties: the objectivity of knowledge and what has been termed "the psychophysical question."

c.1) The Objectivity of Sense Knowledge

The problem of the objectivity of sense knowledge can be developed in the following terms: Does what we sense correspond to *external reality* or is it an internal modification of our senses? Because, if the perceptual process is so complex, might it not be the case that the final sensation that we perceive has little to do with the initial stimulus that triggered it?

Aristotle's response is that sense knowledge is clearly objective. This philosopher distinguishes two fundamentally types of sensible reality: *individual sensibles,* which can be perceived by a single sense (light by the eye and sound by the ear) and *common sensibles* that are perceived by various senses (as shape and movement).[13] According to Aristotle, the knowledge that both provide is objective, and responds to the reality of what things are. Subsequently, modern philosophers such as Locke or Descartes accepted this division but with a change in nomenclature. Common sensibles (movement, figure, duration) came to be called *primary qualities* while individual senses (color, flavor, etc.) came to be called *secondary sensibles.* And, while it was thought that the knowledge of primary qualities was objective, it was thought that secondary qualities were a pure creation of the mind: what we grasp was no more than interior modification of our senses.[14]

Which of these two positions is correct? In my opinion, it is Aristotle's position that is correct. My contact with the external physical world is established through the senses and it does not seem that there are strong grounds to doubt their essential objectivity, which can be confirmed both because we are able to adapt to our environment in an efficacious manner and because communication between persons confirms the intersubjectivity of these experiences. Moreover, there is no special reason to doubt the subjectivity of color and not that of movement. In reality, if our senses do not function well, we could never prove it, because we cannot "prescind" of our senses. They are our ineluctable point of connection with the physical world. Not even scientific experiments permit us to overcome this supposed "barrier" since we can only test the results of these experiments through the

---

[13] Cf. Aristotle, *De Anima,* III, I. As we see, there exists a certain analogy between individual sensibles and sensation and common sensibles and perception.

[14] Cf. R. Descartes, *Principia philosophiae,* AT, VIII, 322-323.

senses.[15] Lastly, another argument that usually appears with some frequency, that of errors, does not present any important difficulty because we can only know that we are wrong if we know what is the truth.

In any case, there is in fact a valid point in philosophers such as Locke, Descartes, and above all Kant: the existence of a *constructive* aspect in knowledge that implies, at the same time, some subjectivity and bias. A human being is not a mere mirror that reflects reality, but rather a complex subject who grasps the world through processes that inevitably affect the content of what is known and of what is felt.[16] Thus, in short, and maintaining the essential objectivity of perception, which is a fact or datum of experience, we can affirm along with Pinillos that "it is certain that, in and of itself, perceptual knowledge detects the organization of reality and does not construct it. But the fact that other psychic functions that are intimately linked to perception have the task of mentally reworking representations derived from perception makes learning and thinking rework this and confirms a constructive dimension that is impossible to ignore."[17]

c.2) The Psychophysical Question

The so-called "psychophysical question" arises from the following question: What is the relationship that exists between neural processes that are generated in our body by a physical stimulus and the final subjective fact of sensation? Or, in other words, *how is it possible that a physical stimulus can ultimately be transformed into a subjective sensation?* Developing this question can seem unsolvable and lead us back to the subjective vision of knowledge, which would not be something objective, but rather a construction of the human mind. But, in reality, this position proceeds from a *mechanistic* vision of both human beings and of perception, which is understood exclusively as a conjunction of physical or neural reactions connection to one another, begun by a physical stimulus and terminating in the brain. However, although perception is certainly that, it is also much more; is it a process that is realized *by the subject* in his or her integrity. Because, and it is very important not to forget this, the brain does not see, nor do the eyes see; it is the subject, the person, who sees. And, precisely because it is the subject who performs this action it can be considered as a cognitive

---

[15] Technical or scientific instruments allow us to *amplify* the range of our sensory perception, but they do not allow us to dispense with the senses.

[16] We will return to this same point, from another perspective, when we treat intellectual knowledge (cf. Ch. 5).

[17] J. L. Pinillos, *Principios de psicología*, 151.

and intentional process, and not merely chemical, physical or neural. The subject who senses and perceives, intentionally appropriates the world through organic faculties that receive external stimuli.

The question, therefore, more exactly, would be the following: How is it possible that the person can have subjective sensations from physical stimuli? The response is in part simple and in part very complex: because there are some organs that allow this to happen: the sense organs. What is the nature and organization of these organs? Are they merely physical? No. Not even merely somatic, however evident the physical-corporeal dependence may be. If I close my eyes, I do not see. But the senses are not only this; they have a psychological dimension that establishes – in a mysterious way, yes – the connection between the physical modifications of the world (or of the subject) and the person as such. It rains and I see the rain through my eyes, but it is not the eyes that see it, for they are nothing without the rest of the body and without the subject. The eyes are the mediators between physical reality that happens and the spiritual dimension of the subject, and it is from here that we can deduce its nature. *They are organic faculties of the person, that is to say, capacities of the subject linked to a sense organ.* If the sense organ fails, the capacity is annulled, but the faculty as such is not merely corporeal because in this case it would be unable to connect the spiritual dimensions of the subject with physical reality.

3.2 Memory

We may define memory as *the ability to store in some hidden place in the soul the experiences of various kinds that we carry out or which happen to us along with their content:* from sensations and perceptions to much more complex realities and structures such as scientific knowledge, language, and lived or affective experiences. Thanks to memory we can remember, that is, return something to mind and therefore, bring back in a nonmaterial way what has happened interiorly across the course of our life.[18]

a) The structure of memory

The internal structure of memory is complex, but, thanks to the experimental work of psychology, we have taken many important steps that permit us to understand the elements that are the components of memory. Concretely,

---

[18] A brilliant description of the memory is performed by St. Augustine in *The Confessions*, Book X, Ch. 8: "On the admirable virtue and faculty of the memory."

according to Atkinson and Shiffrin,[19] human memory is divided into *three related structures* linked by control mechanisms.

The first structure constituting memory is called the *sensory system or registry* where we first register (hence its name) all of the sensory information that arrives at our sense organs. In reality there is a register for each organ. The so-called iconic register (i.e. sight) corresponds to vision, sound to the ear, etc. In the sensory register is stored all the information that proceeds from the senses but it remains there for a very short period of time, on the order of one second. During this time, the subject has to perform a process of control and selection by means of attention so that the information moves to a second structure: short-term memory. The rest of the information is lost and unrecoverable.[20] This can seem negative at first, but it is necessary because, if human beings were to record everything they see, they would die soon due to the saturation of unnecessary information, as happened to the protagonist in a story by Borges.

While the sensory register can be practically considered as a mirror, a mere reflection of reality, *short-term memory* is a properly mnemonic structure in which the individual stores specific selected memories from among many others. In this memory, information undergoes, moreover, processes of elaboration through mechanisms such as organization, repetition, or recovery. All of these operations have as the common objective enabling the person to arrange this information so that it is available whenever desired, and to make best use of the capacity for retention. Short-term memory begins to decay in fifteen seconds to two minutes, and, during this period, the subject must also decide if this information is to be stored in *long-term memory*, the deepest, most complex and persistent form of memory that we possess.[21] If information

---

[19] Cf. R. C. Atkinson y R. M. Shiffrin, *Human memory: a proposed system and its control processes*, in K. W. Spence, *The psychology of learning and motivation*, vol. 2 (New York: Academic Press, 1968). This model is the most established one, since it has a solid experimental basis. Another model of memory has been proposed by Craik and Lockart, who consider that there are different levels of processing of the information which enters into the system, which are hierarchically structured. For a synthetic and precise vision of this whole question, cf. J. Beltrán, *Para comprender la psicología*, 181-199, and J. L. Pinillos, *Principios de psicología*, 385-405.

[20] Parts of information can, in any case, remain at an unconscious level and be recovered later by different procedures.

[21] Some psychologists consider that there are two types of long-term memory. *Procedural* memory, which stores habits and behavioral functions, like driving a car, on a long-term basis (memory of how), and *declarative* memory, which specializes in storing stimuli and other cognitive functions (memory of what).

moves, through repetition or other mechanisms, to this mysterious internal place of storage, it can remain there for days, months or years, constituting the essential basis for human activity. At the same time, it will always be in conflict with another typically human phenomenon: forgetting.

b) Memory and Personal Identity

The usual function assigned to memory is that of an *archive of information*. But, this being true, and precisely for this reason, memory is also essential in a much more important question: the formation and constitution of *the personal identity of the subject*. This quality is already manifest in the control processes through which the person decides – at least in part – what sector of information will be stored interiorly and will contribute, therefore, to the constitution of one's subjectivity and be a benchmark in one's future activities. Attention to what we like or are interested in, for example, will make some things be recorded immediately or intensely while that which is not may fall by the wayside and have no trace in our memory. From a different point of view, the voluntary effort to learn develops our long-term memory, permitting us to have more intellectual and experiential resources throughout our life.

That our memory forms a part of us is also highlighted by traumatic events. Some bumps or accidents block memory from a physical point of view but others can block it from an emotional point of view because the subject, not being able to consciously assimilate an experience, sends it to the unconscious or tries to cancel it out. This phenomenon, on the other hand, is not something exceptional, but is a general human tendency that can be demonstrated, for example, in the fact that, over time, it is easier for us to remember what is pleasant than what is unpleasant.

But the most direct relation between memory and personal identity is manifested in the fact that in the memory we find, not just objects or experiences, but *ourselves*, as Saint Augustine long ago indicated. "There too I encounter myself and recall myself, and what, and when, and where I did some deed, and how I was affected when I did it."[22] If we had no memory, we would not know who we are, or where we came from. As man is a temporal being, projected into the future and fleeing from the past, he needs memory to constantly recover what he leaves behind and thus establish a dialogue with what we were and, in some way, we still continue to be.

---

[22] Augustine, *The Confessions of St. Augustine*, trans. John K Ryan (New York: Image Books), Book 10, Chapter 8, 237.

3.3 Imagination

Imagination is the last component of sensation and is distinct from perception in many ways, but above all, in its distance from objects. Perception is a present knowledge that only occurs when the object is actually present. Imagination, in contrast, is a *representative* knowledge that re-presents or re-produces *an object interiorly in a way independent of its physical presence.* It is precisely for this reason that imagination is more diffuse and imprecise than perception and is subject, with greater ease, to error or deformation.

Diverse types of imagination exist in human beings and psychology usually gives the following classifications[23]:

- post images: these are not images in reality, but sensory experiences that continue for a time after the disappearance of the stimulus. An example would be the image in black that remains on our retina after having directly looked at the sun for a few moments;

- images of memory: this is the classical concept of a memory, the image we remember of something after we have seen it;

- hypnogogic and hypnopompic images: these are the images related to dreams, and, more specifically, phenomena of a hallucinatory type that are produced at the beginning and the end of sleep, respectively;

- eidetic images: these are more precise images, almost as real as perception, but are given only to some persons;

- images of imagination: these are malleable forms of memory that can move far from the original perception and that may or may not be subject to voluntary control.

There are also other phenomena related to the world of imagination. *Synesthesia* consists of a specific sensory modality that gives rise to a sensation of another type. For example, certain pieces of music, such as

---

[23] Cf. J. Beltrán, *Para comprender la psicología*, 239-244. It is a wide classification which includes both normal and special imaginative processes.

Vivaldi's *Four Seasons*, can awaken visual images. *Hallucinations* are false or apparent perceptions (perceptions without objects). The subject is convinced that he or she is seeing something that does not really exist. *Illusions*, in contrast, are incorrect perceptions, in other words, they manifest a distorted perception of something that is really present. Finally, the so-called *body image* makes reference to the idea that we all have of our own body, of its structures and dimensions. It can also be interesting to add that *not all imagination is visual.* We have the ability to reproduce interiorly not only visual images, but sounds, etc.

Of all these types of images, those that have the most relevant and habitual function in the course of daily life are those that are called images of memory and imagination. In these are rooted what can be termed *the anthropological functions of imagination,* which are, essentially, the following:

1) Images of memory are essential for the *continuity* of sensation. Although we may not perceive a rose directly, we can continue speaking about it and thinking about it because we have its image within us. They also allow us to "re-cognize" objects: if we have in mind the image of something (a face, for example) when we see it again, we will recognize it because we will identify it with the one we keep inside.

2) Imagination has, moreover, an important *creative* function (images of imagination). Thanks to it we can create new objects and situations, and even invent nonexistent worlds. The possession of a powerful and creative imagination is, therefore an authentic gift and an essential quality in professions such as those practiced by novelists, designers, screenwriters, inventors and artists. Two magnificent examples of the power of imagination are J.R.R. Tolkien's *The Lord of the Rings* and J.K. Rowling's *Harry Potter.* The authors of these novels created authentic parallel worlds, with their own laws, characters, territories and languages, capable of evolving in time without losing their internal coherence. This is only possible through a great imagination.

Imagination also logically has a negative aspect, that, if not controlled, can lead to living in an invented world that does not correspond to reality and that, sooner or later, can cause disorders in a person.

3.4 Tendencies[24*]

Human beings, in addition to their cognitive relating to the world, *also interact with it and transform it.* The human being is not a mere receptacle of external forms, but an organism which has needs and aspirations, desires and projects. Human activity is multifaceted, and we will explore it progressively. Here we will begin with the most elemental or primary aspect that corresponds to the dimension, also elemental, of knowledge that we have just studied. This aspect is the inclinations or basic dynamisms that we discover in ourselves and come to light through a cursory examination of our experience. Our body needs nourishment, has sexual impulses, has to be protected from danger when it seems threatened, responds aggressively to certain diseases, etc. What are the characteristics of these impulses? Are they similar to or distinct from the instincts of animals? What role do the cognitive-voluntary levels of the person play in them? What are the principal tendencies? These are the questions that we must unravel.

a) Animal Instincts and Human Tendencies

At the outset, and in an attentive analysis, it can seem that human tendencies and animal instincts are similar since, for example, human beings experience hunger and seek to satisfy it, just as animals do. But a deeper analysis quickly discards this possibility.[25] "The different features of instinctive behavior," Beltrán explains, "are: innate behavior (therefore not derived from learning), stereotyped (expressed through fixed and invariable patterns), specific (shared by all the members of a species) and unintentional (necessarily triggered in the presence of an adequate stimulus, in such a manner that, as we have indicated, it moves inexorably toward its consummation). On the one hand, instinct has a clear survival value and is easily satiated; on the other hand, when the instinct has been satisfied, it is more difficult to stimulate it

---

[24*] We translate the word "tendencias", used by the author to describe the basic dynamisms of the person, with "tendencies", even though we could choose others like trends, impulses or even inclinations. With this choice we want to show, in any case, that these dynamisms are flexible and not determined and automatic like those of animals (translator's note).

[25] Time ago, the instinctive explanation of human behavior prevailed in psychology (behaviorism), but currently it has given way to a more realistic version of the dynamisms of the tendencies.

again. It is evident," the author concludes, "that *in human beings there are scarcely any fixed patterns of action, as happens in animals.*"[26]

In human beings, in effect, practically all of our behavior depends on learning; a child must learn almost everything including things as elemental as eating or walking. Moreover, and as the result of learning, the concrete mode in which each person acts varies enormously from person to person and from culture to culture. Lions of all periods in time and all geographic locations hunt in a similar way, that is, they behave stereotypically. In human beings something different happens: hunting technique varies from person to person, from culture to culture and from one era to another. In fact, the majority of people today do not hunt; rather they obtain their nourishment in highly sophisticated ways that would be unimaginable to persons living two thousand, or five thousand years ago. Lastly, human behavior, even in those cases where it is a matter of material necessity cannot dispense with the will nor with intelligence except, perhaps, in the most exceptional circumstances. Hunger is an essentially biological need, but the human satisfaction of this necessity is always voluntary, which separates human beings and animals. An animal that is hungry always eats unless it cannot because it is physically impeded. Instinct is the final mechanism that determines its activity. In human beings the situation is different. A hungry person will tend to satisfy his hunger, but this activity will previously pass through a kind of checkpoint, the subject's decision, which can be either favorable or contrary depending on other criteria: moral, aesthetic, etc. These reflections lead us to the conclusion that the dynamic sensible tendencies of human beings are not instinctive and therefore we tend to use other names to designate them: inclinations, tendencies, impulses,[27] appetites,[28] etc.

b) Characteristics of Tendencies

Having considered what tendencies are *not*, we must describe their characteristics in a more positive fashion.[29] Their principal features, as already pointed out in the previous consideration, are the following:

---

[26] J. Beltrán, *Para comprender la psicología*, 157 (the italics are ours). The notions of instinct, inclination and appetite are studied in detail by A. Malo, *Antropologia dell'affettività* (Rome: Armando, 1999), 105-209.

[27] A precious analysis of why the human sexual dynamism should be characterized as an impulse and not as an instinct is offered by K. Wojtyła in *Amor y responsabilidad*, 57ff.

[28] The term appetite, which comes from the Latin *appetitus*, has as the linguistic inconvenience that it is used with some frequency in the sense of being hungry, rather than in the sense of an impulse.

[29] Cf. R. Yepes, *Fundamentos de antropología*, 43-44.

- *Plasticity:* human tendencies, unlike instincts, are flexible and varied. If we consider nutrition, for example, we see that people eat many different types of food that differ across cultures, following social rules that vary by time and place; furthermore, we prepare food, that is, we cook it, invent new dishes, etc. We satisfy our needs in a flexible and sophisticated manner that reflects something that does not exist in the animal world: the culture of eating and the art of gastronomy.[30]

- *Variability:* tendencies are not only flexible; they are also variable. This means, on the one hand, that tendencies can grow or diminish in intensity, but above all, that human begins can, in a certain way, *create or eliminate necessities*. A lion sated is a lion satisfied, and will remain so until it is hungry again. But for human beings the situation is much more complex: my satisfaction depends in good measure on my expectations and my customs. A poor person is satisfied much sooner than a rich person with an exquisite palate that is satisfied only by certain delicacies. Furthermore, I can make into a necessity something that really is not one in and of itself, such as walking a specific number of hours along a determined route, sleeping in a peculiar fashion or listening to the music of Ed Sheeran. The cause of this is the fact that they are sought in human subjectivity. Animals do not have, properly speaking, subjectivity, and therefore, their desires are essentially identical to and correspond to their vital necessities. But each person is distinct, and this means that, within a common framework, each person has different things they need.[31]

- *Open schema:* I have already alluded to this characteristic which distinguishes human beings from animals. If an animal is hungry or in heat it will seek and try to satisfy these needs in an automatic fashion. But in human beings this process does not activate itself automatically because the satisfaction of an inclination implies another aspect: the cognitive-voluntary

---

[30] The same can be said, for example, of the sexual impulse or of aggressiveness.

[31] Ortega has investigated the peculiar characteristics of human needs, both in themselves and in relation to animals. Cf. J. Ortega y Gasset, *Meditación sobre la técnica*, 17-41.

dimension that has the last word and that will decide how an impulse is to be satisfied or, more importantly, *if* it will be satisfied. I can be hungry but, if I know that I should not eat because I am on a diet, I decide not to eat. I can feel a strong sexual impulse on a specific occasion but, since I know it would be a wrong moral choice, I decide not to act on that impulse.

- *Necessity of learning and formation of habits and patterns of behavior:* One might think that an advantage of instinct is that it does not require learning. Ducks do not have to learn to swim and moles do not have to learn to dig. They are genetically programmed to do what they do. Human beings, in contrast, are genetically programmed for virtually nothing, and therefore have to learn practically everything, including how to satisfy our most basic impulses. This is a complex task that is realized only over many years, during which persons learn to establish stable patterns of behavior that become automatic and that greatly facilitate living. We can mention things as elemental as walking, eating, or the actions we engage in daily to wash ourselves. If we were to have to think each and every day how to do these things, our life would be exhausting and elemental. We would always be starting from scratch. Learning and the formation of habits and patterns of behavior free us from conscious attention to these laborious tasks. Some of these can seem exclusively mechanical, such as driving on certain occasions, but they always depend on the overall activity of the self, which intervenes if it is considered necessary.

Chapter 4

Affectivity

4.1 Introduction

The world of the senses communicates and introduces us to other worlds of personal reality: feelings and affectivity. With regard to these, we must first affirm that this is an *essential* dimension of the person. We cannot imagine a person without affectivity, without feelings; such a person would be lacking something fundamental, something that would make them less than human in a very profound sense. A perfect being, but one that did not have feelings would be considered lacking, truncated, inferior to us. This is a recurrent theme in science fiction movies (*Blade Runner* is an example) in which a supposedly superior robot strains to attain the "imperfection" of human feelings as something highly valued as it can make them more powerful or immortal. The replicants in *Blade Runner* desire to be able to suffer and to love, to rejoice and to feel sorrow, to be surprised or disappointed and it seems to them that these would be preferable to all the powers they possess if they could have these experiences. In the same way, we cannot envision a life without feelings as something desirable even if all of our necessities could be met otherwise. To feel, in the broad variety of possibilities included in this word so pregnant with meaning, is an essential key to our existence.

a) Philosophical Analysis of Feelings: Problems, Concerns and Distinctions

Curiously, philosophy, for centuries, has not given much attention to feelings, and even less to the nucleus that seems to be the key in which they are rooted, the heart, despite this being an omnipresent reality in our daily lives. The reasons for this are many.[1] The term feelings *signifies too many things* and, at the same time, philosophy has identified it with its most basic meaning from an ontological point of view: corporeal sensations or passing feelings seen as irrelevant, such as anger or melancholy. It has considered, and with reason, that such events are not very important in personal life and, consequently, has neglected them or has dedicated only a residual attention to them.

The philosophical study of feelings has also been impeded by an *inadequate focus*. Von Hildebrand has pointed out, for example, that philosophy has

---

[1] Dietrich von Hildebrand, *The Heart* (South Bend, IN: St. Augustine's Press, 2007), 3ff.

tended to study feelings as realities in themselves, separated from what causes them, and warned that to act in this fashion causes us to lose the meaning and importance of feelings. If I am suffering a deep pain or great sorrow over the loss of a friend, and, instead of reflecting on this phenomenon in a global way, I center myself in the sorrow as such, in the mere feeling of sadness considered in an isolated way, my affectivity is reduced to something subjective and irrelevant. My feelings, which were a reaction of my whole self in the face of a loss of someone loved and valued, end up being converted into a morbid fascination, interior, introverted and passing.

Another reason the philosophical study of feelings has been limited is that such study has *centered its attention on the possible deformations of affectivity.* A person's feelings can get out of control and give way to false and inauthentic postures. There are persons who exaggerate their feelings. Others have reactions of a histrionic type, an affectivity that is a reaction disproportionate to the circumstances. And others, finally, can fall into sentimentalism, the desire to feel for its own sake, in an uncontrolled dependency on feelings or as an introverted recreation in states of subjectivity. All of this is certainly possible, but it does nothing to help us make sense of feelings. That a reality can be deformed or exercised in a defective fashion is not to say that it does not have value and dignity, for if we reflect in this way, what can be said of intelligence or of freedom? Have not some committed great outrages thanks to these? Yet intelligence and freedom do not cease to be extremely worthy and relevant.

Feelings present, furthermore, additional problems: *they are fluid and variable.* In the face of realities such as the body or freedom, affectivity presents us with a variable and turbulent force, which makes it difficult to understand to the point that it has been said, somewhat sarcastically that "the whole world knows something about emotions, but no one knows exactly what." The problem of developing a classification of feelings is a good demonstration of the difficulty that presents itself in attempting to make a rational and systematic description of this human dimension. The difficulty is also reflected in the multiplicity of words that are used to describe feelings and the lack of precision in each of these: emotion, passion, commotion, feelings, affect, sensation. These terms can mean many things according to the context in which they are used. And this is not so much a defect of language itself, but rather of the strategy that is employed in order to serve this reality. The semantic flexibility of the lexicon is precisely what permits us, in a way suitably adapted to the context, to reflect all or almost all possible emotional conditions.

b) Affectivity as an Autonomous and Original Dimension of the Person

The scant attention that philosophy had paid to affectivity for the reasons just mentioned has had this result: the confusion of affectivity with other areas of human activity, and its undervaluation. This is clear in the case of Aristotelian tradition, which has identified feelings in a unilateral way with human tendencies. Aristotle, in particular, designated the term passion (*páthe*), "the movements of the sensitive appetites for the apprehension of good and evil, with some corporeal mutation of a natural state to an unnatural one," a definition that has two fundamental implications: 1) an excessive identification between feelings and tendencies[2]; and 2) the exclusion of feelings from the field of human spirituality and its confinement to the area of sensibility. Von Hildebrand has explained emphatically. "The abstract systematic thesis which has traditionally gained currency as being the Aristotelian position toward this sphere unequivocally testifies to a disparagement of the heart. According to Aristotle, the intellect and the will belong to the rational part of man; the affective realm, and with it the heart, belong to the irrational part of man, that is, to the area of experience which man allegedly has in common with the animals."[3]

This way of understanding feelings was modified in an important way by Descartes through his insistence on the *subjective* aspect of affectivity. And it is here that we come across a central point for the comprehension of feelings. It is clear that, according to the Aristotelian line, feelings are linked to the attainment of objectives and to our relation with the world, but the nucleus of affectivity is not in impulses or tendencies, but rather in subjectivity. Feeling is, fundamentally, living oneself, being aware of one's own intimacy and its many modifications and vicissitudes.

This connection between feelings and subjectivity led, at the time, to other very important consequences: the dissociation of feelings from intelligence and above all, from will. Affectivity begins to be considered as an *autonomous and original* reality that can be understood in itself, and not with reference to

---

[2] Along this line, Yepes, for example, defines feelings as "felt tendencies." Cf. R. Yepes, *Fundamentos de antropología*, 57. Lyons makes a specific critique of this position, which does not prevent him from positively assessing Thomas Aquinas' and Aristotle's theory of feelings (especially the latter) and considers them basic points of reference of the cognitive current of interpretation of feelings. Cf. W. Lyons, *Emoción* (Barcelona: Anthropos, 1993), 50ff.

[3] D. Von Hildebrand, *The Heart*, 4.

other aspects of the person.[4] Affectivity cannot be considered a mere product derived from impulses or tendencies or will, it cannot be identified with wanting or desiring, but rather it is an originative dimension not reducible to the others: the experience of feeling, of emotion, the life of affectivity.[5]

These are the key points from which we begin our analysis of affectivity: autonomy, originality of the world of feelings, and the consideration of feeling principally as lived experience (*vivencia*). And, within this broad framework, following von Hildebrand and in part also Scheler, we can distinguish three essential levels in the affective world of the person.[6] The first level constitutes corporeal sensations: feeling cold or hot, feeling relaxed, tense or irritable. They are, in a clear sense, feelings, but at the most basic ontological level. In the second place we encounter what we normally consider to be feelings, which consist basically in psychological reactions: anger or fear, sadness or joy, sorrow or disappointment. And, lastly, there is that aspect of affectivity that reaches persons in the center of their soul, in the heart, and therefore has a strong spiritual character.[7]

---

[4] It seems that the moment of transition in which affectivity begins to have its own autonomy must be attributed to "Kant, who, influenced by Nikolaus Tetens, intervened decisively with his intellectual authority in the legitimation of a new taxonomy that added to the classical cognitive and appetitive processes, others that he designates with the name feelings (*Gefühle*). According to the new point of view, feelings cannot be defined by reference to knowledge or action." This new mentality, Pinillos continues, was developed and strengthened, ending with 'the declaration of independence of feelings that occurred in the eighteenth century." (J. L. Pinillos, *Principios de psicología*, 547-548). A very rich analysis on the evolution of feelings and their interpretation across history is offered by J. Marías in *La educación sentimental* (Madrid: Alianza, 1993).

[5] Cf. B. Moreno, *Psicología de la personalidad. Procesos* (Madrid: Thomson-Paranfino, 2007), chapter 4: "La personalidad emocional." "Feelings cannot be dissociated from their character as feelings. That is to say, they cannot be replaced by the will".

[6] For von Hildebrand we are using the aforementioned work, *The Heart*. For Scheler, the basic reference text is M. Scheler, *Nuevo ensayo de fundamentación de un personalismo ético* (Madrid: Caparrós, 2001), 444-465. This is a translation of his major work, *Formalism in Ethics and Non-Formal Ethics of Values* (Evanston, IL: Northwestern University Press, 1973).

[7] Lyons (*Emoción*, loc cit., 7-73) identifies four principal currents of interpretation of affectivity: theory of feelings, behaviorism, psychoanalysis and cognitive. According to this classification, the position that is adopted in this text takes basic elements from the first, highlighting the subjective character of feelings, and the fourth: cognitivism. A detailed analysis of the first two currents can be found in A. Malo, *Antropologia dell' affettivittà*, 9-57.

4.2 Corporeal Affectivity

The world of affectivity begins very close to the most essential and primary structures of the person: the body and the senses. And the polysemy of feelings already appears here. To feel hot or cold is, in a certain way, a feeling; so is to feel well physically, to feel awake, active, excited. These are real sensations that affect our subjectivity but that have a status very distinct from the experiences that we most habitually classify as feelings: fear, sadness, joy. Therefore, it is essential that we clarify this complicated terrain, circumscribing it adequately.

a) A Terminological Question: Sensations or Feelings[8*]

Above all, we must resolve a certain terminological question: which word most adequately describes what we are considering here: sensations or feelings? In reality, there is no response that is completely adequate. If we refer to "action" as such it is clear that we must use the verb "to feel" (*sentir*), for that is the term univocally employed across the world of affectivity, from feeling a pinch to feeling a deep joy. If, however, we refer to the "fact" which, therefore, requires a noun, then things change because we have two different words available: sensation and feeling (*sentimiento*). As they refer to psychological phenomena the question is clear: we must use the word "feeling." But, if we refer to the corporeal realities, the situation is made much more confusing. If I feel good physically, is it a matter of a sensation or a feeling? If I affirm that it is a matter of a sensation, perhaps this word is somewhat lacking. In contrast, in the face of very elemental corporeal sensations such as pressure on the body, to utilize the word feeling does not seem to make much sense.

As we can see, the problem does not have an easy solution, but, faced with the necessity of choosing, we have decided to use the term "bodily affectivity" (*afectividad corporal*) and to utilize the terms "sensible feelings" (*sentimientos sensibles*) and "bodily feelings" (*sentimientos corporales*) to refer to the realities that we want to encompass with them. In each case, what is important and decisive is to grasp the essence of the phenomena that we want to describe, independently of the name or label that we assign to it.

[8*] We reproduce here the reflections of the author for the Spanish language that can be applied, in quite a similar way, to English. In any case, and to avoid mistakes, we sometimes accompany it with the Spanish expression (Translator's note).

b) Sensible Feelings (*sentimientos sensibles*)

At the corporeal level there exist, fundamentally, two types of feelings (or sensations). The first is linked to sensations that are captured by the organs of the senses and with other bodily receptors and that integrate experiences such as pain and pleasure, hot or cold, kinesthesia, that is to say, the sensation of movement, etc. These are characterized above all by being *corporally localized and extended* and they affect the person through that mediation. It is not the Self which feels cold, but rather my body, and, moreover, and it is also felt on a specific surface of the body: on the hands, in the ears, or on the whole body because I am in the middle of a snowstorm without adequate clothing to protect me. Thus, as Scheler indicates, these feelings are referred to "the self in a doubly indirect way. We do not find them immediately adhering to the self in a purely psychological sense as, for example, sadness or melancholy, depression or joy, nor immediately filling the bodily I and adhering to it, as authentic bodily feelings do."[9]

Sensible feelings, moreover, are present, that is to say, they give themselves in the present and in relation with the stimulus that produces them. We can remember or recall them but they are by then other feelings. It is not the same to suffer pain as to recall pain; it is not the same to feel pleasure and to remember pleasure. In order to feel with the senses (*sentir sensiblemente*) the physical object that provokes them must be present and for this reason the feeling can only be experienced in the presence of what provokes it. Also, they are not meaningfully connected, or only in a very weak way, with other personal realities. Regret, for example, speaks to me simultaneously of a fact from the past, of my actual situation now and raises possibilities of action for the future. But the pleasure that is derived from a meal is something much more given and punctual, which is basically exhausted in itself without referring or introducing meaning in other parts of life. Finally, sensible feelings have little effect on attention. Joy or sadness seem to become distorted if the person focuses attention on their existence. Sensible feelings, in contrast (cold, sadness, pleasure), are less affected by increasing attention to them and, once again, the cause may be attributed to their proximity to the physical-material world.

c) Bodily Feelings (sentimientos corporales)

The second type of body affectivity is comprised of those feelings that can be characterized by *affecting the body in its totality and not being localized.* There

---

[9] Scheler, *Ética*, 450.

are, for example, sensations that my body provides me in certain circumstances and as a result of specific situations. I have just gotten up and I feel obtuse and fuzzy, unable to concentrate or respond. Or after practicing sports with intensity I have taken a warm and comforting bath and now I "feel" very good. Or, on the contrary, I find myself at the end of the day and I am tired and without reflexes, wanting to go to sleep to regain strength. These are all examples of bodily sensations-feelings, of situations in which my body finds itself and about which it sends an overall message that I receive immediately because, as we know, there is no real separation between me and my body. If my body "feels" a certain way I also feel the same way. Bodily feelings affect, therefore, the self, more than sensations, but not as much as a state of mind. The reason ultimately, is that they are, as von Hildebrand has written, "the voice of my body" but not the voice of my Self.[10] It is not the same thing to be comfortable or uncomfortable as to be sad or hopeless; in the first case it is a matter of an essential bodily situation, and in the second, of a situation of the self.

Different from sensible feelings, bodily feelings are characterized by their unitariness since they do not impact only a specific area, but are rather a global state of the body. It is precisely for this reason that sometimes they also give information about our environment that can merge with our bodily situation: the vigor of trees and the transparency of water flowing in a stream can unite with my vital sense and transmit to me the impression of bodily wellbeing and positivity.

Now, some final considerations on bodily affectivity. Both bodily and sensible feelings, despite having a mainly organic dimension, cannot be identified with animal-like sensations. "It would be completely erroneous to believe that human bodily feelings are the same as those of animals. For the bodily pains, pleasures, and instincts that a person experiences display a radically different character from that of animal. Bodily feelings and urges in man are certainly not spiritual experiences, but they are definitely personal experiences."[11]

On the other hand, we have seen that both types of feelings influence the person, but there are situations in which *this influence can be especially important* and difficult to control.

The first can happen in some individuals who can have *an excessive dependency on sensations* such as panic or pain or need special conditions in order to work with a minimum of concentration because each small

---

[10] D. von Hildebrand, *The Heart*, 23.
[11] Ibid.

movement or noise distracts them. These reactions are rare but can also occur in normal persons when they are placed in extraordinary conditions such as particularly painful illnesses or in cases of torture in which the pain can become unbearable and completely dominate the person.

The second case of dependency occurs when certain bodily changes induce a *psychological change* without the person coming to realize that the origin of the change is not psychological but bodily. This can happen, for example, in things as elemental as changes in atmospheric pressure that can induce in us specific states of mind: depression, bad humor, or in contrast, elation. In these cases, it is important to detect the cause to avoid situations of confusion or helplessness since the person can begin to inquire why they are in that state and, by not finding a psychological reason, cause a mental problem or exacerbate the situation in which he is found.

4.3 Psychological Affectivity

a) Emotions, Feelings and Passions

We have already mentioned the terminological problem that develops for bodily affectivity. Now, we must face the same problem for psychic affectivity, although here the question is somewhat different. Previously we were led to the convenience or inconvenience of using the verb *to feel*, now the problem is that there are quite a few words that can be used in this field – emotion, feeling, affect, commotion, passion, etc., which makes it necessary to determine with some precision the meaning before entering into a detailed anthropological analysis. In this text, and drawing in part on the dictionary of the Royal Spanish Academy (RAE), we have integrated *the principal elements of psychological affectivity into three principal categories: emotion, feelings and passions.*[12]

According to the dictionary of the Royal Spanish Academy, an emotion is a "state of mind produced by impressions of the senses, ideas or memories that frequently are translated into gestures, attitudes and other forms of expression." More specifically, we will understand emotion as *a subjective, lived experience possessing a specific intensity, present character and obvious physiological manifestations*. If I am given some bad news, for example, I am

---

[12] This categorization is complex and semantically questionable (one could perhaps use other words in order to indicate the same realities) but *its fundamental objective is to establish some basic phenomenological categories able to minimally discriminate the world of affectivity*. A different option, for example, is that of Lyons, who considers emotion the general condition of the person while reserving the word feeling for subjective experience.

moved, my pulse and my heart rate accelerate, I become tense, etc. However, over time (short or long) the emotion as such disappears or loses intensity, and in some cases gives way to a deeper, interior and more stable sensation: a feeling. Emotion, moreover, by being a reaction to an event, is intentional, that is to say, it exists in relation to the object that provoked and caused it.[13]

Feeling is different from emotion in that it is more persistent, deeper and more spiritual, and its external manifestation is much weaker.[14*] It is a *habitual* state of soul, of the self, rather than a reaction before something that happens to us. Joy, for example, is above all a feeling, rather than an emotion. I am joyful as a stable situation, not as a briefer emotional response. And this is manifested in my attitude, serene, confident and happy but not strident. Feeling is also different from emotion in that its intentionality is less strong, which is not to say that it does not exist. But it is a matter of a state of soul (and not of a reaction), its relation with the object that causes it is much more indirect. Moreover, on other occasions, it is the result of many causes, which makes it much more difficult to identify. In fact, sometimes we realize that we are sad but do not know why, and must make an effort in introspection and a retrospective analysis in order to identify the causes.

In any case, *the difference between emotion and feeling is not as clear as it might seem.* It is clear that true joy, for example, is usually given as a state of soul. But there are also times in which we feel a great, intense joy, and in this case it shares the characteristics of emotions: intentionality, physical manifestations, as jumping about, crying, etc. All of this means that, although we distinguish between emotion and feeling along the lines we have established, in practice, especially taking into account the complexity and turbulence of the world of feelings, it is never easy to establish a clear line between the two. For this reason, and for simplicity, in what follows *we will use the word feeling in order to refer in general to psychological affectivity*, and only when precision requires it, we will distinguish between feeling as a state of spirit and emotion as a more time-limited and specific affective reaction.

---

[13] "Feeling (emotion) is intentional, for you feel something, but its intentionality is very peculiar because, if it on the one hand designates the felt qualities of things, of the world, etc., on the other hand it manifests the manner in which the self is affected by the world. In the same experience an intention and an emotion coincide...in this way one could say that the objective and subjective moment of feeling are welded together." (J. Vicente and J. Choza, *Filosofía del hombre*, 239-240).

[14*] The Royal Spanish Academy defines it as "impression and movement that cause in the soul something spiritual," The reader is referred back to Burgos' anthropological model of person; these terms and the experience to which they point occur at the level of psyche, in the tridimensional levels of body, psyche and spirit (Translator's Note).

Lastly, *passion* (*pasión*) is the usual word in the lexicon of affectivity and some philosophical conceptions, such as Descartes', have globally identified with feelings. However, in contemporary language, we generally understand passion as an emotion or feeling that is particularly strong or disorderly. This is what is found in the RAE, which offers the following definitions: "Any perturbation or disorganized affection of the spirit," "very lively inclination or preference of one person or another," and "vehement appetite or taste for a thing." Passion, in short, is *an especially strong affective experience that possesses the capacity to sweep the person along after it.*

b) What Feelings Are[15]

b.1) Corporeality

In the first place, feelings have a physiological and organic component. If I am walking at night alone on a deserted street and I become aware of a motorcycle behind me, that begins to follow me slowly, my body reacts in a very specific way: my heart rate accelerates, my mouth becomes dry, my muscles tense and there are knots in my stomach. I am feeling an emotion (in this case, an unpleasant one), and a part of me, my body reacts physiologically. This reaction can have the positive effect of helping my response in the face of what provoked my emotion, and we can consider it, therefore, an adaptive reaction. But this is not always the case. If the fear that is generated inside me is excessive, it can block and impede any response. In a similar fashion, if a person blushes, what is usually achieved is to increase the embarrassing situation that produced this blushing in the first place.

Psychologists have attempted to establish whether each feeling produces some specific physiological reaction. There are some indications that it could be the case that some feelings are generally associated with specific body reactions. One who is angry, for example, can be "red as a tomato" while one who is afraid feels their chest heaving and a knot in their stomach. But, despite these indications, persons are sufficiently complex, so that in practice, *it is very difficult to associate specific feelings with specific patterns.* Even similar physiological reactions can occur in completely different feelings. For example, one can become as pale in fear as in anger, which means that it is not possible, in the end, to discriminate feelings based on their bodily reactions.

---

[15] Cf. D.G. Myers, *Psychology* (Worth Public Inc, 2011) and C. Castilla del Pino, *Teoría de los sentimientos* (Barcelona: Tusquets, 2000), 17-34. This last study offers very important reflections on feelings, but is mediated by the strong Freudian orientation of the author.

The bodily dimension of feelings has, moreover, another important aspect as important as the physiological reaction: their *outward manifestation or expression*. Feelings, as distinct from cognitive processes, can be characterized as being exteriorized and being expressed bodily. It is not only a matter of their being manifested outwardly through uncontrolled organic reactions as when one becomes red with shame, but rather, feelings by their very nature tend to be expressed. If I am happy, I will smile or laugh aloud or, if I am angry, I may sulk and adopt a particular facial expression. In the same way, if I am panicked, I can make many kinds of gesticulations: I may hide, or cover my face with my hands so as not to see what is happening, etc. Such reactions refer to body language, which we discussed earlier (cf. Chapter 2.3b). Covering my face when I am afraid obviously means an intention to protect myself, and a gesture of anger is a bodily transmutation of anger and the energy it possesses. Therefore, paying attention to the person's body can give us many indications of their mood states.

In any case, the relation emotion-bodily expression is not always straightforward.[16] Bodily movements (of the hands and arms, the back, etc.) do not necessarily have a univocal meaning and can vary across times and cultures. To strike the hand against the chest is a symbol of repentance in the West, and is used, for example, during mass. In Africa, however, it means the opposite: the exaltation of the self and the strength of the individual. With respect to the face, however, there is a greater universality of meaning that has been confirmed in experimental studies of adults and babies. It seems, in fact, that basic feelings (happiness, anger, surprise, etc.) are expressed universally in the same way so that persons from very different cultures can determine unmistakably the emotion that is expressed on the faces of children and of adults from other cultures.

Finally, in the relationship between emotion and expression, we cannot fail to mention the possibility of *simulation*. A person can simulate bodily feelings that they do not have in order to deceive those around them (or to entertain, in the case of actors). Therefore, if on the one hand it is said that "the face is the mirror of the soul", it must also be said that "there's no art/ to find the mind's construction in the face."[17] It takes a special sensitivity, an empathy, to

---

[16] Wittgenstein has interesting reflections on feelings and emotions and on their manifestation of verbal expression. Cf. Ludwig Wittgenstein, *Philosophical Investigations*, trans. G.E.M. Anscombe (New York: The Macmillan Company, 1953), no. 244 ff.

[17] W. Shakespeare, *Macbeth*, Act 1, Scene IV, 12.

get to know with certainty the feelings of the other person through their expression, something in which women seem to excel at.[18]

b.2) Inner Experience (vivencia interior)

The bodily reaction is, in any case, the reflection of something deeper and more decisive: the internal *experience of feelings*. Affectivity, as we have seen, is, above all, something that affects my subjectivity, my Self, and therefore I experience it as something deeply personal and intimate. Feelings have been defined as "states of the self" (T. Lipps) or "states of subjectivity," and this is probably a good definition, however desirable it may be to have greater precision that is not easy to attain given the elusiveness of feelings. I can be happy about some news that has been given to me (emotion), or over a global situation in my life (feeling), and, in each of these two cases, this fact produces in me a specific bodily manifestation. But what is essential in this situation is that it presupposes particular attitude and situation of my Self; it is *a state of my interiority*. To be happy means that I feel happy with the world, that the events that take place fill me or that I know how to face them, that I am surrounded by people who love me, or that I have just won the lottery, that is to say, that I smile at the world and so my subjectivity is confidently open to the outside world. In contrast, if someone suddenly scares me, I am shaken inside because my inner equilibrium is broken. There is something or someone that can hurt me in some way that I neither know nor can control, and my experience of this situation is the feeling of fear, an experience that, because of the unity of the person, results in a bodily reaction: I react with fright, protect myself with my hands in order to avoid what may happen to me, or scream.

Feelings and emotions are, therefore, and in different modes, *the way in which my subjectivity confronts the events of life and reacts to them*. For emotion, we have spoken of a circumscribed and temporary reaction, but for feelings, we have a more sustained response that constitutes a state of mind, and is, therefore, more persistent and enduring to the point where it may exert a determining influence on my personality.

The experiential (*vivencial*) and internal dimension of feelings gives them, moreover, an *intimate and internal character that is difficult to communicate*

---

[18] Body language, moreover, can affect the development of emotion, something referred to by Darwin in his pioneering study, *The Expression of Emotions in Man and Animals* (1872). If I give free reign to my anger, it can increase and exacerbate, but if, contrarily, I try to calm down (for example, counting to ten), my anger can diminish.

and that leads to a paradoxical situation. On the one hand, it tends to be communicated to others, but on the other hand, this communication is complex because personal experience is unique and intimate, and can never be transmitted in a completely adequate fashion.[19] I can show another person a chair or other object and discuss the objectivity of our knowledge based on an experimental verification of what we see but, how do I discuss *my* pain, or *my* joy? Even more so, how do I know, if I express what I feel, that others can really comprehend it or that I have described it in an adequate manner? The intimacy and the relative incommunicability of feelings creates, consequently, a mysterious, enigmatic and ambiguous world in which it is never possible to definitively hit bottom and in which uncertainty always plays an important role.

c) The structure of the Experience of Feelings (*experiencia sentimental*)

We turn now to another question. What is the place or role of feelings? How are they generated? What is the relationship that is established between corporeality and lived experience (*vivencia*)?[20]

c.1) The Theories of James-Lange and Canon-Bard

Independently, the American psychologist William James and the Danish psychologist Carl Lange proposed, at the end of the nineteenth century and the beginning of the twentieth, a first interpretation that, in principle, appeared to conflict with the rules of logic and common sense. For these psychologists, *emotion arises after the physiological changes* that are produced in the body; in other words, the stimulus is first, the physiological reaction comes after, and then emotion, which takes place when the subject becomes conscious of these changes. If, for example, I have to swerve sharply to avoid an oncoming car, first I swerve my car, and after this I become conscious that my body is completely tense and trembling, and after this, as a consequence, I feel fear and dread. The synthetic and paradoxical formulation of this theory was given by Williams James himself: "we do not cry because we are sad, but rather we are sad because we cry."[21] In its favor, this theory has, among other

---

[19] Castilla del Pino distinguishes two aspects in the expression of emotion: the appeal by which I try to achieve something and which ceases when the goal is reached (the cry of a child), and communication, by which I establish a two-way affective relationship with another person.

[20] See W. Lyons, *Emoción*, cit.

[21] W. James, *Principles of Psychology* (Dover Publications, 1950). James was one of the first psychologists, to the point that he is permitted to say, "the first psychology conference that I attended was the first of its kind."

reasons, the fact already mentioned, that physiological control can modify the entity of emotion. If I become calm, excitement disappears, but if I become excited, it increases.

The James-Lange theory seemed inadequate to many psychologists, among them Cannon and Bard, who proposed an alternative theory.[22] In the first place they argued that physiological reactions are not precise enough to be depended on in the determination of emotion. We have already seen that fear and anger produce seemingly similar organic symptoms, and on the other hand, it seemed impossible to maintain that all of the complex world of affectivity could be reduced to interpretations of doubtful exactitude about specific organic reactions. But, moreover, and above all, it was the experiential fact that emotion is not merely consciousness of a physiological reaction, but much more; it is an internal experience. For this reason, Cannon and Bard added to the physiological element a mental component so that the structure of emotion could be explained as follows: A stimulus produces, simultaneously, two types of nerve impulses, one of which is directed to the cerebral cortex and produces a mental reaction, and the other, directed to the sympathetic nervous system, produces an organic reaction. Both reactions had the same origin and were simultaneous, but they were not linked to each other. In other words, returning to our example, when there is a motorcycle behind me on a darkened street, my heart begins to beat faster and I feel fear, but one is not the cause of the other.

c.2) The Two-factor Theory of Schachter and an Integral Vision

The theory of Cannon-Bard was an important step in advancing the understanding of the structure of the emotional process but raised a fundamental question: what was the role of cognition? That is to say, did they have a sense that physiological reactions happen independently of knowledge of the situation of fear or were they rather the logical reaction of the organism in the face of this situation? Today, the general consensus is that cognition, that is to say, memories, interpretations and perceptions, constitute an essential part in the formation of feelings which, evidently, does not mean that one can prescind from the physiological aspect because both are mutually integrated with one another. Stanley Schachter was one of the first to formulate this position convincingly indicating that *all emotion is comprised of two factors: a*

---

[22] "This thesis has been demonstrated to be false, but at the time, at the end of the nineteenth century, it implied the recognition that feeling was not only the mental experience, but *also* the experience of the changes that the subject perceives in the rest of the organism." (Castilla del Pino, *Teoría de los sentimientos,* 23).

physical response with a cognitive label, that is to say, an interpretation of the phenomenon; and that both interact with each other.

How this interaction is carried out specifically is what is difficult to explain since it is the person as such who reacts to the stimulus and does so by activating all their powers and capacities. The structure that seems most logical is the following: in the first place, a stimulus causes a feeling reaction of the person but only to the extent that it is detected and known as such. If I do not realize that someone is following me then no reaction and no emotion is produced. Now, if I do realize I am being followed (cognition), a bodily and psychological reaction occurs simultaneously since both form part of the structure of feeling. I feel fear because I know that someone is following me and that because of this, I am conscious that I am in danger, and my body reacts physiologically. These two aspects arise as two dimensions of a single real emotion and at the same time interact with each other. Bodily consciousness of fear – my legs tremble, my heart beats faster – augments my feeling of fear, and if I do not control it, it can cause me to freeze or induce panic.

Furthermore, this interaction can be prolonged over time through elaboration of what are termed *secondary feelings or meta-feelings*. If I have fallen into panic at sensing the motorcycle behind me, and then it turned out that it was someone who wanted to ask me about an address, when I remember this fact I will feel ashamed and I will blame myself for my cowardice or nervousness. The primary feeling (fear) subsequently provokes a secondary or meta-feeling (shame). If, instead, I reacted with a cool head and with composure then later, when I remember the incident, I will feel pride or an elevated self-esteem. In either case, what is important to remember is that the meta-feeling is distinct from the feeling: the dread remembered is not the dread felt at the time.

d) The Affective Structure of Reality

Feelings are states of the self but not as forgotten or inalterable islands and they are configured according to the way in which subjectivity reacts to the external world. For this reason *they constitute one of the principle modes of connection that we have with the world*. We relate to the outside through knowledge, but we bond through affectivity and freedom-will. The lattermost represents and constitutes the definitive expression of our wanting but many times what it does is to activate desires of our feelings, of the *architecture of feelings*, of what pleases or is disagreeable to us, understanding this "taste or liking" (*gusto*) in a broad sense, that is to say, not as a mere sensory pleasure, but as agreement or disagreement with our subjectivity. Affectivity, in effect, largely determines what does or does not interest us, what we accept or reject, what we consider our own and what is outside the center of our interests.[23] This presupposes, in other words, that each subject, attaching to certain objects and rejecting others, affectively structures the reality that surrounds us, endowing it with subjective tonalities in accord with our preferences.

One may perhaps ask if this structuring is a positive or a negative thing (in the sense, for example of whether or not it subjectivizes reality) but this would be the wrong question. The affective ordering of reality is, above all, *a fact*, something we all inevitably do because it responds to an intrinsic characteristic of our personal being. As soon as the child is born, he begins to classify reality according to his preferences. Perhaps he likes chocolate but not milk, and these objects quickly pass from neutral to having an affective coloration that accompanies a valuation and a specific attitude or attraction or rejection. These simple objects will be followed by others more valuable and more complex (school, activities, hobbies, friends, etc.) until, in the end, he develops a subjective and affective criterion for ordering reality. In other words, the world, for each person, is affectively labeled in a unique way that conditions their activity.

It is important to emphasize that *this structure does not respond, fundamentally, to logical or rational criteria, but rather to affective preferences*, to taste, which should not be viewed as something negative, but rather as a property of personal life that introduces diversity and a-logicity into the world.[24] To like one person but not another is not something that can be (nor should it be) reduced to logic; it is of the affective and empathetic order, and it acquires its value and meaning in this dimension. In the same way, to like soft colors or bright colors is something that does not have (nor does it have to have) a logical explanation, rather it is situated in the field of preferences of subjectivity and sensibility. And the fact that feelings are distinct from logical rationality does not mean that they are irrational nor that reason cannot or must not say anything about them, but *rather that they are feelings and not reason*, in the same way that the body and tendencies are not reason. And that is why they also have a character of ultimacy and radicality in their own sphere. This does not mean, however, that the person should not sometimes go against their feelings (if they are incorrect or unrealizable, for example). It means, rather that affectivity cannot be reduced to reason or to simple tendency.

---

[23] Cf. C. Castilla del Pino, _Teoría de los sentimientos_, 55-59 and 75-96.
[24] D. Von Hildebrand offers in _The Heart_ a very interesting and deep catalogue of affective modalities.

e) The importance of Taste and of Education of Feelings

The necessity of educating feelings is born, fundamentally, of the impossibility of the architecture of feelings being the only and definitive criteria of the tastes and preferences of the subject. In some respects (perhaps in many), these preferences can in fact be considered unquestionable to the point that it can seem almost irrational to purport to question them from the external world. It would be absurd, for example, if a person *had* to like to go on vacation to the beach instead of to the mountains or that he *had* to like the color blue instead of red. But, this being certain, it does not occur with all preferences and affective attitudes.

There are, for example, *affective attitudes that are too much or too little developed*.[25] A person can have a meager affective register and be incapable of valuing the details of delicacy or of education. This is an objective shortcoming and a limitation for the person. And one can also have *ethically incorrect* affective preferences. I can like drugs, excessive drink or robbery but, however much I may like them, I must not do these things because feelings are not the whole of the person. And this means that, on occasion, I must act contrary to my feelings for the general good of the subject. Behaving otherwise would be to let oneself be swayed by comfortable and superficial sentimentality. Here, the role of intelligence is crucial, in that it shows the truth about the person, as is the role of free will, which makes the subject capable of opting for this truth against feelings that are perhaps strong but wrong.

Counteracting feelings, however, is a difficult task and even more difficult to maintain over time because affectivity is one of the decisive driving forces of life.[26] Our activity in many cases is done because "we like" (understood as taste, as we have said, in a broad sense) and, when this does not happen, we abandon it. Many sacrifices that we make are motivated by "taste." Maintaining a pleasing or aesthetic appearance often requires great sacrifices for many women, but they "like" to because they want to feel beautiful, and the same thing happens with athletes in their training, or with countless parents in their family duties. "Taste" in short is an important part of our life and we do not go systematically against it because, feeling it to be a vital necessity, systematic dissatisfaction inevitably produces important internal fractures: sadness, anxiety, depression, etc.

---

[25] Marías has lucidly warned of the risk that our society runs, despite all the potentialities it has to achieve a deep and developed sentimental experience, of falling into a primitive and superficial emotionalism. Cf. J. Marías, *La educación sentimental*, 273ff.

[26] This is especially evident in incendiary passions that lure people toward the object of their desires in a way that is uncontrollable, obsessive and irrational.

Does this mean that affectivity should be left to itself? No, it means, rather, that affectivity has its own rules and its own power and that, instead of direct confrontation (which, in some cases, is both necessary and inevitable) the most productive and valuable action is education (or reeducation if this is the case). It is necessary to educate persons to like what is good for them, what is affectively elevated and rich. In this way, affectivity can unfold with spontaneity and the person benefits from this unfolding. This task must be done principally in childhood and in adolescence because this is when the subject shapes and forms his personality. After this period, it becomes a case of reeducation that is much more difficult, though not impossible, because forming is different from modifying something that is already consolidated.

In the education of affectivity reasoning is very important because it shows the person the truth and the appropriateness of behaviors that are proposed, and it also plays an essential role in the virtues because acquiring them is attained through the practice of appropriate behaviors. But in this area it is crucial to note that the force of reason is limited. From reason and logic we can come to know what we should do, but this does not mean that these types of actions are "liked" or implicate the person emotively, and thus it is fairly probable that in the end the action may not be realized. In order to truly educate affectivity *what is fundamental is to get the person to experience adequate emotions* so that the person may be affectively attached to them and introduce them into the person's universal axiology. Only then can an adequate sentimental and psychological architecture be constructed.

4.4 The Heart and Spiritual Affectivity

a) The Characteristics of Spiritual Affectivity

There is finally, a third type of affectivity that is higher than corporeal affectivity and feelings and that can be called spiritual affectivity. This affective modality reaches the deepest levels, or the highest, of the person, and touches the heart. An attack of anger affects us and can even alter us in a significant way, but it does not move us or reach the deepest layers of our being. It remains at a superficial level, perhaps like a great storm that changes the surface of the sea but never reaches its depths. In contrast, the death of a loved one, of a friend, touches the deepest fibers of our being, but not through our intelligence or our freedom, rather through the other spiritual nucleus that persons possess: the heart.

In his phenomenological analysis, Dietrich von Hildebrand describes *three types of spiritual affectivity*.[27] The first is constituted by *affective responses to value*[28]. When a person is faced by a value, she can respond positively to this offer that the world makes to her, and then positively engages her affectivity and her heart. She responds to value not only with her intelligence and freedom, but also with her heart, and thus is united in a much more powerful way with the object that provokes the emotion because it is loved with the heart.

Second, spiritual affectivity arises not by our own action, but from feelings that arise in our interior from the *contemplation of the actions of others*. We see an act of heroic or valiant humility and our emotions, our feelings are "affected by" this action that the other person has done and in which we see a brilliant shining forth of human dignity. The reverse can also happen too. Atrocity and barbarism can carve a notch deep within us that shows us the depth of evil or degeneration that human beings can descend to and consequently, it troubles us and alters us in our depths.

Third, there are poetic and *aesthetic feelings*. These are, according to von Hildebrand, "an immense variety of feelings which play an enormous role in poetry. They are feelings such as sweet melancholy and tender sadness and vague longings. Again, there is the feeling of an indefinite happy expectation and all sorts of presentiments, and the feeling of the plenitude of life. There are also anxieties and restlessness of heart as well as torment of heart, and many other varieties of feeling. A characteristic of this wide assortment of feelings is that they are not formally intentional. They do not respond to an object. Nevertheless, they have an inner relation to the objective world and are mostly linked to intentional feelings as their resonance board. They have a mysterious, secret contact with the rhythm of the universe, and through them the human soul is attuned to this rhythm.

These feelings are all dwellers in man's heart. They are meaningful, and it is unjust to regard them as something unserious, or even something contemptible or ridiculous. They have their God-given function; they form an indispensable part of man's life *in statu viae*, reflecting the ups and downs of human existence – a characteristic feature of man's metaphysical situation on earth."[29]

---

[27] See D. Von Hildebrand, *The Heart*, 21 ff.

[28] A detailed exposition of Von Hildebrand's conception of value in D. Von Hildebrand, *Ethics* (The Hildebrand Project, 2020), Part I.

[29] Von Hildebrand, *The Heart*, 39. Although what we have strictly called feelings are situated on a psychic level in principle not spiritual, here we also use the term because of the continuity of affective experiences and the difficulty of pigeonholing them in a rigid way.

b) The Heart as Spiritual Center

The existence of this set of affective-spiritual experiences leads, finally, to the heart, the great forgotten of philosophy, as its center and root. It is very curious that a reality so present in personal and communal life has awakened so little attention in the philosophical world.[30] And this is most curious if we compare it to love. We love with the heart, but while love has been much studied (though not as much as intelligence) it has not been the same with the heart. However, it is clear that the heart is neither the will nor can it be identified with the self. The will indicates energy, tenacity, ambition, power, so one can have an iron will and an atrophied and deformed affectivity. And the self, which is our central nucleus, is not the heart either, something that is highlighted by the body references that we intuitively make. Our self as the center of decisions we instinctively place it in the head, but the heart resides in our chest and there is where we are moved for better or for worse.

What, more precisely, is the heart? We can understand it in a first sense as *the root of all affectivity,* as the ultimate source of our world of feelings. This description is correct, but what interests us more deeply is the heart as the reality responsible for spiritual affectivity, that is, as the nucleus of the most profound experiences of the person.[31] In this second sense, the heart must be understood as *one of the spiritual centers of the person* (along with intelligence and freedom), a center that, on some occasions, is the deepest and most decisive element of the self.[32]

This can happen, for example in *love.* We fall in love with the heart, a process in which intelligence and will are not decisive. There are no reasons to explain why we fall in love with one person instead of another, nor is it possible to fall in love through force of will. Love follows other paths, both dark and powerful, that drag the will along with it because we can fall in love with the wrong

---

[30] This has not occurred in religious tradition. The Bible, for example, speaks of the heart over a thousand times.

[31] The *Catechism of the Catholic Church* defines it this way: "The heart is the dwelling-place where I am, where I live; according to the Semitic or Biblical expression, the heart is the place 'to which I withdraw.' The heart is our hidden center, beyond the grasp of reason and of others; only the Spirit of God can fathom the human heart and know it fully. The heart is the place of decision, deeper than our psychic drives. It is the place of truth, where we choose life or death. It is the place of encounter, because as image of God we live in relation: it is the place of covenant." (no. 2563).

[32] "In man there exists a triad of spiritual centers – intellect, will and heart – which are ordained to cooperate and to fecundate one another." (D. Von Hildebrand, *The Heart,* 19).

person and we can also be incapable of falling out of love. Herein lies the incendiary force of passion.

The heart is also decisive in *happiness*. José-María Escrivá has said this in a beautiful way: "What is necessary for achieving happiness is not a comfortable life, but rather a loving heart."[33] With an iron will one can achieve wealth, power, prestige, but none of these are necessary for happiness, this is a prerogative of the heart. And the same thing happens in personal relations. In the I-you relationship, in the non-instrumental or professional relationship, but in the one that confronts us with the depth of another person and his mystery, the decisive thing is that hearts meet and are able to communicate.

This preeminence of the heart: does this mean that it is situated above intelligence and freedom? Yes and no. In human beings – as we have said – there exist three spiritual centers, intelligence, free will and the heart, which are configured or conform simultaneously to the radical center that is the self. These three centers are always present in each fully human experience but this does not preclude that, depending on the type of action or experience at hand, one can take primacy over the others. In the ethical dimension, primacy belongs to freedom because, as we shall later see, the capacity of self-determination is rooted there (cf. Chapter 6.2). But in other cases, as in love and friendship, it is the heart that is decisive. The heart has the final word. This may perhaps appear to be a risky statement but it is something that should not surprise us since Christianity has maintained this for millennia. Saint Paul affirms it without hesitation: "And now faith, hope and love abide, these three; and the greatest of these is love."[34] And, going far beyond this text, the statement of St. John stands impressive: "God is love."[35]

---

[33] J. Escrivá, *Furrow* (New York: Scepter, 2002) no. 795. In this author there is clearly a differentiated treatment of the will and of the heart, which can be appreciated in texts such at *The Way* and *Furrow*, which dedicate specific sections to each of these dimensions in human beings.

[34] 1 Cor 13:13 (NRSV).

[35] 1 Jn 4:16 (NRSV).

Chapter 5

Intelligence

5.1 What Does Knowing Consist of?

Intelligence and the correlative intellectual knowledge are one of the great marvels which nests in the interior of the person. Essential for our life, quotidian and habitual, it is, like all of the radical and primary realities, something difficult to explain. In a first approach, we may define it as the capacity the person has to go out of himself, transcending, in order to gain access to the world that surrounds him, understand it and possess it in an immaterial way. Indeed, through knowledge, in a mysterious but real way, the human being goes out of himself and "becomes other things"…without being them. "I am" the street which I see before me with its trees, its sounds and its cars, its backlights and its chiaroscuro. I understand it, I know it, I gain access to it and, in this sense, I possess it. The street is inside me because, if it were not, how could I know of its existence if it is beyond and I am not there? But I only possess it intentionally, immaterially, because, in spite of it all, I am not the street, nor the blue of the sky, nor the green of the tree. I am just a person who contemplates and knows. This is the mystery of knowledge.

Knowledge is not a quality exclusive to intelligence; we have already seen that sense knowledge exists. But, with intelligence, human knowledge acquires its plenitude and reaches the maximum of its perfection. What are the principal characteristics which differentiate it and place it above sensibility? There are essentially two.

We may call the first *immateriality*. To know something with the senses we must be in physical contact with the reality in question and, in addition, we only perceive its sensible aspects: smell, color, figure, etc. Intelligence, however, does not need physical contact to understand something; but, in addition, it reaches external realities in a much deeper way because it permits us to access *what things are, their essence*, their fundamental and primary being. If I do not have a rose near me, I will never breathe in its perfume; I have to draw close enough for the aroma to reach me. But intelligence does not have this problem. It would know what a rose is, even if all the roses in the world disappeared. In addition, neither smell nor color nor figure allow me to comprehend that I am before a determined type of flower which is a rose. I reach the essence of things only through intelligence.

The second characteristic of intelligence is *reflexivity*. Thanks to its immaterial character (relative independence of matter) it can return upon itself, that is, act upon its own action. We think about the fact that we think, or at least we can, while we never sense the fact that we sense. I do not smell my smelling or see my sight. But I do think about the fact that I think. For Aristotle, this characteristic was so transcendent that he defined God as thought of thought.

Immateriality and reflexivity lead us to affirm the *spirituality* of intelligence and of the person who sustains it, a spirituality which must be understood as a mode of being superior to corporeality or materiality. Through intelligence, I am capable of going out of myself and accessing the world, and of introducing it into myself without transforming myself into it. I understand, even though I have nothing before my eyes; I return over myself, defying the laws of extension and I encompass the world with my intellect, which can go wherever I want even though it is finite. This spirituality, however, does not imply a total independence from matter, since, as we have already indicated, the human being is an essentially bodily being and intelligence utilizes and needs an organic-corporeal basis in order to become active. Without a brain, there is no intelligence. But intelligence is more than the brain because the brain does not return over itself, while intelligence does. Thus, it is superior, it is spiritual.[1]

a) Knowledge as Light

Traditionally, and especially in rationalism and the Enlightenment, the symbolism of light has been used to explain knowledge. *Intelligence is like a spiritual light.* Just as light allows us to physically see the world with extraordinary perfection which includes the hues of the colors, lights and shadows, volume and distance, intelligence plays the same role in another dimension: it allows us to understand the complexity of the world with its richness and its mysteries, objects and persons, its elemental facts and sophisticated cultures.

Intelligence, in addition, is similar to light in the fact that *it does not affect the object of knowledge.* Light illuminates objects, but it does not deform or modify them; it is like a transparency which allows one to see, but leaves the reality intact. Its task is to highlight and illuminate it, so that the eyes can perceive and admire it. Something similar occurs with intelligence: it does not modify the object, because it encompasses and possesses it in an immaterial way. When I

---

[1] A good updated exposition of the mind-brain problem may be found in J. J. Sanguineti, *Filosofía de la mente*, 171-265.

know something, I do not establish any physical contact; I simply open myself to it in such a way that it comes to form part of me, but without altering it. From the perspective of light, finally, it has been habitual to consider intelligence as a fundamentally *passive* faculty (in contraposition to the will, which would be the active faculty), through which the subject by opening himself to the world, receives what the world is and what is in the world.

The metaphor of light is basically correct, but incomplete.[2] Thus it is necessary to complement it with another image: that of interaction. The symbolism of light places in perfect relief some characteristics of intelligence, but *it forgets the presence of the subject* who knows. In the cognitive process, the human being would be like a reflecting surface without subjectivity: a mirror which would perfectly absorb reality. Now, the problem is that this is not the real cognitive process. It is not a mirror which knows, but a subject who is affected by what he knows, who interacts with reality through that knowledge and who frequently decides what he wants to know and the way in which he wants to know.[3] Thus, it is necessary to introduce the symbolism of interaction.

b) Knowledge as Interaction

The paradigm of knowledge as interaction places in relief, in the first place, the fact that through knowledge the subject goes out of himself and opens to the world, which implies performing an activity which implicates *the entire person*. I do not know through an automatism of nature; rather, I know because I need, yearn and desire to know, since I am an incomplete being who needs the world around me – persons and things – to develop, perfect and enrich me. In knowledge, my destiny is in play and, thus, although I may have aspects of passivity, since I do not create the world, but rather find it, it is also *an active, complex and costly process* in which the subject must invest his vital energies and put into movement sophisticated strategies (studies, work, investigation, orientation, changes of place, money) in order to perform it in the most perfect way possible. This process, on the other hand, never occurs independently and individually, but rather it is mediated *socially* by persons, cultures and institutions which constitute the vital means in which the person grows and lives.

---

[2] A sharp criticism of the limits of the epistemological project of rationalism and the Enlightenment is offered by A. MacIntyre, *Three Rival Versions of Moral Enquiry* (London: Duckworth, 1990).

[3] "Reality is 'that which I find, just as I find it.' This means, in turn, that I am an ingredient of reality, that it is chimerical to omit the self surreptitiously when one speaks of reality." (J. Marías, *Antropología metafísica*, 151).

In addition, although the process of knowledge is immaterial, *the known objects modify the inner world of the person*, who should activate some type of response in the presence of them. There is knowledge which hardly requires interior adaptation (for example, quantitative knowledge); but, on other occasions, what is known (a truth, a person, a fact) can affect life in a profound and even decisive way. Then, a time of assimilation, of sedimentation is necessary. For example, living in a new country, with different customs and a different mentality to those of the home country can open endless questions and possibilities which must be weighed, pondered and calibrated in order to integrate them into the existential patchwork. And an affirmation, a theory which appears to be true but at the same time opposes one's deepest convictions, can create a grave interior conflict. And, in extreme cases, if there is a lack in the ability or flexibility to modify one's interior structure and adapt it to these new data, the subject may reject their very existence as a survival mechanism.

These examples, and others which could be added, reflect what we wanted to place in relief: the cognitive process does not operate only as light, but also as interaction. The principal reason is that *the knower is not a spiritual faculty, but a concrete subject through a faculty*, a subject who is vitally dedicated to that activity and has to integrate it into the entirety of his actions, objectives and desires.

c) Objectivity and Subjectivity of Knowledge

The presence of the subject in cognitive activity poses numerous questions, but perhaps the most interesting is the following one. If the subject intervenes in this process, does this not automatically put in danger the objectivity of knowledge? Or, in other words, does what is known not depend on the subject who knows?

The fact that the subject intervenes in knowledge is, above all, a fact. *The knower is the self, the person.* And this fact inevitably introduces a subjective factor into knowledge: subjects are different, see the world with different eyes and from different perspectives. How, then, may we safeguard the objectivity of knowledge? It is a very complex problem which has given headaches to philosophers for centuries and whose final resolution is more proper to an epistemology[4] treatise.

---

[4] N. T.: The original Spanish text uses the term "gnoseología". In Spanish, this is the term normally used for the philosophy of knowledge, while "epistemología" is the study of specifically *scientific* knowledge. However, since in English, "gnoseology" or "gnosiology" are not common, we have opted for the general English term for the philosophy of knowledge.

Therefore, here we limit ourselves to indicating some key points which allow one a glimpse of how the problem should be addressed. The points basically consist of finding an equilibrium between two possible extremes: radical subjectivism and radical objectivism[5].

In the process of knowledge we find, on one hand, the fact of objectivity.[6] With this we mean that the realities of the world have their own entity, independent of the human being, which we can know in its fundamental aspects without deforming it by our subjectivity. That this objectivity is a fact and not a mere opinion can be deduced, in addition to our firm conviction that things are in fact so, from the *possibility of interpersonal communication*. When we speak and communicate, we transmit to other subjects information about things or persons (intentional objects of our knowledge) that we have acquired and elaborated. That the persons with whom we establish that communication are capable of comprehending us and responding to us in a meaningful way necessarily implies that they are understanding, in its essential aspects, the same as we are, which, at the same time, implies that knowledge is not merely subjective (I understand something but from a unique perspective), but inter-subjective (others understand basically the same as I do) and, therefore, objective (things are, objectively, just as we know them).

Now, the fact that objectivity exists in knowledge *does not mean that knowledge is completely objective* or, said differently, that it is *exactly the same* in all subjects. And this, for many reasons:

- Each subject knows a *partial* aspect of reality which does not completely coincide with that of other subjects, beginning with something as simple as the perspective of a chair or of a person in a classroom.

- We have *different intellectual abilities*, and thus the understanding of the same reality is different and not just in what refers to the profundity of comprehension, but the

---

5 "Objective language only captures a shred of real life" (Martin Buber, *Yo y tú* [3rd ed.] [Madrid: Caparrós, 1998], 23). English version: *I and Thou*. Translated by Walter Kaufmann (New York: Scribner's Sons, 1970).

6 This point is key for the rejection of idealism, the philosophical vision which supposes, with different variants, that reality is a product of the human mind. This position has been criticized by many authors. Two particularly important texts are: Etienne Gilson, *Methodical Realism* (Front Royal, Va.: Christendom Press, 1990) and J. Maritain, *The degrees of knowledge* (Notre Dame, Ind.: University of Notre Dame Press, 1995).

content of what is understood. A person with musical sensibility can perceive in a melody aspects which another person would not even think exist, while the second person might be able to describe in a mathematical problem relations and virtualities unimaginable for others.

- There are *very complex realities*, with many facets (persons, theories, etc.) in which a criterion of objectivity cannot be applied in a simple way and which, therefore, are open to being understood from different points of view.

- One knows in a determined *social context* and, more concretely, as MacIntyre has insisted, in a specific *epistemological tradition*, which implies that each subject elaborates some determined guidelines of access to reality, in concordance with that tradition.[7]

All of this leads us to conclude, on balance, that knowledge is an objective process because it allows us to know things as they really are, but, at the same time, it has a subjective dimension, because it is the subject who knows and who intervenes in such important questions as the election of the field of knowledge, the selection of some aspects over others, the level of comprehension, etc. Expressing it paradoxically, we could say that it is necessary to maintain a certain dose of subjectivism in the human cognitive process in order to give an objective account of it.

5.2 How We Know: Integral Experience

Knowledge is a very complex process which begins with integral experience and develops through comprehension in a continual process of going and coming, always wrapped in the mystery of what is real.[8]

---

[7] From a systematic point of view, this topic is developed in A. MacIntyre, *Three rival versions of moral Enquiry*, and from a historical point of view, that is, analyzing different types of epistemological traditions and their evolution in A. MacIntyre, *Whose justice? Which rationality?* (London: Duckworth, 1988).

[8] We explain the cognitive process according to the path of integral experience which can be found synthetically in K. Wojtyła, *Persona y acción*, 31-58, and in detail in Juan Manuel Burgos, *La experiencia integral* and in *The Originary Source. A Theory of Knowledge* (in press). We should not forget, moreover, that the cognitive process is evolutive and passes through different phases before reaching its maturity, as Piaget demonstrated.

a) Integral Experience

The human cognitive process begins with experience, which is *the primary lived process of contact with reality,* our door of entrance to the world. With experience and through experience we appropriate what exists, which in some way comes to form part of us. Now, authentic human experience is *integral,* which means, among other things, the following:

- It is a *primary and lived* process. It is primary because it is the basic and direct mode of access to what exists.[9] It is lived because it is not merely cognitive; it is the human action through which our personal totality enters into contact with reality and appropriates it. Sometimes we experience new things (for example, a trip to another country) which impact us in a special way, but we are always experiencing because it is our mode of access to what is real.

- Experience is *simultaneously subjective and objective.* Two different types of experience exist. The experience of ourselves, in which we experience our inner world, which is subjective and unique. And the experience of the exterior world (of others or of our own body) which is objective, in the sense that it reflects something external to our subjectivity, which other can also verify. But these two types of experience always occur in the person simultaneously and in a unitary way. "The experience of anything that is outside of the human being is always associated with a certain experience of the human being himself. Because the human being never experiences anything external to himself without, in some way, experiencing himself simultaneously."[10]

- Integral experience is the path of *all* knowledge. Scientific experience is a part of experience, that which refers to the sciences.

---

[9] By experience, we do not mean here the knowledge of someone who knows something very well (who has much experience), as Zubiri does in *Inteligencia y razón* (Madrid: Alianza Editorial, 2008), 228-258, but, on the contrary, the primary facts which, accumulated, proportion him with that knowledge.

[10] K. Wojtyła, *Persona y acción,* 31.

- Experience is the result of *the combined activity of the senses and of intelligence.* We do not know first with the senses alone and later with the intelligence. The experiential activity is personal and, therefore, *the entire person always intervenes from the start,* with intelligence, memory, sensibility, in addition to the emotions, tendencies, etc.[11] For that very reason, experience is not a superficial activity, which remains in the phenomenon, on the surface of existence, as the empiricists thought; rather, it has an ontological scope. It reaches the nucleus of reality.

b) Comprehension

Experience is like the raw material which the human being needs in order to comprehend reality, but that material needs to be classified, organized and related in order to be able to be understood in profundity. We call this process *comprehension.* It is composed, in turn, of two fundamental processes: induction and exploration.

  b.1) *Induction:* experience is always changing, it never repeats itself. Both our subjective experience, regarding our feelings and our life, and the experience of the world and of things. No two experiences are exactly the same. Therefore, in order to comprehend it in depth we need to stabilize it, categorize it and universalize it through ideas or notions, such as dog or man, which allow us to fix its concept and refer to it in a stable way. The idea or notion "dog", for example, does not refer to any concrete dog, but to the essential characteristics common to all dogs. Thus, one can say: this animal is a dog and this one, too; that is, unite, relate and coordinate experiences. Notion are, then, "units of meaning" which surpass the multiplicity of what is real and play a key role not just in comprehension, but also in communication, since we can only understand each other if we have

---

[11] This is also Zubiri's position, developed through his concept of sentient intelligence: "Sentient intelligence is not a sensible intelligence, that is, an intelligence poured into what the senses offer it; rather, it is an intelligence which is structurally one with sensing. Human intelligence senses reality. It is not an intelligence which begins by conceiving and judging what is sensed." (X. Zubiri, *Inteligencia y razón,* 351). If this initial intervention of intelligence is not accepted, the most logical way out of the problem of knowledge is the Platonic way, which is the one adopted, for example, by St. Augustine: "the sciences do not enter the memory through the ministry of the senses, but rather they *come out* of another cavity deeper than itself." (St. Augustine, *The Confessions,* Book X, Chapter X). And it is also, in a different sense, Kant's solution.

cognitive schemes which, without separating themselves from experience, are inter-subjective and universal.[12]

b.2) Exploration or investigation. With induction we are capable of setting in place concepts or ideas, but life does not stop, and we accumulate new experiences which demand that we define those concepts, enrich them or relate them with new ones. To that end, it is necessary to return to experience, explore it and investigate it, checking whether the concepts or ideas which we had elaborated are correct and, if not, improve them and enrich them, and also elaborate new ones.

We see, therefore, that the process of comprehension is *a going and coming from experience to experience*. Integral experience gives us the content, induction classifies and organizes it and then we return again to experience in order to check its validity or continue enriching our knowledge.

One of the most spectacular results of comprehension is *science* in all its versions: scientific-experimental, philosophical, social, mathematical, etc.[13] Sometimes, one falls into the error of considering it to be a simple logical-formal construction, but, in reality, it is a very complex activity which implies all of the cognitive facets of the person: intuition, induction, judgment, experimental proof, etc.

c) Types of Knowledge

All persons have a similar intellectual activity, but, at the same time, *the intelligence of each person is different*. Psychology has established methods and tests to measure the intelligence quotient (IQ), but the difference does not only affect the intellectual capacity, but many other aspects. There are people highly gifted for determined areas which, however, are incapable of performing simple operations in other areas. Some people have a great ability for reasoning and other are very intuitive. That is, *there are different types of intelligence*.

The principal and most habitual distinction is that which is established between *theoretical intelligence and practical intelligence*. The first is principally contemplative; the second, operative, directive and creative. "The speculative intellect," Maritain explains, "knows only to know. It aspires to see and only to see. Truth, the apprehension of what is, this is its only goal, its only life. Practical intelligence knows in view of action. From the beginning,

---

[12] Cf. K. Wojtyła, *Persona y acción*, 47 and J M. Burgos, *The originary source*, for a explanation of "notion".

[13] M. Artigas, *Knowing things for sure. Science and truth* (University Press of America, 2006).

its object is not the being to be apprehended, but the human activity which must be directed and the human tasks which are to be performed. It is immersed in creativity. Its entire life consists of modelling intellectually what will be placed in existence, judging about means and ends, directing or even governing our powers of execution."[14]

But, in reality, there are not just two types of intelligence, but many: numeric and abstract intelligence, proper to mathematics; organizing intelligence, necessary to put businesses and projects in movement; theoretical intelligence, indispensable for the comprehension and elaboration of structured doctrines; aesthetic intelligence, proper to artists; masculine and feminine intelligence, etc. [15] This diversity is, moreover, logical, because, as we have been insisting, intelligence is not an autonomous and isolated entity, but a property of the subject.

Finally, we want to emphasize that one must *avoid the error of identifying intellectual activity with conceptual reasoning*, because the latter is only one part (although important) of cognitive activity. Performing abstract reasoning is a sophisticated way of exercising intelligence, but it is not the only one, and probably not even the best or the most perfect. Intuition, the knowledge which immediately understands the one and the multiple, the whole and the details, is much more perfect. In addition, this identification leaves out of intellectual activity those processes in which reasoning is not the most significant part. But drawing a picture or writing a poem, for example, are fully intellectual activities and, on some occasions, especially elevated and creative, and it matters little if there is not much reasoning capability, because that intellectual activity does not consist only of reasoning, it is also expressed and manifested in a sublime way in the contemplation of beauty or in technical and artistic creation.

5.3 Truth

a) What is Truth?

"What is truth?" The question that Pilate asked Jesus in the Praetorium before his Passion has been formulated by human beings of all times because the answer is essential. Truth is our point of reference and, if it did not exist or we

---

[14] J. Maritain, *La intuición creadora en el arte y en la poesía* (Madrid: Palabra, 2005), 87. English version, *Creative intuition in art and poetry* (Cluny Media, 2018).
[15] This view has become a common approach now thanks to the work of Howard Gardner, *Multiples Intelligences* (Basic Books, 2006).

were not able to know it, we would find ourselves questioned in our deepest roots. We would not know what to do or how to act. Pilate did not wait for Jesus' response and he went away. But Christ had already answered on another occasion: "I am the way, the truth and the life."[16] Truth was he himself, a person, although divine. It is a response that can orient one's entire existence, but, evidently, it is not a philosophical response, which is what we are looking for here.

What, then, is truth from a philosophical or anthropological point of view? The most adequate definition up to now has been given by Scholasticism: truth is the *correspondence between the mind and reality*.[17] Truth occurs when the idea that our intelligence has of an aspect of reality, and that aspect of reality, coincide; or, in other words, when our knowledge corresponds to what things really are. Aristotle explains it with great clarity: "Someone is adjusted to truth when he thinks that what is separated, is separated, and that what is together, is together, and someone errs when his thought is in contradiction with things... You are not white because we think you truly are white; rather, because you are white, we, those who affirm it, adjust ourselves to the truth."[18] This is the nucleus of the question of truth and the key element for founding the objectivity of knowledge. Human knowledge is objective because we can know with truth; that is, we can and really do know how things are.

All of this being true, the simplicity and beauty of this Scholastic definition should not mislead us. Truth is not so simple, or at least on many occasions it is not so simple. If it were so evident or direct, it would not pose the problems which it in fact awakens. It would be enough to recognize it and accept it. But we know that that is not the case. Truth is, on many occasions, difficult to reach and to establish; it is an *ideal* to which we aspire. Thus, it is necessary to go deeper into this question in order to not be satisfied with a solution that may be excessively simple if it is not presented with the necessary depth.

---

[16] John 14:6

[17] Cf. Thomas Aquinas, *De veritate*, q. 1, a. 1. There is a classical distinction between ontological truth (truth as reality, linked to the transcendental *verum*) and logical truth, truth as adequation. Here we will only refer to the latter because it is the one that has anthropological relevance. Heidegger's critique of truth as adequacy in *Being and Time* is interesting, but it does not justify its substitution by truth as revelation as he intended.

[18] Aristotle, *Metaphysics*, 105 1b 3-9.

b) The Complexity of Truth

We can address this problem by posing the following question: Is truth one or not? The correct answer seems to be the affirmative. If reality is one, truth also has to be one: things are in a determined way or they are not. Therefore, we will know with truth if we know things in the concrete way in which they are, which is singular. Truth, therefore, is one.

This resounding affirmation is true in an *ideal* sense, but we should nuance it in order not to fall into a simplistic vision which may be counterproductive. Things, for better or for worse, are not that simple, as is reflected, certainly in an exaggerated way, by the following poetic line: "nothing is true nor lie, everything is according to the color of the glass through which it is seen." What does this mean from a philosophical point of view? Let us look into it with some detail.

Above all, it is necessary to look deeper into the concept of reality. In an instinctive way, when we apply the Scholastic definition, we tend to imagine it composed of *simple physical objects* which do not pose difficulties. If there is a table here and I ask myself if there is a table or not, there is, evidently just one true response: yes. There is no room for nuances. But the problem is that reality is not always so gracious[19]. It is possible that it is not so simple to determine its exact color, although it evidently has a color, its origin or its chemical composition. And, if from a table we move on to *complex realities*, like persons or theories, the question becomes even more entangled. Is the Grand Unified Theory of physical forces true? Is the foreign policy of the United States correct? What is the best philosophical theory? What is freedom?

Faced with problems of such magnitude and complexity, it is clear that no one can claim possession of the complete and unique truth. And not only because these problems are inevitably addressed from a personal position that raises the question of interpretation[20], but because no one is capable, due to the limitation of human intelligence, to comprehensively address issues of this magnitude. Therefore, in most real situations, which are complex situations, the person will be able to arrive at *authentic but partial truths,*

---

[19] "In real life as opposed to the simple situations confronted in logical theory, one may not always be able to respond in a simple way whether a statement is true or false." J. L. Austin, *Cómo hacer cosas con palabras* (Buenos Aires: Paidós, 1971) 189. English version *How to do things with words* (Cambridge, Harvard University Press, 1975).

[20] See M. Beuchot, *Tratado de hermenéutica analógica. Hacia un nuevo modelo de interpretación* (5ª ed.) (México: UNAM, 2015).

which must be contrasted and completed with the authentic but partial truths reached by others.

Another aspect one must take into account when speaking of truth is the difference between *facts and actions*. Facts are, in their essence, irrefutable. It is unquestionable that the Real Madrid soccer team has won the Champions League twelve times. It is a manifest truth. But what is not so clear is what it has to *do* to win another one. Should it contract defenders or forwards? Should it keep its coach or replace him? Should it use the rhombus or the double pivot in its game scheme? It is complicated to respond well to these questions. To begin with, one must know about soccer; but, in reality, this is not what is crucial. What is decisive is realizing that, properly speaking, *just one true response does not exist* because there may be many paths that lead to the desired objective. The same thing occurs if we ask how to get to Santiago de Compostela from Madrid. There is not one unique true response, but many.

What is in play here is *the difference between practical truth and speculative truth*, a matter already posed by Thomas Aquinas and which, among others, was developed by Maritain: "For speculative knowledge," he explains, "truth is the correspondence or conformity of the intellect with being, with that which things are. But how could this be for practical knowledge? For practical or creative knowledge there is nothing preexisting to which the intellect can conform itself. The thing does not exist yet, one must put it in existence."[21]

This distinction also affects *the relation between a principle and its applications*. Principles are singular, but their consequences are not. The same principle can be put into practice in different ways, which does not necessarily mean that just one is true or correct. For example, two Catholics with the same beliefs may consider that they should act in different ways in determined social or political circumstances, and both are coherent with their beliefs.

In summary and to conclude: truth is one and consists of the correspondence with reality. This correspondence is, in some cases, simple and, in others, much more complex and partial, so that complete truth presents itself as an ideal to be reached. On the other hand, this characterization only refers to theoretical truth, since practical truth, which tells us how to do things, can be plural.

---

[21] J. Maritain, *La intuición creadora en el arte y en la poesía*, 162. Cf. Thomas Aquinas, *In VI Ethic.*, lect. 2, nn. 119-127; Cajetan, *In I-II*, q. 57, a. 5, *Commentaria in Summam Theologiae, S. Thoma Aq.* (Rome: Leonina, 1891), y G. A. McCool, *From Unity to pluralism. The internal Evolution of Thomism* (New York: Fordham University Press, 1992), 127.

c) Objections to Truth

Maintaining a balanced position regarding truth is not always simple and, in fact, throughout history some have opposed the notion of truth from different points of view. We will now briefly indicate some of them.

Skepticism is a position which denies that truth can be known. Total skepticism is a theory easily criticized because it is very difficult to deny truths about facts, especially about elemental facts. If someone denies, for example, that one can know with truth the existence of determined material objects, it is probable that we would begin to question the state of that person's mental health. But the question is very different if we face a more subtle and sophisticated skepticism which does not deny the existence of the truth of elemental facts, but rejects the possibility of reaching truth in questions like the meaning of human life, moral truths, the interpretation of history, etc.[22]

Skepticism applied to religious truths and, in particular, to God is called *agnosticism*. The agnostic is different from the atheist in the fact that the former does not deny the existence of God, but rather affirms that one cannot know if God exists or not. If this affirmation is made with honesty, it is a respectable position, since the topic is not banal.[23]

Relativism is a modality of skepticism which applies above all to practical and ethical truths. Currently, a very potent relativism exists on the moral level. It is not infrequent to consider morality as something merely personal, where universality and objectivity have no place: each person would have the right to act, above all in the area of sexuality, according to one's own ethical and behavioral rules. It is an erroneous position because it opposes the notion that human nature is common to all human beings, which implies, in turn, the existence of certain common rules of behavior.

d) The Search for Truth

Knowledge of truth forms part of the project that each person wants to forge of himself. It is for that reason that it is not something neutral which implicates just the intelligence: it is *an activity of the person* who requires specific attitudes in order to culminate successfully: a disposition to learn, effort and perseverance, attention, etc. These attitudes, which operate in

---

[22] An especially sophisticated version of skepticism is that of David Hume, *Enquires concerning the human understanding and concerning the principles of moral*, Chapter X (Oxford: Clarendon Press, 1927).

[23] An agnostic proposal (although it almost touches atheism) is that of J. A. Marina, *Dictamen sobre Dios* (4th ed.) (Madrid: Anagrama, 2002).

every cognitive process, are especially necessary when something particularly relevant is in play.[24]

Above all, in order for the person to really know the truth it is necessary for that person to *be prepared to accept it freely*, because otherwise the person will end up interrupting the process of knowledge or deforming it. A truth which is too hard, or which compromises us is like the light of the sun that blinds us. We instinctively cover our eyes to protect ourselves, or we look in another direction. "Why does truth generate hate?" St. Augustine asked. "Why does the man who proclaims the truth become for them an enemy, loving, as they do, the happiness which is nothing but the joy of truth? There is no other answer than this one: [...] they do not want anyone to deceive them, but they want to deceive. Thus, they love truth when it is discovered, and they hate it when it discovers them. The pay which it will give them will be to discover them against their will."[25]

When truth is particularly hard, an exercise of moral authenticity and personal commitment will, therefore, be necessary, which will lead the person not to turn around and look the other way, eluding reality. In other occasions, time and a slow process will be needed and, if we are accompanying someone on this path, comprehension. Other times, on the contrary, it will be necessary to confront people with reality because perhaps only that somewhat rough exercise can pull them out of their cowardice or their distraction. But, in any case, *truth can never be imposed* because the dignity of the person implies that it can only be accepted freely. Truth should show itself in its splendor for the person to realize that accepting it compensates him, because that is the correct path to orient his life and to grow as a person.[26]

A frequent obstacle in the process of seeking truth are *prejudices* which we may define as erroneous or unjustified convictions which impede us from approaching reality in an objective way. The psychologist Allport defined them as "an antipathy based on a defective and inflexible generalization directed toward a group or an individual for being a member of that group."[27]

---

[24] Furthermore, the search for truth is a collective process which can only occur in the framework of a community. The role of the social dimension in scientific knowledge has been emphasized among others by R. K. Merton in *The Sociology of Science: Theoretical and Empirical Investigations* (Chicago: University of Chicago Press, 1979) and T. S. Kuhn, *The structure of scientific revolutions* (Chicago: The University of Chicago Press, 2012).

[25] St. Augustine, *The Confessions*, Book X, 23-24.

[26] Cf. John Paul II, *Veritatis splendor*.

[27] Cf. G. Allport, *The nature of prejudice* (Anchor, 1958).

Now, it is important not to confuse prejudice (in the negative sense we just defined) with pre-judgment (a previous vision or pre-comprehension of a determined problem). We all judge what is new from the starting point of already acquired knowledge, but this does not necessarily harm intelligence. On the contrary, it is an entirely indispensable help. Otherwise, we would have to start always from zero, which would mean that we could never advance. Contemporary hermeneutics (like Gadamer and Beuchot) and also postmodernity have insisted a lot on this point, emphasizing against rationalism that it is not possible to face problems from an absolutely cold and independent perspective, without presuppositions, because the human being always understands things from the particular tradition in which he has been formed and from the mental structures which he has forged throughout life. "Long before we understand ourselves in reflection," Gadamer explains, "we are already understanding ourselves in a self-evident way in the family, society and State in which we live."[28] In conclusion, the problem is not posed by the previous presence of structures and knowledge, but by their possible deformation; it is then that they become authentic prejudices which block that access to truth.

In order to overcome prejudices, it is important to possess *a critical spirit*, that is, a mentality that leads us to go deeper and to pass over opinions that are well-established but incorrect or atmospheres of opinion which criticize events, persons or institutions without firmly founding their affirmations.[29] But it is also important to have an *open* attitude which allows us to grasp the positive aspects that are to be found in all doctrines and attitudes. A systematically closed and cautious posture regarding what is new or distinct harms personal development and leads, perhaps slowly, but inexorably, to an enclosure from the exterior world, a result of the rejection of all information that could alter one's own system of beliefs. In addition, that attitude radically impedes the elimination of prejudice, because all information which weakens

---

[28] H. G. Gadamer, *Verdad y método* (Salamanca: Sígueme, 2012), 344; English version, *Truth and method* (London: Sheed and Ward 1989). Eugenio Trías, *Pensar la religion* (Barcelona: Destino, 1997) has signaled the great importance that religion has in determining that *humus* of meaning in which we live and from which we think, and has criticized postmodernity, which accepts the narrative structure of intelligence but does not dare to recognize that a very important part of that narration depends on religious "revelations". For postmodernity's position, cf. J.-F. Lyotard, *The postmodern condition. A report on knowledge* (Manchester: Manchester University Press, 1984).

[29] A deformation of the critical spirit, in the sense in which we use it here, would consist of a systematic and preconceived doubt of everything, or in a twisted attitude that always seeks an ulterior reason behind what appears.

the prejudice is rejected before it can penetrate into the individual, since his system of defense identifies that information as a threat and eliminates it.

Openness, in any case, does not mean *naïveté* or helplessness. There are false doctrines and there are professionals in confusing others for their own benefit, a problem that has recently become extremely serious in social networks. For that reason, it is necessary to have an attentive attitude which may lead one to distinguish the true from the false or the deformed, and the hypocrite from the mistaken. In this difficult task, it is always useful to count on people of trust who can simplify the work for us.

Finally, in the path of the search for truth, our *personal truth*, which we may also call *vocation*, is especially important. Within the multiple truths that exist in the world, some mark our orientation in some essential aspect: profession, marriage, a decision of a religious type, etc. It is particularly important to find them, accept them and put them into practice, because there we wager our destiny. To reject a known vocation can imply an irreparable rupture in the fabric of our life and a weight on the rest of our days. To accept it may be, on the contrary, the initiation of a path of fullness. And it is here that Christ's emblematic phrase returns, although it seemed to have been discarded from our reflection: "I am the way, the truth, and the life." The truth, in its deepest sense, is necessarily linked to a holistic vision of life in which the religious dimension stands out (cf. Ch. 15.2). And it is also linked to concrete persons, because our existential itinerary is not constructed by objects, but by men and women whom we love and who therefore define our life. In the case of Christianity, both dimensions coincide.

Chapter 6

Freedom

6.1 What does it Mean to be Free?

Freedom is a magic word which convokes hearts. Who does not feel an interior vibration when it is mentioned? Or, who does not rebel interiorly before the possibility – even if only the thought of it – that the country where one lives could be invaded by a foreign power? Freedom seems to touch the nucleus of the person more decisively than intelligence does, and for this reason unravelling its deepest meaning is an inevitable task in understanding the human being.

But, what exactly does it mean to be free? What is the human mystery hidden under so valued a word? At first glance, it does not seem easy to establish it, since the phenomenology of freedom is very wide. Freedom suggests independence, openness, autonomy, ability to choose, power, want, love, will. I am free when I choose and when I can choose; I am free because my will is free; since I am free, I can love, and because I am free, I am responsible. Freedom is also openness to what is new, and it is lack of constriction: not being tied down by bonds or by material or spiritual chains.

What, then, is freedom? What is accessory and what is essential in such a wide framework of possibilities? What is the nucleus that may allow us to affirm that the centrality of what is human lies in freedom?[1]

A first approach to the idea of freedom is given to us by the notion of *openness*.[2] To be free is to be open and capable of interacting with the world in a quasi-infinite way in coherence with the spirituality of the human being. In contraposition to the fixism of material reality, the person is open to the multiplicity of what is real (cf. Ch. 2.3). Even his body, as we have seen, is prepared for this possibility. But this explanation, although not false, is too generic. It does not reach the depths of the question, nor does it satisfy our

---

[1] The valorization of freedom has been growing in the West since the Renaissance, but the apex of this tendency can be found probably in Romanticism, philosophically thematized by German idealist philosophy. For Hegel, freedom is "the most sublime principle of the new times," *Jenner Systemenwürfe* III (Hamburg: F. Meiner, 1987), 262-264, quoted in D. Innerarity, *Hegel y el romanticismo* (Madrid: Tecnos, 1993), 25.

[2] Cf. A. Millán-Puelles, *La libre afirmación de nuestro ser* (Madrid: Rialp, 1993).

expectations. No one gives their life for a generic openness. To understand in profundity the enigma of freedom, it is necessary to go further.

Another step is offered by the idea of *choice*. Freedom is choosing. I am free because I can choose, from all the possibilities which are presented to me, the one which I desire, the one that I want, because I, as the final absolute instance, establish it. Is the essence of freedom not here? At first glance it could seem to be so; freedom is certainly choosing and, the greater the ability to choose, the greater the freedom. In addition, I cease to be free at the exact moment when I cannot choose, when someone imposes his options on me or confines me in a closed space from which I cannot leave. But, although it may seem surprising, freedom does not fundamentally consist in choosing. Identifying freedom with choice means implicitly accepting that it refers *only to actions* and not to the person as such. But this is an error, as Max Scheler signaled: "'free' is originally an attribute of the person, not of certain acts (like wanting), nor of the individual. A human being's actions can never be freer than he himself."[3]

Freedom is, then, openness, but not just openness; it is choice, but more than choice. Where, then, is the nucleus of freedom? Karol Wojtyła has indicated it in an accurate and profound way: freedom is, above all and fundamentally, self-determination and, more precisely, *self-determination of the person through his actions*. Freedom is the ability that the person possesses to dispose of himself and to decide his destiny through his actions. This is the nucleus of freedom, its essential structure.[4]

---

[3] M. Scheler, *Zur Phänomenologie und Metaphysik der Freiheit*, Obras, I (Bern: Francke, 1957), 174.

[4] In the explanation of freedom, I follow K. Wojtyła, above all in *The Acting Person*, although some developments may be found in other texts, such as *El hombre y su destino* (Madrid: Palabra, 1998). De Finance has approached the idea of self-determination, but does not develop it systematically and ends up staying with the concept of "determined indetermination" *Essai sur l'agir humaine* (Rome: Presse de l'Université grégorienne, 1962). Mouroux, however, has understood the nucleus of the question: "Free will is just a means for freedom: *being able to choose is at the service of being capable of fulfilment.*" (*Sentido cristiano del hombre*, 195, and more generally, 195-257). Isaiah Berlin maintains a similar position (although he develops it above all in the political arena) through his elaboration of the "two concepts of freedom." By "negative freedom" he understands that human beings possess a determined area in which they can be what they want; that is, they are not subject to coercion, and by "positive freedom," the ability of the human being and of peoples to direct and govern themselves. It is "the freedom which consists in being one's own master and the freedom that consists in the fact that other human beings do not impede me from

6.2 "I want something": The Essential Structure of Freedom

The essential structure of freedom can be summarized in the expression: "I want something." Through freedom I, in the first place, choose an object, a "something" of the many things that exist in the world. But that "something" does not remain outside of me, but rather, it impacts my self and modifies it. More still, in reality, I am the one who modifies myself when I perform the action of wanting, when I introduce into the world the action "I want". Freedom, then, is made up of choice and self-determination, and since the latter is the more essential aspect, we will begin our analysis with it.[5]

a) Freedom as Dependence on One's Self: Self-Determination

a.1) Conditions of Self-Determination

In order to understand self-determination, it is necessary to take as a starting point a series of prior concepts: the first is *self-possession*[6]. Self-possession means that the person is master of himself, independent and autonomous, and is not radically at the disposal of another, but rather of himself. Self-possession leads to self-dominion – understood, not in a psychological sense, but in a structural sense – and both together make *intimacy* possible: I am my own, and for this reason, as a necessary condition for being my own, for possessing myself, I have my own space in which I live and inhabit, and in which I decide my destiny. According to Yepes, intimacy is "an *interior space* which no one can possess if the person does not desire, and in which I am, in some way, at my own disposition. I am independent, autonomous, I can enter into myself, and there no one can capture me or take my freedom from me. It is an inviolable interior space, which can be defined, then, as a *possessing of*

---

deciding as I want." These two aspects have a certain correspondence with the dimensions of self-determination and freedom of choice. Cf. I. Berlin, *Cuatro ensayos sobre la libertad*, 43-74, and 215-280 (English version: *Four essays on Liberty* (Oxford: OUP 2002).

[5] The question can be, and has been, posed as to whether will and freedom should be analyzed as separate entities or in a unitary way. In this text, following Wojtyła, we are not going to take on a differentiated treatment of will, but rather we include the dynamism of the will within the whole of free action through which the person self-determines. The reason is that the will's "I want" is identified in practice with the exercise of freedom. In the person there is no voluntary wanting which is not free. Thus, a possible option – it is the one that we have adopted – is to study both aspects unitarily in the mechanism of elective self-determination.

[6] "A person is someone who possess himself." (K. Wojtyła, *Persona y acción*, 168)

oneself in the origin, being master of oneself, and, in consequence, of one's own manifestations and actions."[7]

Torture consists precisely in the attempt to violate that intimacy, to break that self-dominion and that self-possession in order to submit the human being to another will, that of the torturer. But self-possession is so radical that strictly speaking is can never be broken. Cervantes said, through Don Quixote, "I know well that there are no spells in the world that can move and force the will, as some simpletons think; I know well that our choice is free, and there is not an herb or an enchantment that can force it."[8] But it is possible, however, to submit the person to such a degree of violence that either the person is incapable of resisting it and cedes to the torturers' desires, or the violence breaks the person's psychological structure in such a way that he loses self-dominion and responsibility from the point of view of their exercise. What is broken, then, is not the constitutive structure by which the person possesses himself, but the physical or psychological levels through which that structure is manifested and expressed.

a.2) Characteristics of Self-Determination

It is precisely that dominion of the person over himself that makes possible the essential dimension of freedom: self-determination. "Every truly human 'want'," Wojtyła indicates, "is precisely self-determination [...] and it structurally presupposes self-possession. In effect, one can only decide about that which one really possesses. And only he who possesses can decide. The human being decides about himself through the will, since he possesses himself."[9] Freedom essentially consists in this deciding about oneself, but that decision is activated in concrete actions. When I want something, I choose an option, but what I do is I fundamentally make a decision about myself: to be a professor or a journalist, to work, to rest, to play, to love or hate are decisions about the world, but they are, above all, decisions about me and my destiny.

One of the first consequences of understanding freedom as self-determination is that *it impedes understanding will merely as a faculty.* A faculty is a determined capacity for action, and the will is a faculty. But free will is not just that, but much more, it is the ability that the person has to determine himself as a consequence of self-dominion. It is not, therefore, a

---

[7] R. Yepes, *Fundamentos de antropología,* 160.

[8] Miguel de Cervantes, *Don Quixote,* Chapter XXII.

[9] K. Wojtyła, *Persona y acción,* 168. See also Romano Guardini, *Persona e libertà. Saggi di Fondazione sulla teoria pedagogica* (Brescia: Scuola, 1987), 97 ff.

mere property of the person's acts, and not even a property of the person as such, but rather a mode of being. Another important and at the same time surprising consequence is that, contrary to the more habitual interpretation, freedom does not consist in independence, but rather in its opposite, in dependence, but not dependence on the objects, but dependence on oneself. *The person is free because he depends on himself* and this is so because he possesses himself. "In the abstract, freedom is independence, lack of dependence. But, on the contrary, lack of dependence on the self in the dynamization of a concrete subject is equivalent to lack of freedom, the lack of its real foundation."[10]

Curiously, *the self-referential aspect of freedom, which is the principal aspect, has been, however, the most overlooked aspect.* "In the philosophical and psychological tradition, this 'I want' has been examined, probably excessively, from the point of view of the external object, considered thus in an excessively unilateral way as 'I want something,' and perhaps not sufficiently from the point of view of the internal objectivity, as self-determination, as a simple 'I want.'"[11]

Literature has sometimes also followed the same tendency, but not always. *The Lord of the Rings*, for example, is a marvelous hymn to freedom; to self-referential freedom as well. Sauron's ring, which symbolizes and incarnates the power to which all beings aspire, always imposes a radical choice: for or against the ring. But everyone knows that they are not simply choosing an object, but that they are facing something much deeper: the decision about their destiny: the shadows of Mordor or the light of Rivendel. To opt for the possession of the ring is to opt for darkness, but not only external darkness; internal darkness as well, because it implies passing over to the dark side, deciding that from that moment on, one does not just want to live in darkness, but, in some way, to be darkness as well. And opting for the destruction of the ring means, on the contrary, deciding that one wants to continue in the light, that one wants to be true, fighting on the side of truth, despite the suffering or the difficulties that it might bring with it.

A final question which it is well to indicate is that *the capacity of human self-determination is limited.* The human being cannot redo himself completely at will, because human nature is not modifiable: I cannot fly, I cannot live 200 years, I cannot cease being human. One could object that these limits do not have their origin in freedom, but rather in corporeality, which is what restricts my will's possible options. But this is not entirely true. Corporeality is not a

---

[10] K. Wojtyła, *Persona y acción*, 183.
[11] Ibid., 175.

weight on freedom, but on the contrary an inevitable means for its expression. I swim, I run, I think, and I live thanks to my body, which is, therefore, the conditional of possibility of my freedom. A different issue is that my bodily structure is limited and constrains me to a range of possibilities which I cannot go beyond; but, without that body, freedom simply would not exist. In conclusion, freedom is self-determination made possible by my personal structure (bodily, psychological, and spiritual) and, at the same time, it is limited by that structure.

b) Freedom as Independence of the Objects: Choice

b.1) The Voluntary-Elective Dynamism

Self-determination can be defined as the vertical dimension of freedom. The "I want" directed toward myself, which deepens and elevates my being, is in this sense vertical. Now we must consider the other aspect of freedom which, by contrast, we can identify with the horizontal dimension: I want "something," an object, thing or person, which is before me, in front of me and outside. That is to say, the choice.[12]

The elective dimension of freedom, although it is inseparable from self-determination, has a practically opposite structure. Above all, it is always *intentional*, that is, it is exercised over a concrete object. Whenever I choose, I choose something; a choice without an object makes no sense.[13] In addition, although it is free, it is free in a very different way than self-determination. Freedom of self-determination consists in dependence on self; freedom of choice, on the contrary, consists in *independence of the object*. I am free because no object, as elevated or beautiful as it may be, determines me to choose it. I choose because I want to. Wojtyła has summarized this very graphically in a phrase that reflects the interior experience that we all possess, and which says: "I can, but I am not obligated." No object can obligate me to act.

In contraposition, the effective choice of an object places into relief another characteristic of freedom: *its causal origin in the self*. A choice implies the causation of an action by which the subject freely directs himself toward the

---

[12] Classically, freedom of choice is divided into: 1) freedom of *exercise* (to do or not to do: the dominion over the action as such); 2) freedom of *specification* (to choose this or that: dominion over the object of the action). In freedom of exercise, a reference to self-determination may be intuited, but only slightly, because, in reality, the subject, the self, hardly appears in this classification which is centered on action and the object.

[13] Here, we understand 'object' in its technical sense, that is, as an external reality (*objectum*), not in the sense of a thing. Object is any reality that I choose.

object and appropriates it to himself in one way or another. And only if we are conscious of the fact that the action is produced inside of us, that we are its origin because we have caused it, do we speak of a free action. Thus, it is much more adequate to describe voluntary action as a *response* to a good than as a mere *tendency* to a value, because, although the latter description reflects a real aspect of the voluntary dynamism, it mutes the essential aspect: that it is a *free* tendency, that is to say, one caused by the will and which proceeds from the subject.[14]

The reverse of causality is *responsibility*. I am responsible for my actions simply because they are mine, because I have placed them into existence. Without me, they would not have arisen and thus I am responsible: they are *my* actions. Thus it is clear that there is no hiatus or separation between freedom and responsibility, but rather they are two sides of the same coin. To be free is to make actions arise from the self, and to be responsible is to recognize that those actions have arisen from inside me, that is, that they are mine.[15]

b.2) The Problem of Determinism

Curiously, although freedom of choice is a fact that we *experience* every day, there are those who deny its reality for different motives.[16] *Determinism*, in concrete, *consists in postulating a primacy of the object over the human being*. Taking as their starting point the irrefutable fact that we always choose for some motive, some philosophers have concluded that the human being is determined by the motive of the choice and, thus, is not free. Freedom would be a mere appearance: a self-deception without a real basis. There are different types of determinism according to whether one or the other cause is considered to be the determinant of the will: social conditions, the genetic basis, psychology, the pleasure impulse, etc. But all these coincide in the key

---

[14] For this reason, Wojtyła indicates that the description of the will as a "rational appetite" can present problems, since "the term 'appetite' in our linguistic meaning seems to indicate exclusively what 'happens' in the human being and that, therefore, it is not in the sphere of conscious decisions. For the same reason, the expression 'rational appetite' seems fairly strange, almost like an internal contradiction, which does not seem to occur in the Latin expression 'appetitus rationalis' due to the more neutral character of 'appetitus'." (*Persona y acción*, 193)

[15] A different question is the *ethical* attitude to be adopted. Despite being intrinsically responsible for my activity, I can ignore my acts in practice, thus becoming an *ethically* irresponsible subject.

[16] Hume, for example, rejects the idea of causality and with that automatically eliminates freedom. Cf. D. Hume, *Enquiries concerning the Human Understanding and concerning the Principles of Morals*, Chapters VI-VIII.

point: the subordination of the will to the object of choice.[17] An example: if I like sweets, and especially nougat, I am *determined* by them. In reality, it is not I who chooses nougat, but rather, in a certain sense, it chooses me. And the experimental proof would come from the fact that whenever there is nougat, I choose it. It is, evidently, a prosaic example, but we may generalize it consistently, widening it to the principle of pleasure and pain. A determinism which is based on this principle establishes that I will always choose what causes me more pleasure and saves me from greater pain.

Determinism was especially in fashion in the 19th century and at the beginning of the 20th, but it is now more a theoretical argument defended by few and with a scarce social weight. Therefore, we will only note the two reflections that seem most essential to us. The first point is that determinism is correct on one issue, that the object *conditions* freedom. If it is not Christmastime and there is no nougat, I cannot choose it. And if I am a glutton and they put nougat before me, it is very probable that I will end up eating it. The object conditions the choice, since I am inevitably influenced by the array of possibilities that I find or which I am able to access. If we return to Tolkien, we find that Sauron's ring and the power that it incarnates, determines and conditions the life of all of the beings in Middle-earth. Frodo, the small hero, strongly wishes never to have found the ring, and the wizard Saruman and the creature Gollum, on the contrary, would give their life to have it in their power. In any case, their life is marked by the existence of the ring, by its power and by its attraction. But the question is that, by affirming this, we have not even touched the essence of freedom. This is what determinism does not see and which, however, Tolkien reflects admirably.

The ring can attract almost irresistibly, but in this *almost*, small and imperceptible, is where the essence of freedom is put into play. Because, as powerful as the ring may be, it is not enough so to force anyone's freedom. It is each one who decides in the end, and Tolkien seems to indulge in placing each one of his characters in front of the ring: Gandalf and Galadriel, Bilbo and Boromir, in order to obligate them to make that decision. But no one is chosen by the ring; rather, each of the characters chooses it or rejects it through their own action which arises from the depths of their self and in which no one can substitute them.

Definitively, and returning to our problem, determinism is correct regarding an accidental fact, the conditioning of the will, but it is incorrect in what is essential, because it does not realize what is most important, that *the free,*

---

[17] See J. De Finance, *Ensayo sobre el obrar humano* (Madrid: Gredos, 1966), 257-295.

voluntary action proceeds from the person, because the person gives origin to it and *causes* it. In other words, the real cause is confused with the condition[18] and, by eliminating the causality, also cancels in one instant responsibility and morality. Isaiah Berlin has seen this point with special lucidity. If determinism were true, he affirms, it would be necessary to radically change our conception of the world as we know it, since concepts as essential as justice, freedom, morality, responsibility, etc., would have an entirely different meaning from the one they are normally given; or better, they would not have any meaning. Now, he adds scathingly, "the behavior, in reality, of those who defend [determinism] and their reluctance to confront what in this case would be the cost of the unity of theory and practice indicate that, for the moment, one need not take too seriously this theoretical defense."[19]

c) Freedom as Dependence on Self through the Objects: Decision

Finally, we must consider how self-determination and choice occur *simultaneously*, in a necessary and unitary way, in the key moment of freedom which we call *decision*.

The process is the following. When I decide to perform a determined action:

1. I choose one possible option among many others (choice, intentional dimension);

2. by choosing, I dispose of myself in relation to that concrete option and I determine myself in a determined direction.

If, for example, I decide to do something as simple as eating an apple, I am choosing one option among other possible ones. The first of them will be whether to eat or not to eat, or to eat a pear instead of an apple. This is the intentional-horizontal dimension. But, although at first sight it may not seem like it, I am also deciding about myself. I have chosen an apple because I like apples and I have decided to give myself a treat, or because it is good for me for intestinal reasons, or simply because I was hungry and that was what was at hand. In any case, the essential fact is that I decide about myself in the act of deciding about the object. And the same thing occurs in more transcendent decisions. When I choose a profession, I opt among the set of possible jobs, but simultaneously I am making a disposition regarding myself in relation to

---

[18] K. Wojtyła, *Persona y acción*, 205.
[19] I. Berlin, *Cuatro ensayos sobre la libertad*, 32.

the future and I am establishing what I am going to be: a professor, an engineer or a drawer.

Finally, it is important to note that the existence of the two dimensions of freedom is not accidental in the sense that they in fact exist, but they might not. *On the contrary, we must say that real freedom is only possible thanks to the simultaneous existence of both*, since each one of them makes the other possible.

Self-determination is possible because freedom of choice exists; that is, because my will is independent of the objects. If my will depended entirely on the intentional object, I could not exercise my self-dominion. If, returning to the examples we have used, I were completely determined by eating pears, the area of food would be excluded from my self-dominion. I would always have to eat pears, independently of my desires. In the same way, if I were determined by being an architect, I could never freely determine my professional future. I could not decide what I want to be in the area of work. In turn, independence of the objects of wanting is possible thanks to self-possession. I do not necessarily depend on any object, because I fundamentally depend on myself. *By possessing myself I am not possessed by anything*, I do not radically depend on anything, I am independent and, therefore, I can elect what I decide.

d) On the Object of the Will: The Notions of Good and Value

We are now going to make brief mention of two manifestations under which the object of will can be presented. Classically, the will has always been associated with the good, even through its very definition. "The good is what everyone desires," Aristotle affirms.[20] However, in recent centuries, the notion of value has acquired relevance, coming even to displace the notion of good.[21] Why has this occurred? The fundamental reason, in the aspect we are considering, is that value gives force to the personal and subjective character of the good, something that the traditional notion had left a little mute.

The good, from the classical perspective, is what is convenient to beings. It thus fulfills an essential function in ethics: to show that an objective order exists to which the person must adapt in order to be able to perfect himself and to act correctly. If the person follows that order he does the good; in the opposite case, he does evil. This perspective is perfectly correct, but on

---

[20] Aristotle, *Nicomachean Ethics*, Book I, 1.

[21] A brief historical summary of the notion of value is offered by B. Mondin, *L'uomo: chi è? Elementi di antropologia filosofica* (Milano: Massimo, 1989), 307-312.

occasion its objective and universal character has been taken to extremes, causing a series of problems. Above all, it leaves little explicit room for *freedom* since it gives the impression that that objective order is the same for everyone or, in other words, that there is a good which perfects the person *independently* of who that concrete person may be and what his life project may be. But this way of posing things is inadequate. In a multitude of questions, and not only irrelevant ones, there is not an objective good that the person has to know and discover, but rather it is the person who, through freedom, determines it. There are people, for example, who have a very specific professional vocation which, so to speak, is waiting to be discovered and accepted; but in many other cases, this is not so. The profession one chooses is the result of a multitude of different types of options which one chooses throughout life. The second negative aspect of this position is that it does not make explicit the lived relationship of what is convenient with the *subjectivity* of the person, with the self. The good may appear to be something that is imposed from outside, like an order which the subject has to accept and assimilate, whether he likes it or not, but which does not arise out of the subject's interior or implicate him in a lived and affective way.

So, then, the notion of value has taken its place and has become generalized precisely due to its ability to respond to these problems. Let us look at it in some detail. Above all, *value can be defined as a specific good in that it is assumed by a determined person in his lived and affective universe.*[22] And, developing this definition, we have the following points:

a) Values are specific goods that have a direct relation with the lives of persons: the family, education, safety, love, beauty, ecology, etc.

b) They are assumed by the person who considers that they benefit him and constitute something valuable for his existence.[23]

c) They implicate affectivity; they are felt to be one's own and their loss or gain affect the subject's lived universe.

---

[22] Cf. R. Yepes, *Fundamentos de antropología*, 136 ff.

[23] "In order for there to be a value, it is necessary that it be recognized and appreciated by the subject." (J. de Finance, *Ensayo sobre el obrar humano*, 83). This author proposes a relation between value and good similar to the one expounded on here.

d)   They are criteria of action. We move and strive to attain values
     that we consider relevant in our life.

e)   They vary from person to person. Not everyone has the same
     tastes, nor do we desire the same things, nor do we have the
     same culture. Each person builds the universe of his own
     values, accounting for many parameters: the education
     received, what prevails in society, personal experiences and
     the mark they have left on us, etc.

Values, thus described, respond to the problems which an excessively
objectivistic vision of the good posed: they are open to freedom and implicate
the subject personally. But now, to turn the sock inside out, we could ask
ourselves if this description, in turn, presents a series of problems and, in
particular, if it leaves too much space for subjectivism and *relativism*. In the
end, if each person builds his set of values, can he not include those which he
desires, based solely on his preferences? To the extent that we have defined
value as a good, this is not possible; values are realities (objects, situations,
persons, etc.) that are ethically correct.[24] What is possible is that, through
deformation or interest, attitudes or customs may be generalized, which are
called values and which, in reality, are countervalues: freedom understood as
an absolute value, sexuality considered as a mere instrument of pleasure, etc.
It is in these cases when the notion of good shows all its usefulness, since it
reminds us that the person has a specific nature, which may not be
manipulated and which imposes on the person some general lines of ethical
action which are not completely subjected to the choice of the will. Good and
value are, then, two notions which complement each other, since they place
in relief different aspects of the motives which drive the human being in his
search for happiness.

6.3 The Self-Fulfillment of the Person through Freedom

Until now, we have looked at freedom in its essence, in its anthropological
structure. But freedom is not just essence, it has a concrete framework of

---

[24] In this sense, López Quintás explains that, "*values are relational, but not merely
relative*. A value is *relative* to the human being if he decides what is valuable or
insignificant. A value is *relational* if its mode of being consists in driving the human
being's action toward an elevated goal." A. López Quintás, *Inteligencia creativa, El
descubrimiento personal de los valores* (Madrid: BAC, 2002) 453. On the hierarchization
of values, see ibid., 450-458.

implementation and personal conditions which favor or hinder it. If I am in jail, my essential freedom does not change, but I am less free: I need space, air, light, sun, and thus I long for freedom. If I am a drug addict, I do not cease to be free, but, as a matter of fact, I depend on a drug; my freedom is eroded, consumed, and I am less free. If I am efficient or virtuous, on the contrary, I can do many things, achieve more, which implies that, in some way, my freedom grows. In conclusion, my freedom affects my life and the conditions in which I live affect my freedom. These are the aspects which we should consider in order to complete our exposition of this topic. We will begin by analyzing how the decisions I adopt from day to day configure my personality and my life project, and we will do it, in the first place, from an overall perspective, which we have called *existential*, and later on we will refer to the specifically *ethical* aspect.

a) Existential Self-Fulfillment

Freedom, by being a disposition of ourselves – self-determination – modifies us throughout our existence or, to say it differently, we modify ourselves through freedom. As St. Gregory of Nyssa says, "each one of us makes himself through his own decision... and we are in a certain sense our own parents, since we make ourselves as we desire."[25]

Above all, choices form our *personal identity*: we choose one profession or another, we dedicate ourselves to one task or another, we travel to this or that country, we work with effort or we do not. All this little by little forms what we are from the starting point of two elements: what we are at birth and what we receive from the environment, and the *life project* that we have elaborated and which constitutes our point of reference in making decisions. We are something, but we want to be more and to be different and that is the path which we follow thanks to freedom.

Choices also form our *realm of life*: our profession forms our work world and our social relations; the city (and country) in which we live also affects us in multiple questions (commuting, tiredness, possibility of progressing or, on the contrary, limitations to our abilities); the group of friends is essential in our life and we choose it, just as the family we have created or in which we live. All this cumulus of circumstances depends, at least to a certain degree, on the decisions we make, and these, once adopted, condition, in turn, future decisions, because they configure our framework of relations: if I have gotten married and am a father, I am different from how I was before, and the

---

[25] St. Gregory of Nyssa, *Vita Moysis*, PG XLIV, 327b.

decisions that I make in the future will be conditioned by this fact. In the same way, choosing a profession depends on me, but that decision will condition me. Freedom thus creates the *narrative character of existence*, that is, the fact that in order to comprehend a person it is necessary to know his past, because the human being is not something merely given and factual, but rather a biography and a history which has been forged on the basis of decisions.[26] This means, from another point of view, that one may not identify decision and commitment with limitation of possibilities. *The essence of commitment is not the limitation of freedom, but positioning of life*: it closes some paths, but it opens others.[27] If I decide to get married, for example, and I make a commitment in the creation of a family, I impose on myself, evidently, a series of limitations, but I also create a new realm of freedom and of development that the person who has not made that decision does not possess.

To choose, in addition, means *to gamble, to take a risk*. No one assures me that my choices are adequate or correct, or that they actually lead to the predetermined goal. Therefore, the existential unfolding of freedom is always linked to happiness or frustration to the extent to which I grow closer to or farther from my life project: I have the house I want or I do not; I have married the right person or I have made a mistake and now I find myself in a dramatic situation; I want to ascend professionally and I achieve it or I am unable. Here is the dramatic part of life, the risk and the inevitability of freedom which the existentialists emphasized so forcefully. I am free, even if I do not want to be and I am condemned to choose because my destiny depends on some decisions which I inexorably have to make, since not deciding is also a decision.

However, in daily life, this dramatic character is not so frequent. On the contrary, our life can be, even more so than we would desire, mundane and bland, ordinary. But, whether the routine has a meaning or becomes loathsome depends, above all, on the existence of a defined life project (goal, ideal, vocation) which orients and gives meaning to the daily choices. If I am sure about what I want to be, if my life has a project and a meaning (at least in

---

[26] "Since we necessarily orient ourselves toward the good, we determine our place in relation to it and in that way we determine the direction of our lives, we inevitably have to understand our lives in a narrative way, as a search. But we could perhaps begin with another idea: since we have to determine our place in relation to the good, we cannot cease to orient ourselves toward it, and for that reason we are to see our life as a story." Charles Taylor, *Sources of the Self* (Cambridge: Cambridge University Press, 1990), 51-52.

[27] "The human being makes himself day to day through his freedom; but *yesterday's freedom weighs on today's freedom*, and the latter prefigures and modifies tomorrow's freedom." (J. Mouroux, *Sentido cristiano del hombre*, 212).

a general way), my daily decisions will be the steps on the path that lead me to that goal. On the contrary, the lack of a life project can give existence a sad and empty, hopeless tint. I choose because I have no other option, because I must move ahead toward a destiny that I do not know, and which perhaps does not even interest me.

This lack of ultimate meaning affects people of our time ever more forcefully and leads to a *paradox*: the coexistence of a very perfect and developed realm of life – good working and economic conditions, large and inviting houses, satisfactory social relations (at least on a superficial level), etc. – with the lack of a life project with an *ultimate*, that is, transcendent, dimension. The result is that many people know perfectly what to do with their life each day and where they want to go professionally and perhaps on a human level, but they do not know what is the ultimate meaning of their existence, that is, what they are living for in a *radical* way. And this lack, sooner or later, will end up mining away and weakening the impulse which moves them, since they act and live, perhaps with extreme efficacy, but with a deep unsatisfaction at base. Here is an important element in understanding the increase in emotional problems or some types of depression.[28] The solution necessarily passes through a strengthening of the religious sense, since the ultimate reason for life is only found in a transcendent reference point (cf. Ch. 15.1).

b) Ethical Self-Fulfillment

Within the existential unfolding of freedom there is an especially important part which is the *moral dimension*. The human being, by acting, poses for himself the dilemma of the choice between good and evil, and that decision, due to the self-referential character of freedom, also returns and affects the subject. By choosing good or evil, one does not just act well or poorly; rather the human being *makes himself good or evil*, modifies his moral being through the exercise of freedom.[29]

Above all, the human being modifies his being through *concrete actions*. If I choose to steal, knowing that I should not, I act against my conscience and, thus, I do evil. But the evil does not remain outside of myself as if it were merely external – the theft (the horizontal-intentional dimension of freedom) – rather, it enters to form part of me, making me, in some sense, evil (the

---

[28] "Around 20% of neuroses are conditioned and caused by a feeling of lack of meaning, which I call existential emptiness." Victor Frankl, *Psicoanálisis y existencialismo* (Mexico: FCE, 1987), 32.

[29] This topic basically corresponds to ethics, and so here we will only offer a sketch.

vertical dimension of freedom). Logically, I do not make myself evil in an absolute way; I can annul that decision, return what was stolen, ask forgiveness, and then freedom acts in me in the opposite direction, undoing the deformation that I had forged in myself.

But what happens when I make many decisions in the same direction? What occurs is that I determine myself in a *stable* way in order to act in a certain direction, good or evil; that is, I develop what are classically called the *virtues* (good operative habits) or *vices* (evil operative habits).[30] If, instead of stealing once, I do it habitually, I become a thief and that means that my ethical structure is stably deformed (a vice) in such a way that I tend to steal "naturally".[31] Does one lose freedom here? In the strict sense, no. The thief steals because he wants to, but he has, so to speak, a *deformed or diminished freedom* which moves him to do evil and that makes it difficult for him to do good. There is a loss of freedom linked to a diminishment of self-dominion, which is normally known as being a "slave of the passions." A person who habitually acts in an evil way ends up diminishing his self-control and being a "slave" of that which he desires.

Here, as well, we can have recourse to Tolkien. The magic ring constitutes the point of inflection of freedom. If I do not cede to its attraction, I maintain intact my self-dominion and my ability to decide. On the contrary, if I cede and submit to its power, I end up being a slave of the ring and, thus, of Sauron. From then on, the ring (that is, Sauron) will dictate to me what I should do. Theoretically, I always have the possibility of rebelling, but in practice it will be ever more difficult, because remaining on the dark side weakens me and enslaves me. The creature Gollum represents perhaps the example *par excellence*. When Gollum found the ring, he was able to choose and he did: he opted for the ring. But, little by little, the ring consumed his will

---

[30] Cf. Thomas Aquinas, S. Th. I-II, q. 55, a. 3. Abbà and MacIntyre, among others, have made important contributions to the theory of the virtues. See, in particular, G. Abbà, *Lex et virtus. Studi sull'evoluzione della dottrina morale di san Tommaso d'Aquino* (Rome: LAS, 1983), G. Abbà, *Felicità, vita buona e virtù. Saggi di filosofia morale* (Rome: LAS, 1989) where an abundant bibliography on the debate between the ethics of duty and the ethics of the virtues is also offered, and A. MacIntyre, *After virtue. A study in moral theory* (Notre Dame, Ind.: University of Notre Dame Press, 2007).

[31] The self-determining character of the virtues is explained by the philosophical tradition indicating that the virtues constitute something like a "second nature" which is superimposed on the basic nature of the person and they move him to act in a certain direction, since, as is known, nature is the principle of operations. A precise and precious analysis of some virtues can be found in J. Pieper, *The four Cardinal Virtues* (Notre Dame, Ind.: University of Notre Dame Press, 1990).

and his being until Gollum's life became identified with the search and possession of the ring: "my precious."

Something similar, but inversely, occurs when a person develops a virtue. If I habitually help others, I become someone with solidarity and then it is easier to act with generosity because my being is already oriented in that direction. Just as in the previous case, there is not a loss of freedom. One always acts because one wants to. Here, on the contrary, one must rather speak of a development and perfection of freedom that leads me to dispose of myself in such a way that I perfect myself ethically and I help others in a consistent and habitual way.[32]

6.4 The Social Conditions of Freedom

Freedom is an eminently personal reality, but since we are not lost islands or castaways without relations, it has an important social aspect. Some of those aspects, like the systems of government, basically correspond to political theory, but others touch anthropology, if not completely, at least in a relevant way: What are the adequate social conditions in order to be able to say that I am really free? What happens when my freedom clashes with that of my neighbor? Should any decision be admitted because it proceeds from a person? These are key questions which we will take on, grouping them into two large topics: the social conditions that are required for the dignified and adequate exercise of freedom and the principal problems which that exercise implies.[33]

a) The Social Conditions for the Exercise of Freedom

a.1) The Ability to Exercise the Fundamental Freedoms

First of all, society *should permit the exercise* of freedom in its different dimensions: expression, movement, education, religious freedom[34], etc. Only if the law permits people to decide freely about these fundamental aspects is

---

[32] "The habits are intrinsic super-elevations of living spontaneity, living developments which make the soul better in a particular order and which fill it with active sap: *turgentia ubera animae*, as John of St. Thomas calls them." (J. Maritain, *Art et scolastique*, Oeuvres Complètes, vol. I, 628).

[33] We will return to this topic from another perspective in Chapter 13.

[34] Some principles of religious freedom were already formulated by Locke, who affirms: "tolerance toward those who dissent from others on religion is something so in conformity with the Gospel and with religion that it seems monstrous that there are human beings who are blind to so much light." (J. Locke, *A letter concerning toleration* [Merchant Books, 2011], 8).

one in a free society. In current democratic societies, the right to exercise these freedoms is included in the society's Constitution and laws. The United Nations, as is known, in 1948 made a Declaration which includes the fundamental rights of the human being; rights which any legal code which legislates taking into account the dignity of the person should include.

If the system of government does not allow the exercise of these freedoms, then it is a tyrannical government, of which there exist multiple modalities.[35] In some cases it may have its origin in an accumulation of power by one person or by one group (oligarchy); it may have as a foundation an abstract value which is considered more relevant than individual persons: religion in the case of theocracy, the proletarian revolution in communism, the nation in nationalist societies, etc. In any case, it is a regime with an unjust legal code that limits or impedes the exercise of personal rights and freedoms and is thus a justification for the citizens to attempt to change or eliminate that unjust legal code. In extreme cases – an exacerbated tyranny, the invasion of a country – that fight can and should use all possible instruments: liberation movements or even war.

a.2) The Exercise of Freedom Should Be Truly Possible

But, in order for real freedom to exist, it is not enough for it to be legally guaranteed; *one must be able to exercise it in fact*, it must not be limited in practice. That limitation may have multiple causes. One of them can simply be *the lack of material means*. For example, in a very poor country, freedom of movement can be a mere utopia and be very limited in practice if there are no means to move about or if they are so rudimentary that any trip is full of difficulties and obstacles. But there is also a second possibility; it may occur that *a government uses the restriction of material means to restrict freedom furtively*. On the one hand, it may affirm to its citizens, to the governments of other countries or to the media that in their country there is an ample system of freedoms expressed in general laws, but then impede in practice the real exercise of those freedoms through administrative procedures or other types of difficulties that the everyday citizen cannot overcome. For example, in many communist countries, freedom of movement was affirmed on the level of the law of the State, but then special passes or permits were required in order to go to certain zones, and they were only granted to those favored by the government. And something similar occurs today in many Islamic

---

[35] Despite the passage of time, the Aristotelian description of tyranny and other forms of government continues to be useful and instructive. Cf. Aristotle, *Politics*, especially Books 3-5.

countries. Freedom of religion is theoretically affirmed, but then permits are not granted to build new churches, the possibility of repairing already existing churches is delayed – even for decades –, conversions are prohibited, etc. Freedom is thus reduced to a mere mirage.

Another way of impeding freedom is *limiting the ability to develop for people contrary to the regime in power*. This was the attitude which England adopted during its centuries-long occupation of Ireland. Higher education was for centuries reserved only for Protestants and there was only one university in the entire country, which was confessionally Protestant: *Trinity College*. This meant in practice that Catholics, unless they decided to publicly reject their religion, were practically condemned to illiteracy. And, evidently, from an ignorant and illiterate social condition it is very difficult, not to say impossible, to effectively exercise one's own rights and freedoms.

b) The Problem of Social Control of Freedom

The second question that we wanted to take on is the social control of freedom. And in the first place we can wonder about the need of this regulation. Would it not be better for each person to act according to his convictions? This is the core of the anarchist ideal, but it is an unrealizable utopia and not only because of the evil in the human heart which would confirm what Hobbes said (*homo homini lupus*) against Rousseau. There are many and important motives that impose the *regulation of freedom*. Let us see the most important ones.

1) *The bad use of freedom.* There are people who exercise their freedom erroneously: stealing, murdering, evading taxes, etc.; and they oblige the society to establish mechanisms which impede them and dissuade them. These means can even include the limitation of freedom because, although it is an essential good, it is not an absolute good. As Isaiah Berlin said, "the freedom of the wolves has frequently meant the death of the lambs."[36]

2) *Personal choices can clash.* In any society, it is inevitable that confrontations will be produced between the desires and interests of different people, so it is necessary to establish a superior authority with the ability to settle the question and

---

[36] Isaiah Berlin, *Cuatro ensayos sobre la libertad,* 53.

decide. The existence of a confrontation does not necessarily imply that one of the sides is wrong or is acting in bad faith. Both may maintain positions that are correct and honorable, but in conflict. A group of people, for example, may think that it is correct and convenient to cut down a forest in order to obtain wood and produce wealth and work in a certain town, while another group may oppose it for ecological reasons. Both positions may be reasonable, but only one of them is possible.

3) *Plurality of Customs and Mentalities.*[37] Confrontations and divergences can also be produced due to deeper questions: customs, the vision of life linked to belonging to different nationalities or religions, etc. It is thus necessary to harmonize freedoms so that life in common may be possible.

4) Finally, the correct exercise of freedom can clash or *enter into conflict with other essential values:* health, security, justice, tolerance, etc. Then it may be necessary to limit freedom in order to safeguard them. In a situation of war, for example, certain freedoms are automatically limited, and currently similar measures have been considered, and in some cases adopted, with respect to terrorism.

All these problems are social constants which are repeated throughout history, in such a way that the human being has attempted to respond to them by elaborating complex social structures or systems of government which have become ever more sophisticated. Let us now look briefly at three basic possibilities for dealing with the regulation of freedom.[38]

b.1) Permissivism: An Excess of Social Freedom

In current societies, freedom is valued greatly. But that attitude is, on occasion, disproportionate and leads to what is called *permissivism*: the

---

[37] Liberalism has insisted on this point. Rawls, for example, affirms that "the plurality of different persons with independent systems of ends is an essential feature of human societies." J. Rawls, *Teoría de la justicia* (Mexico: FCE, 1978), 47; English version: *A Theory of Justice* (Segment Book 2019). But he emphasizes the autonomy and the independence of persons so much that society seems to have "shipwrecked on a desert island with a group of individuals whom I do not know and who do not know each other either." A. MacIntyre, *After virtue*, 307.

[38] The detailed study of this question belongs to political philosophy.

tendency to allow any type of behavior, as long as it comes from a free decision. Permissivism has at base some correct presuppositions: it values freedom and respects plurality and the decisions of others; but it takes little account of the fact that people can use their freedom poorly and that, in certain circumstances, freedom needs to be oriented so that its decisions are constructive for the entire society.

Sometimes, for example, it is necessary to prohibit and cut off certain behaviors (xenophobic and violent acts, thefts, etc.), and not to do so is an act of cowardice and inhibition. In some cases, it will be easy to take those measures because they are unpopular attitudes; but on other occasions, when one knows that the measure is going to cause strong social or political opposition, it may be easy to become inhibited in order not to create problems or political disfavor. This is what happens in some countries, for example, with such a transcendental question as education. Since it is difficult to defend a type of education which implies authority, the existence of rules of behavior, academic demands, etc., in the end, a passive and inhibited attitude is adopted, the inevitable result of which is a drop in the level of education, the discrediting of authority, an increase in classroom violence, etc.

b.2) Authoritarianism: The Repression of Freedom

The option opposite to permissivism is *authoritarianism*, which is characterized by favoring the principle of authority over that of freedom. What is important for this system of government is that the society acts in an established way, even if it does so under pressure and coercion. Authoritarianism, in other words, distrusts freedom (the freedom of the subject, obviously) and limits it and determines from above the lines of social behavior.

There are different types of authoritarianism which go from paternalist systems to dictatorial and repressive regimes. Authoritarianism as such tends to content itself with the citizen's obedience. *Totalitarianism*, its most extreme version, has the pretension, in addition, to achieve internal conformity with the measures imposed by the dictator, because it wants to avoid any possibility of opposition or overthrow. The most efficacious way to achieve it is the mental identification of the subjects, that is, that they consider that their system of government is the adequate one. And thus, in totalitarian regimes, so much importance is normally granted to education and indoctrination. Very recently, due to the unsuspected power acquired by technology, a technological or *digital authoritarianism* is emerging in which citizens are controlled in very complex and subtle ways through the digital footprint they leave on the Internet and the knowledge that the great technological giants (Google, WhatsApp, Amazon, Apple Facebook, Netflix, etc.) have of their preferences, tastes and decisions[39].

Paternalism, which Kant considered, with a little exaggeration, to be "the greatest imaginable despotism," is, so to speak, the "light" version of authoritarianism and consists in limiting the ability for self-determination of the person because he is considered to be a minor and thus incapable of deciding his own destiny. Since it is the mildest version of authoritarianism, it is compatible with the existence of restricted zones of freedom which the authority generously "grants," as long as certain rules, which the authority itself has established, are not infringed. Paternalism is, on the contrary, incompatible with the responsible and mature self-government of a society.

All of these systems have as their starting point a true principle (the social need for authority), but they are essentially unjust because persons have the fundamental right to live in freedom, and society should attempt to restrict it as little as possible. Some, in any case, have wondered about the viability of a moderate authoritarianism. Could an authoritarianism in which a few upright and wise people, interested in the common good, ruled the destinies of the rest not be valid? It may indeed seem logical at first sight that wise and upright people direct the destinies of the less wise – Plato proposed it in *The Republic* – but this outlook does not resist a minimally profound analysis.[40] Because who determines which are the wise and upright people? That is, who decides who decides? In addition, who determines what is just for a society and who determines which decision should be adopted in those questions, which are the majority, in which there are many different correct or possible decisions?[41] And all this, without taking into account the possibility of corruption because, as Lord Acton signaled, "power corrupts and absolute power corrupts absolutely." What happens, then, if the supposedly just people cease to be so?

Unfortunately, history has proportioned too many examples of the terrible situations which can come about through the uncontrolled exercise of the principle of authority. Therefore, Western societies have made a tremendous effort to develop a political system that combines freedom and authority much more harmoniously: the democratic system.

---

[39] Cf. Byung Chul-Han, *Psychopolitics: Neoliberalism and New Technologies of Power* (Verso Books, 2017) and Soshana Zuboff, *The Age Of Surveillance Capitalism: The Fight for a Human Future at the New Frontier of Power* (New York: Public Affairs, 2020).
[40] Dahl calls this mode of government "tutelage", and lucidly poses the aporias which confront it. See R. A. Dahl, *On Democracy* (Yale: Yale University Press, 2015).
[41] Let us remember here the multiplicity of practical truth.

Chapter 7

The Personal Self

When we knock on our front door and a familiar voice asks, "who is it?", w
might simply respond "it is I".[1*] In a certain sense, this response is totally
superfluous. We are all an "I". But, from another perspective, it is the most
correct and radical response to a known and familiar voice, because with that
response I make reference to what is most profound in my being, to my
ontological root and to my personal identity. We touch here the central and
ultimate nucleus of the person, the reality which we call the "I" or the self.[2*]
We have seen that we are body, freedom, intelligence, but we have not been
able to completely identify ourselves with any of these aspects, because what
is most essential in the person does not lie in any of them. It only appears in a
hidden way, as a presupposition and foundation, because when we talk about
the body or freedom, what we are really thinking is: "*I* am corporeal, *I* am
free." And that "I," the ultimate nucleus with which we really identify, is what
we must now consider.

7.1 Consciousness and the Unconscious

a) A Brief Historical Overview

The path that brings us to the self is consciousness understood as subjectivity.
And the fact that philosophy has not understood this aspect with the
necessary depth until recent eras has had the consequence that philosophy
has not occupied itself with the self as such either.[3] Classical and, particularly,

---

[1*] Colloquial English would respond, "it's me." However, this response, apart from being
grammatically incorrect, does not reflect what the author wishes to convey in the
original Spanish (Translator's Note).

[2*] The topic of this chapter according to the Spanish original is "*el yo*". Literally, "the I".
However, we consider that in the majority of the cases, the English word that best
conveys what the author wishes to express is "the self" (Translator's Note).

[3] "The self," Ebner comments, "is a late discovery of the human spirit which reflects on
itself and reveals itself as the idea. Ancient philosophy did not yet know anything about it.
Because it was due to the spirit of Christianity – which is as much as to say, due to the
religious dimension – that for the first time the human being awoke to the consciousness
of himself." (F. Ebner, *La palabra y las realidades espirituales* [Madrid: Caparrós, 1995], 25.)

medieval philosophy occupied themselves with consciousness basically from the point of view of action and its morality (conscience).[4*] In order for an action to have a moral qualification, there must be awareness on the part of the subject, and the philosophical reflection was focused principally from this perspective: consciousness as awareness of the action, as a realization that I am acting and that the action is voluntary. Scholasticism was centered on the object and, for that very reason, it was generally very difficult to be conscious of the subject and his interiority.

The systematic reflection on consciousness as such is properly the work of modernity, and Descartes may be considered as its initiator.[5] The *cogito*, "I think, therefore I exist," is already situated in the proper perspective of consciousness, that is, the interior of the subject. "I, subject, think" is the implicit affirmation in the Cartesian thesis that consecrated consciousness as the first philosophical category. The Cartesian discovery had a transcendental repercussion and filled a gap that the preceding philosophy had not been able to bridge. However, it was quickly frustrated and overwhelmed by its lack of ontological anchorage. Descartes' consciousness hung in the air, it was not rooted in being and, thus, with the passage of the centuries and the developments and elaborations of different thinkers (principally Kant and Hegel), consciousness itself became being, the absolute. Consciousness turned from being a property of the person to being pure consciousness in rationalism and, later on, in Hegel, absolute self-consciousness, the subject *par excellence* in the evolution of what is real.[6]

This position, however, began to weaken in the 19th century. The vindication of the individual by Kierkegaard initiated the crisis of the Hegelian system, and the scientific discoveries regarding different unconscious structures obligated a drastic, downward revision of the notion of consciousness. Darwin postulated that there were uncontrolled mechanisms that determined something as essential as the evolution of species and, consequently, of the human being. And Freud, directly opposed to rationalism on this point, showed, in turn, how within the human being there are unconscious

---

[4*] In Spanish, the same word ("*conciencia*") is used for consciousness and conscience (Translator's Note).

[5] It is not, in any case, an absolute discovery. It is enough to remember St. Augustine's thought, with his profound vision of the interior of the human being.

[6] But, as Millán-Puelles has remembered, "for a being which does not consist in being consciousness, adequate consciousness is impossible. Subjectivity is not integrally transparent to itself because its very essence impedes it, not in virtue of some added obstacle." A. Millán-Puelles, *La estructura de la* subjetividad (Madrid: Rialp, 1967), 151.

dimension, even being important, is not the fundamental one. The essential role of consciousness consists in its constituting *the place of the self and of subjectivity*. What exactly does this mean? It means that we are persons not only because we are conscious of our activity, but also for a much more profound reason, which makes that realization possible, due to the existence of an *interior space* in which we live and inhabit, in which we introduce ourselves and root our experiences, from which our feelings, our loves and our hates arise, and to which they return, once they are mixed and confronted with the world. That *interior space* is like the stage of our life from which the particular psychological phenomena proceed, and to which they return; it is the anthropological place of subjectivity and it is, for that very reason, the philosophical *gateway* of the self which cannot exist if it is not assisted and received subjectivity. And the existence of this space is possible thanks to the fact that the second dimension of consciousness consists "in forming *the lived experience*, which allows the human being to experiment in a particular way his own subjectivity."[8]

Consciousness thus has two dimensions. One by which we recognize our *acts*, and another, the more fundamental one, by which we live them *interiorly*. Both mutually imply each other in real existence, such that it may be difficult to distinguish them; but an attentive analysis clearly shows us the subtle line which separates the two, as occurs when, on contemplating a landscape, we are conscious (1) that we are contemplating it, and (2) that we live that contemplation interiorly.

b.3) *Other* Characteristics of Consciousness

Consciousness, despite its importance, is not inalterable or constant. There are moments in which it disappears entirely (sleep, loss of consciousness due to a blow or weakness, etc.) and others in which it may increase or decrease (drowsiness, drunkenness or tiredness). It is not always clear and lucid. "The clarity of consciousness," Jaspers indicates, "demands that I have clearly before me what I think, what I know and what I want, what I do, what I feel, my lived experience, the attachment to my self, and that it may remain in connection through memory."[9] But this does not always occur. In addition, it is not homogenous. I do not have consciousness of everything in the same way and with the same intensity. There is a central point on which consciousness' beam of light focuses and which I, therefore, experience with particular

---

[8] K. Wojtyła, *Persona y acción*, 86.
[9] K. Jaspers, *Psicopatología general* (Mexico: FCE, 1996), 159. English version. *General Psychopathology*, vol. I. (John Hopkins University Press, 1997).

intensity; but there is also a field or atmosphere around that nucleus that we are conscious of in a much less intense way, because it is unfocused and dark.

It may be interesting to note, finally, that some authors have spoken of a third dimension of consciousness, that of self-knowledge or consciousness' knowledge of itself. But, in reality, here we are not properly before a dimension of consciousness; rather, we are before an activity of the intellect. When the subject knows himself (that is what self-knowledge is), he or she performs an intellectual activity which does not depend directly on consciousness because we have already said that consciousness is neither cognitive nor intentional. In turn, the consciousness of that activity, of that self-knowledge, is reduced to the two dimensions that we have already described: being conscious of that self-knowledge and living it.

c) The Unconscious

c.1) Existence and Discovery of the Unconscious

The unconscious, while it may seem contradictory, is above all a *datum of experience*. It may seem like a contradiction because how can one have experience, that is, consciousness, of something that is unconscious? But this difficulty is quickly overcome if we take into account that not all our knowledge has to have a direct basis; some knowledge can be deduced with certainty from proven phenomena. And this is what happens with the unconscious; there are numerous experiential phenomena which clearly make manifest to us its existence, although in an *indirect way*. Artistic creation is one of them. The artist can work hard to "create beauty," as Maritain would say, but in order to do so, he or she needs a decisive but uncontrollable impulse: inspiration, which hides in the depths of the spirit and arises and manifests itself in an unexpected way. And this means that there is inside of us a psychological dimension which escapes, at least partially, the dominion of our consciousness. The phenomena of hypnosis points in the same direction. A hypnotized subject may perform actions which later he or she does not remember, and even – when he or she has returned to a conscious state – obey orders given during hypnosis, without realizing it.

But in order to show the existence of the unconscious, it is not necessary to have recourse to special experiences. There are ordinary situations in which the unconscious becomes manifest. The birth of an idea or the comprehension of a problem are a few examples. Our minds may go round and round about something, reflecting and thinking, without comprehending a situation until, suddenly, without our controlling that process in a precise way, we understand it or an idea arises which illuminates a determined question (the insight, according to Gestalt). The idea is, obviously, conscious, but the interior process that has produced it is not. In the same way, dreams also speak to us of an unconscious activity, and the activity of memory, like searching for a name that we cannot remember, is clearly the attempt to illuminate a dark recess in which our knowledge and our identity are deposited. It is thus that Jung has called memory "a faculty of reproduction of unconscious content."[10] In conclusion, all these examples, and others which could be added, are to establish a fact: the existence of an unconscious psychological dimension.

The *explicit and systematic recognition* of the unconscious fundamentally corresponds to Freud. The human being has always known or intuited that there are, inside him, dark and minimally accessible zones, but Freud was the first to analyze this question clinically, arriving at the elaboration of a detailed theory which in summary may be described as follows.[11]

The Freudian unconscious is characterized by a non-conscious *psychological* (that is, not motor, vegetative, etc.) dimension of the person which contains, fundamentally, his repressed sex drive energy. All of the impulses rejected by the conscious ego of the person accumulate in the unconscious and there they wait, under the pressure of the subject, until they are liberated in one way or another. One of the forms of liberation is produced when, for whatever reason, the subject suppresses the censure which the super-ego imposes on the ego and then the repressed impulses come to light and are executed. If this does not happen, they try to come out by indirect means like dreams, for example. The subject attempts to actualize and discharge in his non-conscious activity that which he or she cannot do consciously. Thus, Freud developed his theory of the interpretation of dreams as a means of access to the unconscious. Finally, when those repressed impulses do not find any type of release at all, pathologies are produced, which psychoanalysis attempts to cure by accessing the unconscious of the subject, first to know those pathologies and then to neutralize them.

The Freudian theory about the unconscious (as with the entirety of his thought) had a great reception but also numerous criticisms, both within psychoanalysis (the neo-Freudians) and outside it. The neo-Freudians, like Adler, Jung, Horney, Fromm and others, maintained the central thesis but attempted to reduce the importance of the sexual dimension in the formation

---

[10] C. J. Jung, *Los complejos y el inconsciente* (Madrid: Alianza, 1969), 116.

[11] See an appraisal of Freud's theses in J. M. Burgos, *Historia de la psicología* (Madrid: Palabra, 2015), 231ff.

of the content of the unconscious.[12] For Freud, this dimension (*id*) was practically the only important one, which seemed clearly excessive, reason for which his disciples made an effort both to diminish its importance and to incorporate other elements: social relations, the struggle for one's own identity, etc. Jung was another author who also took on central elements from the Freudian doctrine of the unconscious, but made an effort to take away its eminently negative character and incorporate the influence of the collective. For Jung, the unconscious is not only the result of the evolution and personal frustrations of the subject; rather, everything the subject unconsciously receives from his social environment also intervenes in the formation of the unconscious (the so-called collective unconscious).

These contributions, and others which have come after them, have gradually modified the general notion of the unconscious. An important part of Freud's thesis has remained: the existence of the unconscious and its influence on the conscious life of the subject. But the general concept has changed in such a way that, as Myers affirms, "many investigators today do not consider the unconscious to be that region where the passions and repressing censures become agitated, but rather a system where information is processed without one realizing it."[13]

c.2) Topographical Description of the Unconscious

From a descriptive point of view, we may consider the following dimensions or strata in the unconscious:[14]

- *Subconscious:* Included in it are all the aspects of reality which we hardly notice because we are centered on other questions, but which, returning to them, we can easily identify. For example, if we take a walk engrossed in our thoughts we might

---

[12] Other authors, like Frankl and Maritain, have spoken of the existence of a *spiritual unconscious*, that is, an unconscious dimension of the human being in which activities related to spirituality have a place: knowledge, subjective experiences, etc. Although the idea is correct, perhaps the expression is not very adequate, since the spiritual is characterized by self-consciousness. See, for example, J. Maritain, *Creative intuition in art and poetry*, ch. III, and V. Frankl, *Man's Search for Meaning* (Beacon Press, 2006).

[13] D. G. Myers, *Psicología* (Buenos Aires: Editorial Médica Panamericana, 1990), 471.

[14] Cf. C. G. Jung, *Los complejos y el inconsciente*, 89ff. The nomenclature sometimes varies. Kaplan and Sadock, for example, designate these three levels with other names: preconscious, unconscious and deep unconscious. Cf. H. I. Kaplan, B. I. Sadock, *Synopsys of Psychiatry* (Lippincott: Williams and Wilkins, 2014).

not "realize" what we are doing, but, if necessary, we can think about that walk and relate or remember many things that we have done almost without paying attention to them. This dimension of the unconscious may be identified with the low or unclear consciousness to which we have alluded previously and, regarding its content, it is constituted to a great degree by processes that we perform automatically. There are, in effect, many processes that we initially perform in an entirely conscious way, like walking through an unknown place, but, if that process is repeated, our psyche is able to automate it and perform it in an almost mechanical way, so that we save effort and can employ our mind with other activities.

- *Preconscious*: It is constituted by all the processes or psychological content that habitually exist in an unconscious way and which only with great effort or through sophisticated processes (therapy, hypnosis) are able to be elevated to consciousness; for example, long forgotten memories which awaken due to some unexpected and intense event or through hypnosis.

- *Deep unconscious*: It is constituted by the psychological activity of the person which never comes to the surface and which, therefore, we only know in an indirect way.

c.3) The Content of the Unconscious

J. Vicente and J. Choza have distinguished up to five different activities of the unconscious: vegetative, motor, perceptive, affective and linguistic.[15] The vegetative unconscious, for example, would be constituted by the non-conscious psychological activity of the person involved in the control of the vegetative processes. In that same line, the perceptive unconscious would be formed by the non-conscious processes (which are many) that intervene in

---

[15] Cf. J. Vicente and J. Choza, *Filosofía del hombre*, 317ff. Regarding what has to do with the *functions of the unconscious*, Wojtyła notes the following: 1) it shows in a more adequate way the inner potentiality of the subject; 2) it helps one to understand the continuity and inner cohesion of the subject; 3) the continuous relation between consciousness and unconscious indicates to us that the human being is subject to time and the existence of an inner history; 4) it delineates hierarchically the potentialities of the human being (cf. *Persona y acción*, 156-158).

the human cognitive activity: automated mechanisms of perception, uncontrolled processes of selection and processing of information, etc.

This classification is interesting because it allows one to realize the amplitude of the human unconscious, but we are not going to analyze it in detail. For the objectives of this text, it is enough to realize that practically all of life and of human action is a mix of conscious and unconscious aspects. The person is his own master through consciousness, but consciousness always acts in company with a necessary and elusive shadow. It is necessary because without the unconscious, the human mind would not be freed from the multitude of repetitive and trivial tasks which would condemn it to failure and psychological rupture, and it is elusive because what escapes our consciousness is always mysterious and hidden. Freud compared the human mind to an iceberg, in which what appeared (consciousness) was a small part of the whole of the psyche (the complete iceberg of which, as is known, the majority remains hidden underwater). It is probably an exaggerated image, but it reflects a great truth. Underneath the light of consciousness, there is a relevant and influential psychological activity that cannot be scorned or ignored.

7.2 The Self as the Ultimate Nucleus of the Person

Consciousness, we said, is what opens the path to the self through subjectivity. In that inner space, the center of our person is rooted: the personal self, the root of our being, the point of convergence of our life. But *what exactly is the self,* that radical and ultimate trait of the person? We will try to answer this difficult question beginning with a description of its main traits and qualities to finally face its essential identity.

a) Properties of the Self: Self-Consciousness and Self-Belonging

It is not easy to define the self, about which we have, however, daily and essential experience, since we are our selves. What is deeper and more radical than the self? What is more profound or decisive? Through the self, we are subjects and we enter into the category of spiritual beings who transcend the passing nature of things, but grasping its essence and its characteristics is a very difficult task. In any case, we can try to define or characterize the self as *self-conscious self-belonging,* two traits that occur only in humans and not in animals.[16]

---

[16] Uniqueness is also sometimes used to define the Self. And, although we consider this position to be correct, it nevertheless requires a specific characterization of human uniqueness since it can also be considered that, in some way, animals also possess this

We find in this definition two traits or properties. Let us start with the first, *self-consciousness*. The self is characterized by the radical possibility of self-awareness, that is, of becoming aware of oneself in a profound way, of living oneself in the performance of any act or activity. It is easy to verify that whenever we carry out any type of activity we possess it not only in an intelligent way, but also in a conscious way, that is, we live it as something that is ours, in a reflective way. I am aware of everything that I do, live, think or desire at the same time that I do, live, think or desire it. But this awareness does not only mean, as we said previously, that I realize what happens, but that I live it as part of my self. And this is only possible thanks to the existence of the self.

The second essential property of the self is *self-possession or self-belonging*. The person possesses himself thanks to the self. The space of self-consciousness is the space of the self, of which the self is master and lord, and to which no one may gain access from outside in the most radical sense. And, because I am my own master, I may dispose of myself and decide my destiny both from a moral and from an existential point of view. Self-possession resides, ultimately, in the self, not in the psychic level, according to the diagram of the person, and not even in freedom, since freedom is, after all, nothing more than the freedom of a subject capable of self-determination, that is, of a personal self. Freedom only exists in a subject. The self, therefore, is constituted as the definitive guarantor of self-control and self-possession, fundamentals that make self-determination possible.

And, putting both features together, self-consciousness and self-belonging, because they take place simultaneously in the conscious subject, we have this possible description of the self as self-conscious self-possession.

b) Personal Functions of the Self

The previous description could perhaps lead to the conclusion that the self is like a type of autonomous entity which subsists on its own, but this would be an error. The self is not an isolated point in ontological space; the self is always the self of a person, and it only has meaning as such. A "pure self," independent and autonomous, would be assimilated to the Hegelian absolute self-consciousness, but such a reality is an abstraction, a mere idea. What exists is the self of a concrete person who possesses a body, a mind, feelings,

---

uniqueness trait. It is a question, however, that requires further investigation, especially in view of the strength acquired by animalism, valid in some aspects and clearly exaggerated in others.

and who is free. And, although the self is in a certain sense the entire person: "I am my body and my hands and my feelings," it is also clearly distinct from them. My hands are mine, they are part of me, but they are not my self, but a part of my being, situated under its influence. Thus, it is meaningful to pose the question as to which are the *personal functions* of the self, or in other words, what is the function of the self in the entirety of personal activity.[17]

1) Source of activity: the self is the most radical source of the activity of the person, something that is made especially manifest in free actions. It is I who act and who decide freely what I want to do and what I want to be. When, on the contrary, the self is in doubt, the person is also paralyzed.

2) Unicity: the human person is composed of many elements and the center which unifies them is the self. My hands, my feet, my feelings, my actions, my intelligence respond and are coordinated and integrated by an ultimate central and unique dimension: the self.

3) Permanence in time: the person is always the same person, although time may affect him and he or she may change in a deep and radical way, like Theseus' ship. But there is a central element that does not change, but remains, the self. "But behold, long ago did my childhood die, but in spite of this, I live,"[18] St. Augustine affirms, expressing a universal experience.

4) Being a subject: thanks to the self, we are also subjects. By having a unified and unitary activity, and by being, through the self, my own master, responsible for my actions, I become conscious of myself as an entity who is different from the world and confronted by it. I am a subject before the world which is an object (*ob-jectum*), that is, it is in front of me like something radically different and exterior, even if the object is another subject, another self.

---

[17] We basically take this classification from K. Jaspers, *Psicopatología general*, 139-148. Its origin is rather psychopathological, since what Jaspers is seeking in this work is to determine specific pathologies, but that does not mean that it is uninteresting. One may also consult a later work: K. Jaspers, *Filosofía*, vol. I (Puerto Rico: Revista de Occidente, 1958), 419-447.

[18] St. Augustine, *Confessions* I, 6.

5) Personality and identity: I am a subject, I remain in time, I am
    a source of activity, etc., but I am these things in a concrete
    and unique way. There is no other person, no other self,
    identical to mine. I am a unique being because my
    subjectivity is a unique being and because all the decisions
    that I have made about myself are unique.

c) The Self as the Ontological Foundation of the Person

The self is central in the subsistence and identity of the person. Things pass,
actions disappear, the body grows older, but I remain. I am the same human
being (*el mismo*) who was previously 5, 20 or 40 years old, although I am not
the same (*no soy lo mismo*).[19] And this fact brings us to a key problem which
has already been treated when we spoke of the person, but about which it is
now important to return from a different perspective: the question of
substantiality or subsistence, that is, *how it is possible for there to be a nucleus
which is immune to changes in human beings and what that nucleus is.*

The question may be posed initially in the following terms: Is there a self
that is the subject or proprietor of each life, that is, of all the acts and passions,
or, on the contrary, is the self or one's own individuality no more than the
inner linking or interlocking of all of one's experiences? After what we have
said about the self, the answer seems evident. The self is not a particularly
intense set of experiences, as some anti-substantialists like Hume may
maintain, but rather it is much more: it is, so to speak, their proprietor, the
place where they exist and are meaningful. And it is for this reason a root of
subsistence: experiences pass, but the subject, the self, remains.

So far, the question is clear. What now remains to be resolved is *which is the
most adequate notion to describe the substantiality or subsistence that occurs
in the human person.* Classical metaphysics has used two categories to
express this fact: *substance* (what is in itself and not in another) and
suppositum (what is underneath). Both reflect very well the permanence
through changes, but they present a problem: *they are not very adequate for
expressing subjectivity.* "The expression *suppositum*," Wojtyła indicates,
"works for defining the subject in a completely objective way, separating by
abstraction the aspect of the lived experience and, in particular, the lived
experience of subjectivity, in which the subject is given to himself as 'self'."[20]

[19*] That is to say, many of my qualities have changed over time. (Translator's Note).
[20] K. Wojtyła, *Persona y acción*, 89. See also L. Stefanini, *Personalismo sociale* (2nd ed.)
(Rome: Studium, 1979), 46.

And the same thing happens with the concept of substance. Although it is possible to understand its use to define the subsistence of the human person through changes, the possibility that, when using it, we lose sight of the essential subjectivity of being personal should not be underestimated. For this reason, we consider that it is not appropriate, from a personalistic point of view, to use either the term substance or the term *suppositum* to reflect the depths of the human being. At the end of the day, these terms are, in reality, *impersonal* and, therefore, it does not seem that it makes much sense to try to explain the most personal of the human being, which is, precisely, the self, through an impersonal concept[21].

What, then, is the concept that we must use to found the subsistence of the personal being? In fact, when things are analyzed in detail, *it does not seem that any additional concept is needed to found the personal self.* The self is self-founded or, in other words, the self, *understood ontologically*, is the ultimate foundation of personal being. It is not necessary to go beyond the self to found the person, as long as the self is considered ontologically and not phenomenologically or psychologically, as a set of personality traits or characters. It is, in effect, our self that has subsisted over time while all the rest of our personal constitution changes. I am always the same being (*el mismo*) even though I am no longer the same (*lo mismo*).

Having arrived at this point, it might appear that the problem that we had posed has been solved. *The permanence of the identity of the person should be attributed to the self,* understood less as an inalterable substrate, and more as a *personal* reality capable of subsisting through the changes[22]. However, this explanation leaves an important loose end: what happens when the self eclipses? Because, as paradoxical as it may seem, the self, like consciousness, is not a "permanent" reality: it can weaken, eclipse, become psychologically ill

---

[21] A detailed analysis of this problem can be found in my dialogue with John F. Crosby: J. M. Burgos, *El yo como raíz ontológica de la persona. Reflexiones a partir de John F. Crosby*, "Quién, Revista de filosofía personalista" 6 (2017), 33-54; J. Crosby, *On solitude, subjectivity and substantiality. Response to Juan Manuel Burgos*, "Quién, Revista de filosofía personalista" 8 (2018), 7-19; J. M. Burgos, *De la sustancia al yo como fundamento de la persona. Respuesta a John F. Crosby*, "Quién, Revista de filosofía personalista" 10 (2019), 27-44.

[22] "The substantiality of the self should be understood less as a substrate and more as subsistence. As has been affirmed repeatedly since classical metaphysics, the formal constituent of the substance is not to underlie, but rather to subsist. That the living being in general and the human being in particular are substances would not mean, then, so much that there is an inalterable substrate, as that living beings are subsistent. That the living being is always *the same being* (*el mismo*) does not mean that it is also always *the same* (*lo mismo*)." (J. Vicente y J. Choza, *Filosofía del hombre*, 425).

and disappear. Hypnosis, for example, generally supposes a certain weakening of the self, and some mental illnesses (for example, schizophrenia) produce very complex disorders whose common feature is that the self cannot dispose of itself harmonically. But, above such illnesses, there is a much more normal, daily process which makes the self disappear: sleep. Approximately a third of our life goes by without the self being activated and self-conscious. The question that naturally arises, then, is the following: *How can the self be responsible for the subsistence of the subject if it seems that the self does not subsist?*

It is a problem that is difficult to solve, but it does not seem possible or logical to seek a different solution since there are no consistent alternatives to the self as the ultimate foundation of the person. Once the concepts of substance or suppositum have been discarded, we would be left with the possibility of affirming that it is the person himself that constitutes the ultimate nucleus of the human being but, in reality, the person is a complex structure made up of many components, so that trying to found the subsistence of the person in the person would be like begging the question. Which, on the other hand, is confirmed if we attend to a decisive fact: the person dies. And, therefore, if the ontological foundation of the person resided in the person himself, this would mean that he would completely disappear with death, which does not seem to be the case, given the existence of spiritual dimensions in the subject (cf. Ch. 14.3).

It does not seem, therefore, that there is another possibility for the ontological foundation of the subject other than the self. And although its "disappearance" may constitute a problem, if we analyze the matter in detail we can see that perhaps it does not have the radicality that it seems to present at first glance, since the self does not really disappear, but hides or becomes inactive. In fact, if this were not the case, we would have to speak of different people each time the self is activated, or, if we consider that it is the same self, of a kind of "resurrection". But this is not the case, and precisely for that reason the continuity of the subject and the person is maintained. There has not been a disappearance of the self, but only a deactivation. The self, the same self, has continued to be present, only that self-awareness, due to the influence of the human body, has been deactivated. When the body is activated again, the self activates its self-awareness and regains lucidity. We consider, therefore, in conclusion, that the self is the ontological core of the person, since only a personal structure can be the ultimate foundation of the person, and the most radical structure that persons have is precisely the self.

The following adaptation of the diagram of the person (figure 7.1) made by Carlos Martínez) shows in a very graphic way the structural relevance of the self in the entire personal structure.

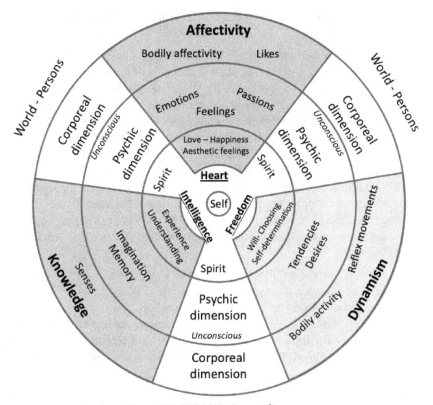

Figure 7.1: PERSON - *Burgos diagram.*

d) Personal Identity: Fact and Process

The self is the center of the person and is thus also the radical place of identity, of *my* identity. Identity is what I am in concrete, as a specific and *unique person* identifiable without error among the billions of people that populate the world. But, although my identity is unique – how could it be otherwise? – it has a *complex structure*. We find, on the one hand, the ontological root to which we have just referred, our radical and unchangeable foundation. I am this person and not another; and it will always be like that, with no possibility of change or mutation. But, at the same time, and on the basis of that unchangeable identity, the person can undergo, and does undergo, important changes that affect her way of being as a person, which varies over time. The person remains the same, but due to internal decisions, external events or the meeting of both, his deep structure changes and, consequently, so does the way in which the person lives himself, understands himself and copes with the world. This process of change, of biographical modulation of the ontological identity, lasts a lifetime and begins in childhood. [23]

In fact, it could be said that, at the beginning of life, the *biographical differentiation* between persons is slight and, in fact, it is easy to verify that all small children look alike; among youth there are also many similarities in character, but then persons become ever more distinct and their inner worlds become stronger and more unique. Personal identity is, therefore, a fact and a process, something given and something to be achieved, a point of arrival and an objective always on the horizon. From the very fact of being a person, I always have an identity, an ontological identity that does not change and cannot change, because otherwise I would become another person. But since I am a temporal being, extended over time, projected toward the future (*futurizo*), as Julián Marías would say, my identity is always changing because time does not stop and it places before me new obstacles and new situations (see Chapter 15).

There are moments in life in which our biographical identity is well established because we have properly assimilated and integrated everything that has happened to us up to that moment in such a way that we live the present with tranquility. We know who we are, how we are and what we want. They are, generally, times of interior tranquility and serenity: the years of maturity, some of the childhood years or a well-accepted old age. And there

---

[23] There are many proposals about the deep structure of the self, both at an anthropological and on a psychological level, such as those of William James or Freud. A more recent psychological proposal is that of Castilla del Pino, which distinguishes the subject, the I's and the self. "The subject as a system constructs the adequate model of the I (the *ad hoc* I) for each situation or context. The subject is describable according to the I's that it constructs, that is, according to its actions. The identity of the subject, the self, is the image that others and he himself form from the starting point of the I which he constructs for each situation." (C. Castilla del Pino, *Teoría de los sentimientos*, 347). This description seems to describe well some experiential data. On one hand, the fact that we can act in quite different ways according to the contexts and the persons with whom we relate, *almost* as if we were different persons; and, on the other hand, the fact that the image we have of ourselves (and that others have of us) proceeds from the set of all those I's that we activate according to different situations. This theory, however, would be invalid if one did not admit the existence of a profound (ontological) self, unique and ultimate (the subject in Castilla del Pino's terminology) which is responsible for all the superficial selves ("I's" for Castilla del Pino), which we construct and according to which we act depending on the circumstances (work, family, sentimental relationships, sports, etc.). That self, furthermore, does not disappear when the superficial "I's" are activated, since the latter are, at bottom, no more than a specific modulation of the profound (ontological) self in a determined circumstance.

are other periods, on the contrary, in which our identity is questioned, in crisis: we do not know what we are, or we do not know what we want to be. The person confronts radical changes which leave her disconcerted and perplexed, and they force her to make decisions that will affect her future, as happens in adolescence. But, in general, all periods of life are decisive, in one way or another, in the formation of personal identity.

The initial moment, childhood, as Freud, Erikson[24] and Piaget, among others, have shown, is particularly important because in those years the basic identity of the person is formed and later on it will be very difficult to change it. But there are also very relevant modifications in subsequent phases. The period around age 40 is particularly significant because it presupposes the change of slope in the horizon of existence.[25] The end of life is already seen, in a distant but real way: thus, it brings with it a profound examination and evaluation of everything previously done and it also permeates the decisions to be adopted with a particular transcendence, because they will not be able to be revoked any more, as was the case in youth. And a great change also happens in the last period, which Guardini has treated so brilliantly,[26] because old age is not simply a life's change of slope; old age means the end and therefore it affects in a radical way the subject's identity, reinforcing it if it is seen as a good consummation of life or, on the contrary, breaking it and fragmenting it if the end is not accepted.

---

[24] Cf. E Erikson, *Childhood and Society* (New York: Norton, 1950).

[25] Levinson's studies from his perspective of the life cycle have contributed notably to the knowledge of this period. See D. J. Levinson and W. E. Gooden, *The life cycle* in H. I. Kaplan, B. I. Sadock, *Synopsis of Psychiatry* I, 1-13.

[26] Cf. R. Guardini, *Las etapas de la vida* (3rd ed.) (Madrid: Palabra, 2000).

Part III.
Spheres of Human Acting

The structure of personal being has shown us the essential skeleton of the person, the elements of which he is composed and the relations and dependencies between them. But the person is not merely structure, he is dynamism and activity, he is action. The person acts, and by means of his action, he creates an unsuspected world which transforms the entity of things. Cities, highways, crops, instruments, technology, art, science are the result of the acting of the human being who manifests and expresses himself in a multitude of spheres. In addition, action is not just an exterior product, the transformation of the world, it is also manifestation, expression and modification of the person himself who executes it. So, it is a multiform and varied, fascinating and powerful reality.

This is the topic that we are now going to address. First, we will analyze action as such and its relation to the person. Then we will explore two specific spheres: language and work. It is certainly a very limited selection, but inevitable, given the space limitations. In any case, we have attempted to study two topics which seem to us to be especially important and which, in addition, serve as indicators and reference points for similar developments that may be realized regarding other types of activity.

One last issue: the fact that we treat action in a section of this book distinct from that which corresponds to the structure of the person does not mean that it is not an essential dimension of the human being. The person is not a static being who, once constituted as such, acts or does not act as an optional reality. Very much to the contrary, he is an intrinsically active and dynamic being who manifests himself primordially in action, to the point that it can be said that action is the person himself manifesting himself, modifying himself, unfolding himself, and expressing himself. Why, then, have we not included it in Part II, which describes precisely the essential structure of the person? The reason is fundamentally pedagogical. It is not possible to talk about everything at the same time and, although action is intrinsic to the person, it is meaningful to distinguish between some more static aspects and other more specifically dynamic ones. We have collected the first in Part II of the book and we will take on the more specifically dynamic ones in this third part.[1]

---

[1] In any case, there is an important presence of the personal dynamism in Part II through the consideration of tendencies and, above all, of freedom.

Chapter 8

Action

8.1 The Structure of Action

a) Person and Action

In the human being many dynamisms exist – instinctive reactions, vegetative drives, inclinations, tendencies – but none of them is in concordance with what we properly call action. Action does not make reference to any partial dynamism, but to the activity of the entire person as such, to the dynamic and unitary unfolding of the human being.[1]

"I act." In this sentence resides the essence of human action as we want to consider it here. I, as a person, unfold my potentialities and enter into contact with the world and with myself through the mystery of human action.

What is the essence of this reality? It is not easy to respond to this question because, like all deep human realities, it tenaciously resists description and, even more so, definition. But we can say that a key and defining element is *causality* (cf. Ch. 6.2.b). What radically distinguishes human action from any other dynamism that can take place in the interior of the human being is that the subject is the free cause of the action. "I act" means that I, the subject, freely place an action in the world. Without me, that action would not exist

---

[1] Wojtyła distinguishes these phenomena appealing to two different experiences: "something occurs in the human being" and "the human being acts". Only in this second case are we properly talking about action (cf. K. Wojtyła, *The Acting Person*). This work is fundamental for an adequate reframing both of the relation between person and action and of the very conception of action due to the newness which it contributes with regard to the classical perspective. The latter has tended to study action as an external actualization of an already constituted subject. "The objective of our study, entitled *The acting person*," affirms Wojtyła, "is to invert that relation. It is not a dissertation about action in which the person is presupposed. We have followed a different line of experience and understanding. For us, action *reveals* the person, and we look at the person through his action. [...] Action offers us the best access to penetrating the intrinsic essence of the person and permits us to reach the greatest possible degree of knowledge of the person. We experience the human being inasmuch as he is person, and we are convinced of it because he performs actions." (ibid., 42). The classic work of M. Blondel, *L'action* (Paris: 1893) offers a similar perspective.

while, on the contrary, my voluntary determination presupposes a modification in the being of the world which follows its being "placed in existence," as Maritain would say.

Having established the most radical essence of action, we can now ask about the reasons for our activity. Why do we act? Why do we submerge ourselves in a sometimes even unbridled and voracious dynamism? First, we do it out of *necessity*. We cannot not act, because the structure of our being is dynamic. We are movement and we are obligated to act, to the point that, as we know, omissions are also a specify way of acting that consists of the decision to do nothing. But human activity is not, evidently, a mechanism, an end in itself, but rather what permits us to achieve our fullness, our self-realization, that which we intuit in our interior that we should be, but we have not yet obtained. From this point of view, *the reasons behind acting are as numerous as the aspects of human nature with which they correspond.* I can act in order to achieve what I am not and what I believe I should be, in order to test myself, in order to create or to destroy, in order to possess or to give, in order to transform the world or society or to perform that particular type of activity which consists of repose and quietude. In any case, I seek a certain fullness, an object, a longing, something that I did not possess before and that I consider favorable to me from some point of view. This is the essential spring which lances the fascinating mechanism of human action.

b) The Objective and Subjective Dimensions of Action

The structure of human action is highly complex, to the point that an entire branch of philosophy, *action theory*, exists to study it. Here we will limit ourselves to the description of the two most essential dimensions that we can discover within it and which correspond with the two dimensions of freedom that we have already studied above.[2]

The first of them, the *objective* dimension, arises on contemplating the transcendence of the person over his action and fundamentally corresponds with the intentional dimension of freedom. When we act, we seek our own fullness, but by way of something that cannot exactly be identified with us, since we are not our actions. "I act" means that I cause the action, that I produce or generate it; and this implies, in turn, that it is distinct from me. It

---

[2] We will not consider, for example, intentionality, the scope of action, finality, motivation, voluntariness, etc. Some of them are addressed in ethics. Some useful references are: J. de Finance, *Essai sur l'agir humaine* and G. E. M. Amscombe, *Intention* (Cambridge: Harvard University Press, 2009).

accompanies me inseparably, but it cannot be identified with me. Under this aspect, action appears as a product, as an objectifiable fact, as a reality distinct from my being and, for that very reason, with the capacity to interfere and modify the world in which it arises. A worker who builds a building, for example, is acting, but his action is distinguished from him. At the moment in which he builds, he transforms the world which surrounds him, but he can stop doing it; then, he continues being himself and the action remains objectified in the task he has realized. Therefore, from this perspective, action is fundamentally *transitive*, since it does not remain in the subject, but rather is transferred to the world and its objects (or persons).

The objective dimension of action shows, in addition, the primacy of the person over his acting (the classical *operari sequitur esse*). The action is essential, but the person is more essential, and has an ontological priority. If the action disappears or is completed, the person still remains. It is important, however, to not understand this priority in the sense of an unreal "staticness" of the person. It makes no sense to speak of a person who does not act from the first phases of his existence, but in that acting there is an ontological priority of the subject-person.

But action is not only objective, it also has a *subjective* dimension. The phenomenon "I act", just as we saw with the phenomenon of the will, "I want," presupposes a subject who performs the action but who, at the same time, is modified by it, because the action, in the end, is never separated from the person. The "act of building" does not exist, but rather "someone who builds"; the "act of running" does not exist, but rather "someone who runs" and who, while building or running, gets tired or fatigued, gets stronger or perfects himself. This means, from another perspective, that action, as one can easily intuit, never completely leaves the interior of the person, because it is the person himself, modifying himself, activating himself and developing himself. And it also means that action modifies the world but, above all, it modifies the person because it comes back to his interior, changing it in one sense or another. This quality of action, by which it comes back to the person who performs it, is called the subjective dimension and corresponds with the self-determinative dimension of the will.

From this point of view, and in a different way from what occurred previously, action is *intransitive* because it remains in the subject. And this – it is important to emphasize it because of what will be said below – occurs *in all human actions*. Even in activities as apparently material as construction or other manual or mechanical tasks, one can never prescind from the fact that we are before a *subject* who is acting, that is to say, that that dynamism which modifies matter is the result of a subjectivity that unfolds and which is inevitably modified in turn by that activity. More concretely: the person who builds gets tired, becomes fulfilled or frustrated, reaches his objectives or fails, enjoys or gets depressed.

Finally, one must add that the complete and real action is neither subjective nor objective, neither transitive nor intransitive, but rather *simultaneously possesses both qualities*, just as occurred with freedom. "I act" implies a subject who performs an action which changes the world but also changes the subject himself. In Wojtyła's words: "actions, which are the effect of the operativity of the person, unite in themselves exteriority and interiority, transitivity and intransitivity. Each action contains in itself a certain intentional orientation, is directed toward determined objects or sets of objects, is directed beyond the person. At the same time, action, in virtue of self-determination, penetrates into the subject, into the self, which is its first and essential object. In this way, in human action transitivity and intransitivity are both present at the same time."[3]

c) Unity, Complexity and Integration

Together with the subjective and objective character, it is possible to indicate, in addition, other characteristics of action. On the one hand, it is *unitary*, that is, it corresponds with the totality of the person and is an action of the person as such. Neither the intellect, nor the will, nor the senses act, rather the man or the woman acts as a unitary and individual being.[4] But this very fact places in relief another quality: *complexity*. The human being is a unitary being, but he is at the same time complex and thus action is as well. The human being is a self who causes an action, but in doing so he has to activate numerous mechanisms and dimensions in a coordinated and complementary way, and this is not always simple or easy. It requires a lived effort on the part of the subject. It requires the task of *integration*.[5]

Integration fundamentally implies the need for the subject to include, in a correct way, in his act of self-determination the different aspects of the structure of the person: body, psyche and spirit. And this task, in turn, has two

---

[3] K. Wojtyła, *Persona y acción*, cit., 177.

[4] The self also plays an essential part here (cf. Ch. 7.2.b).

[5] "It does not make sense to continue the centuries-long struggle between the different strands and potencies of our being: life and spirit, will and reason, feeling and understanding, sense perception and intelligence... Nor it is beneficial to concede an exclusive primacy to some of these over the others. What is decisive is to learn to integrate its fields of energy through the force of love, understood as a firm will to create elevated forms of unity." (A. López Quintás, *Inteligencia creativa*, 417, and more generally, 417-438).

dimensions: a psychological one and a moral one. *Psychological integration* implies the achievement of an internal coordination which permits the subject to do what he really desires to do and in the way he desires. If he desires to drive, for example, he needs a period of learning – which affects both the motor aspect and the intellectual one – to be able to do it in a coordinated and effective way, and the same thing happens with the rest of the activities. An adequate and sufficient psychological integration is the result of an entire life of learning, it is entirely necessary for a normal life and its lack can result in different degrees of pathology.

A *moral integration* is also necessary, so that the person may structure himself internally in such a way that it is easy for him to perform good actions (the classical concept of *virtue*). This coordination and harmonization is not always simple because the different human capacities, having a certain degree of autonomy, can become mutually opposed or may attempt to block the self's decisions. Even though I know, for example, that an action is incorrect, the passional impulse can push me to perform it.[6] And, in the other direction, different internal mechanisms – tiredness, arrogance or pride – can impede me from performing actions that I think I should do. Both psychological and moral integration are a task for one's entire life and are never definitively achieved because new behaviors to learn and control, difficulties that did not previously exist, etc., always appear.

8.2 Realms of Activity

a) The Classical Tripartition and its Limits

We can now consider if it is possible to *classify* or in some way order the realms of action. If that were the case, we would be before a very useful instrument for comprehending the human being, since it would tell us a lot about what he is and what he aspires to. The classical tradition made such a classification and divided human action into three major types: making, acting and contemplating.[7] Let us look at the content and characteristics of each one of them.

---

[6] Which does not imply that it ceases to be an action of the self, but rather that the self decides to let himself be pushed. This is perfectly expressed in a liquor advertisement: "Let yourself be taken by your senses."

[7] This classification can be obtained, for example, from Book X of the *Nicomachean Ethics*, where Aristotle assigns the highest place in human activity to contemplation and places in second place ethical virtue. To the latter, one must add the third dimension: producing.

1) Doing or, in a more precise way, production (*poiesis*) is made up of actions in which the subject performs a concrete and material activity that implies a transformation of reality through the elaboration of an object external to the person. Examples are easy to find: making objects, instruments, utensils, working in material professions such as construction, agriculture, industry, etc. The characteristic of these actions is that *they are essentially transitive* since they operate under the domain and direction of the object. The person, in fact, is focused on the realization (production) of the external object which is what determines the beginning and the end of the action. The productive action, in short, consists of the modification of the world by means of the realization of an object.

2) The second category of action is the moral act that Aristotle calls *praxis*. Unlike production, it is not a mere external going out of the subject with the result of a modification of matter. Praxis affects the subject himself because its content is formed by actions of an ethical nature, which imply a decision about good or evil and, therefore, determine the subject's ethical orientation. Praxis, for this reason, does not revert to the material exterior, but to the anthropological and ethical structure of the person and therefore has an intransitive dimension. The human person, through his moral action, becomes good or bad, and, if he repeats the acts sufficiently, virtuous or vicious through the generation of habits. Praxis is, therefore, *basically intransitive*.

3) Finally, Aristotle contemplates a third category of actions: contemplation or *theory*, which constitutes the most perfect level of activity because it is the purest and most disinterested type of action. Production is centered on and dominated by the object. Praxis frees itself to a great extent from that domain, but not completely, since the chain of moral decisions that good and evil impose and the gradualness with which good is achieved, inject an inevitable dose of purpose outside the action that degrades its quality. But in contemplation, in pure theory, nothing is sought beyond the

action itself: the end is integral in the action and therefore, the action is full and perfect.[8] One contemplates to contemplate and the very action is contemplation. For this reason, contemplative action is perfectly intransitive since it remains completely within the subject. For Aristotle, contemplation is, fundamentally, an intellectual activity: the most perfect action of the most perfect faculty.[9]

What assessment can we give to this division? It has some truly valuable elements, but it also presents important problems. With regard to the positive aspects it seems clear that it captures in a lucid way three areas or realms of activity which are truly distinct and about which we can have some sort of personal experience: working hard on something material, doing a good deed, contemplating the sunset or praying with devotion. Also, the distinction it establishes between the transitive and intransitive aspects of action seems to be, and historically has been, a decisive contribution.

But this does not preclude that significant limitations may be indicated as well. The first and principal of them is that, while at first the contrary may seem to be the case, *this classification does not describe real actions, but rather formal aspects present in every action.* In reality, exclusively transitive or exclusively intransitive actions do not exist; rather, in every action (whether it is laying bricks or "contemplating") there is a transitive or objective dimension and another intransitive or subjective one. Every action is performed by a subject who always modifies his own intimate self while performing it (whether more or less is another issue) and who, similarly, seeks an objective through its performance (even in the case of contemplation). All of this means that although the distinction between "acting" and "making" contains valid elements, it can only be accepted if it is understood not as a distinction between two completely independent genera of actions, but as a distinction between formal aspects which can be possessed by one and the same action.

---

[8] "This activity (contemplation) is the only one that seems to be loved for itself, since nothing is derived from it except contemplation, while from practical activities we obtain more or less, other things, in addition to the action itself" (Aristotle, *Nicomachean Ethics*, X, 1177b 1-5).

[9] Thomas Aquinas later rectified this position by introducing the element of love and thus allowing the rectified Aristotelian category to be applied to the Christian notion of loving contemplation of God in heaven. However, the presence of Aristotelian intellectualism is still very strong as can be easily verified by reviewing the *Summa's* questions dedicated to happiness (*I-II*, qq. 2-5).

Nor is it appropriate, moreover, to drastically separate the technical aspects (making) from the moral ones (acting) since in real human actions that separation does not occur. The worker who builds a fence is simultaneously performing a human and a technical task with which he contributes to the wellbeing of others, and the same thing occurs with any other action. It makes no sense to distinguish merely technical or productive actions from others which are moral, above all because they do not exist and, *a posteriori*, because this distinction ends up causing very grave problems when one attempts to reunify the technical sphere with the moral one. In this case, something similar occurs to what we have commented on previously regarding the realms of action. One may, of course, distinguish between the technical and moral aspects of an action, but only from a formal point of view, not as distinct actions.

In reality, and perhaps it is something which has not been sufficiently taken into account by those who have accepted this classification, this division, Aristotelian in origin, is very much linked to the social and cultural circumstances of the Greek and Roman era (and, in part, of the Medieval era which took it up again) and that explains in part the problems which its uncritical utilization implies (cf. Ch. 10.1). The distinction between doing and acting, for example, has its origin in the Greek social structure, which entrusted hard, material tasks to the slaves, while it reserved political and leisure activity to free men.[10] One thus understands that the former was considered the inferior and transitive activity, since it consisted of the production of objects by beings who were not considered persons. And something similar occurs with the overvaluation of contemplation or speculation. On the one hand, Aristotle was conditioned by his vision of the gods. Not possessing the concept of love, the Aristotelian gods could not act, since that would have meant that they sought something of which they lacked and, therefore, that they were imperfect, that is, non-gods. Consequently Aristotle concluded that acting (*agere*) could not be the most perfect activity, since the gods do not perform it.[11] To this is added his intellectualism. Since, for Aristotle, the most perfect faculty is the intelligence, the most perfect act, which corresponds with the exercise of the most perfect faculty, is precisely speculation or contemplation.

That the problems that this distinction posed were not sufficiently recognized by the medieval Christian thinkers who adopted and formalized it can also be linked in part to the social and cultural conditions which

---

[10] Cf. Aristotle, *Politics*, III, 4-5.

[11] Cf. Aristotle, *Nicomachean Ethics*, X, 7, 1178b.

consisted, in this case, of the fact that the majority of these thinkers belonged to religious orders. Since they were not implicated in professional jobs (then in formation), the distinction between the technical and the moral did not pose excessive difficulties and, still less, the primacy of contemplation. On the contrary, the latter was in concordance with the religious ideal of separation from the world and from worldly things in order to concentrate on the "only important thing", and so it appeared to be the more perfect type of activity, in agreement with the Aristotelian tradition, although slightly modified, since Aristotle proposed an almost exclusively intellectual contemplation, something incompatible with Christianity.[12]

b) The Thousand Faces of Human Action

The problems we have just indicated inevitably impose the abandonment of the classical tripartition (although without renouncing its enduring elements) and obliges us to ask if it is possible to establish today a different and better classification of human activity.[13] Our opinion is that it is not. The tremendous complexity of the modern world has multiplied the different types of actions in such a striking way that attempting to box them into closed categories seems like a vain and impossible task. That does not mean that we should renounce the study of action; on the contrary, the effort to understand the human being's activity should increase, but respecting the diverse and differentiated identity of each one of its acts, something that, in any case, is not limited to our era, but has always been a privilege of humanity, as this precious text from the Bible reminds us:

> "To every thing there is a season,
> and a time to every purpose under the heaven:
> a time to be born, and a time to die; a time to plant,

---

[12] We may find a confirmation of the problems which this tripartition poses in the relative sterility of the classical (Aristotelian-Thomistic) tradition with respect to the analysis of human action. This tradition has made profound structural analyses of action and its morality (St. Thomas' *Summa Theologiae* is a pioneer in this terrain), but action as manifestation and expression of the person has rarely been addressed, something which is easy to confirm if one looks, in this tradition, for studies on work, aesthetics, art, or culture. None of these activities can be ascribed directly to any of the previously indicated categories and that may explain, in part, their absence.

[13] Hannah Arendt, in *The Human Condition*, classifies human activity into labor, work and action, but, although her analyses are suggestive, it seems to us that they fall into the same error that we are commenting on here: they reify in types of action mere aspects that really exist but only as modalities of concrete actions.

and a time to pluck up that which is planted;
a time to kill, and a time to heal;
a time to break down, and a time to build up;
a time to weep, and a time to laugh;
a time to mourn, and a time to dance;
a time to cast away stones, and a time to gather stones together;
a time to embrace, and a time to refrain from embracing;
a time to get, and a time to lose;
a time to keep, and a time to cast away;
a time to rend, and a time to sew;
a time to keep silence, and a time to speak;
a time to love, and a time to hate;
a time of war, and a time of peace."[14]

Each one of these actions merits *a distinct and diverse study*, because each one influences the human being and the world in a different way. Making war is not the same as doing politics, being born or dying, loving or hating. Each one of these acts demands a specific treatment that captures the essence which constitutes it and which accounts for the weight that it has in the life and history of humankind. Any other approach seems to us to imply an unjustified reduction of the multiform and splendid world of human action.[15]

---

[14] Ecclesiastes 3:1-8.

[15] An expansion of this question in J. M. Burgos, *Praxis personalista y el personalismo como praxis*, in J. M. Burgos, *Reconstruir la persona. Ensayos personalistas* (Madrid: Palabra, 2009), 97-133.

Chapter 9

Language

The first sphere of action we are going to consider is language, speech. Ever since Aristotle, it has been considered one of the essential characteristics of the human being, but in the 20th century the so-called "linguistic turn" in philosophy has highlighted in a spectacular way this dimension of the being and activity of the human person. Analytic philosophy, originating in the English-speaking world (with names like Peirce, Wittgenstein, Austin, Searle and Grice) has elaborated penetrating analyses of linguistic structures, the speech act and conversation. And, from the point of view of so-called "continental philosophy", the importance of language for philosophizing has also been deeply – even to an almost exaggerated extent – revalued. In this sense, Appel, the main representative of transcendental pragmatics of a Kantian filiation, has indicated that "the fundamental change in the relationship between language and philosophy, which distinguishes the 20th century from earlier centuries, consists of the fact that language ceases to be treated as an *object* of philosophy and, for the first time, it is taken into account as a *condition of possibility* of philosophy."[1]

In a similar, although parallel, line, hermeneutics has insisted on the importance of the linguistic comprehension of reality, but to the point of transforming the philosophy of language practically into an *ontology*. "Language is the house of being," said Heidegger[2] and, even more radically, Gadamer affirms: "The being which can be understood, is language."[3]

These positions, which are clearly excessive and which today may have lost part of their initial force, speak to us, however, of the radical importance of language in human life and make us understand that we are not before a mere *instrument* which the human being can take or leave as one uses a tool; rather, we are before a reality which can be identified with our very being, which modifies us and in which we live. Language precedes us and influences us, it determines our way of seeing the world and our thought, it modulates

---

[1] K. O. Appel, *Die idee der Sprache in der Tradition des Humanismus von Dante bis Vico* (Bonn: Boubier, 1975), 22.

[2] M. Heidegger, *Carta sobre el humanismo* (Madrid: Taurus, 1970), 7. English version, *Letter on humanism*.

[3] H. G. Gadamer, «Hombre y lenguaje», in *Verdad y método*, 149.

our relationships with others and with ourselves, in addition to having in a sense its own independent life: indeed, languages, in a mysterious but real way, create their own laws and subsist on their own as a result of a collective task, impossible to trace in its details.

In a book such as this one, it is evidently impossible to attempt even an introductory study of the multiple questions which language poses. Therefore, we will limit ourselves to three aspects of particular importance for philosophical anthropology: the difference between animal language and human language, the relation between language and thought, and one of the most novel points in language theory which situates us in the sphere of pragmatics and connects with the structure we are giving to this anthropology: the understanding of language as human action.[4]

9.1 Animal Language and Human Language

As we just mentioned, it is almost a cliché to say that language is one of the specific features of the human being, but against this oft-repeated affirmation one may oppose a not less manifest and at the same time contrary fact: the existence of a certain degree of communication among animals which, in the case of some superior species – chimpanzees, dolphins, etc. – can become relatively complex to the point of acquiring features similar to language. But, is the system of animal communication really language? Or, said differently, what is the difference, if one exists, with human language?[5]

a) Experiments with Chimpanzees

The attempt to compare – and in some cases to identify – human language and animal language has not been merely theoretical; rather, some investigators have done very spectacular experiments with chimpanzees in order to attempt to reach the bottom of the question and, more concretely, to attempt to determine if, through training, an animal could learn a human language. If these experiments had worked, that is, if chimpanzees had been capable of communicating in a similar way to human beings, the

---

[4] On the relation between language, thought and word, see the interesting study by E. Gilson, *Lingüística y filosofía. Ensayo sobre las constantes filosóficas del lenguaje* (Madrid: Gredos, 1969), specially, 59-92 and 128-161. English version, *Linguistics and Philosophy: An Essay on the Philosophical Constants of Language* (Notre Dame, Ind.: University of Notre Dame Press, 2017).

[5] Confronting this question is important, not only because it will permit us to recognize once more the irreducibility of the person to the animal world, but also because it obliges us to define the specificity of human language.

insurmountable barrier which distinguished human language from that of animals would have fallen and, perhaps as well, the barrier which separates animals from human beings. The results of the numerous experiments that have been performed along these lines, however, have been rather negative.[6]

In one of the first experiments performed, the Kellogs raised their son Donald together with a chimpanzee named Gua treating them both in exactly the same way. Donald, of course, in time learned English, while Gua never produced human sounds and, although he could respond adequately to some 20 words, his behavior never exceeded that of a well-trained dog. This result could be interpreted, logically, as a confirmation of the incapacity of animals for language, but one might also consider that chimpanzees cannot speak, not because they are not capable of it, but because their phonetic apparatus does not permit it. To overcome this possible obstacle, another family of investigators, the Gardners, trained a female chimpanzee named Washoe to learn sign language. The results obtained were in a certain sense spectacular, since Washoe was able to establish numerous communication patterns with some level of sophistication, but it appears that she never performed any authentic syntactic construction. Something similar occurred with the chimpanzee Sarah, trained by Premack. Through a detailed process of learning, she acquired a vocabulary of some 60 nouns, 20 verbs and 30 other words including adverbs and adjectives which she used correctly. But neither was she able to overcome a key point: to perform a *new* syntactic construction, that is, one which she had not previously learned (something which, however, a child performs easily), which posed the crucial question of whether she really understood what she was saying or her language was no more than the fruit of a complex process of learning through conditioning.

The result of these and other experiments, in the end, was negative with respect to the possibility of identifying animal language with human language, because, while some chimpanzees made spectacular progress, they were only spectacular inasmuch as they were animals, since they never went beyond the first elemental phases of speech which a child learns naturally and without any effort or teaching. And this confirmed, in other words, that the radical separation between human language and animal "language" or communication remained intact.

---

[6] See J. Beltrán, *Para comprender la psicología*, 200 and ff.

b) Characteristics of Human Language

That human language is not identifiable with animal language is, at base, something easy to understand and accept since it is no more than a consequence of the radical difference between humans and animals. Karl Jaspers has explained it with clarity: "Calling out, whistling, blowing, or squawking are not languages and the thundering imitation of the noise of nature is as dissimilar to true language as the repetition of sound by a parrot. Language appears when I accomplish my intention with respect to the object and the meaning in the sound that I hear or emit. *To meaningfully address a distant object by means of the voice: that is the fundamental phenomenon of language.* Thanks to language, sounds cease to be sounds and become phenomes. The organization of audible images is the art of language, which created, from times immemorial, as humanity developed, a reality whose transformation has given life to the languages of all the periods of history. Language is the production of phenomes created while speaking which takes place in the human community. In the words of Humboldt, it is 'a world which the spirit must lodge, through the secret work of its force, between itself and the objects.'"[7]

But, what exactly distinguishes human language and animal language? Some of the principal differences are the following:

- *Productivity and creativity:* Human language is *an open system* that can potentially produce an infinite number of words and constructions, some of them entirely original. "Only language," Steiner reminds us, "knows no conceptual or projective finality. We are free to say anything, about anything or about nothing. No deep grammatical imperative, if it can be proved that one exists, abrogates the anarchic ubiquity of the possible discourse."[8] Animal languages, on the contrary, tend to form a closed system with a fixed and limited repertory of elements.

- *Dual structure:* All human languages are organized on at least two levels.[9] For example, if I say, "tomorrow will be sunny," we

---

[7] K. Jaspers, *Lo trágico. El lenguaje* (Málaga: Librería Agora, 1995), 112-113. (The emphasis is ours.)

[8] G. Steiner, *Presencias reales* (Barcelona: Destino, 1991), 72. English version, *Real presences. Is there anything in what we say?* (London: Faber and Faber, 1989).

[9] The real structure may be much more complex, and grammars (finite state, structural, transformational or others) are charged with unpacking it.

can observe that this sentence is formed by four words, each one of which has a meaning; but we can also say that it is formed by 19 letters (phonological units) which do not have any meaning in themselves. It is precisely this double structure – which does not occur in animal languages and which, evidently, is linked with human intellectual ability – that permits human languages to have an infinite potentiality, since with a small number of unmeaningful sounds (about 50), an indefinite number of words and an also indefinite number of combinations and, thus, of meanings can be composed.[10]

- *Conventional symbolic reference:* The majority of words have a conventional relationship with what they mean.[11] For example, instead of "table" we could call the same object any other name and that is in fact what occurs in other languages. This contributes also to the productivity of language since, if each word had to have a direct relationship with what it means, the number of words would be significantly limited.

- *Distance:* Humans can speak about events and objects that are remote in time and in space. It appears that practically no animal, except perhaps bees, can do so.

- *Cultural formation and transmission:* Human language, as opposed to animal language, is formed and transmitted from generation to generation, to the point that it is only meaningful as a collective task. No language is the product of one person alone or of one generation, and less still in the case of important languages which have a millennial history. In a certain sense, language is configured as a reality which is external to the individual human being (this is its objective dimension), which precedes him and into which he is introduced when he is born and little by little over the years acquires through a complex process of learning, which is in

---

[10] It is a structure partially similar to musical language, which allows one to express any song through combinations of individual sounds.

[11] Conventional is not equivalent to arbitrary, since each word has a history behind it, which links it, for diverse reasons, to its meaning.

part extremely mysterious.[12] Animal languages have nothing
to do with this complex process.

9.2 Thought and Language

The second question that we are going to address, and which has been widely
discussed from fields so diverse as psychology, linguistics and philosophy, is
the relationship between language and thought or intelligence. *What is
previous or primary, language or thought?* We will briefly expound the
principal positions and, at the end, indicate the one which seems to us to be
the most balanced and correct.

a) Thought Depends on Language: Linguistic Determinism and Relativism

Some psychologists, among them Sapir and Whorf, have maintained the
thesis that thought depends on language, a position that has been called
linguistic determinism. Sapir initially maintained a moderate position,
indicating that language influenced thought; but Whorf radicalized that
position, affirming that all the high levels of thought proceed from language.[13]
A derivative of determinism is so-called linguistic relativism, which affirms
that different languages lead to different worldviews.

Linguistic relativism is based on the idea that language is prior to individuals.
The child, when he is born, is introduced into a cultural world which precedes
him and which is configured by specific linguistic structures which not only
influence, but structure his mode of thinking in a specific way. In this sense, one
may observe, for example, that English-speakers not only have a different
phonetics from Spanish-speakers, but that their grammatical structure is
different, their linguistic terms of reference are different, and therefore so is
their conceptual world, since words determine concepts. In addition, and at a
more elevated level, one may also observe that the essential categories of their
cultural world are mediated by a different literary tradition which presents

---

[12] How the child learns to speak is a question which has been widely debated by
psychology, but which still remains open because of its complexity, since it affects such
profound and varied questions as the structure of intelligence and of language, the
psychological evolution of the child, etc. Especially well-known in this sense is the
debate between Skinner and Chomsky. The former sustained that the child learns to
speak, fundamentally, through a behaviorist type of learning, while the latter insisted
that the child possesses some innate internal structures which enable him to
understand language (the so-called innatist theory). R. Bayés, *Chomsky o Skinner. La
génesis del lenguaje* (Barcelona: Herder, 1977).

[13] Cf. B. L. Whorf, *Language, thought and reality* (Martino Fine Books, 2011).

different cultural models and models of understanding the world. It is not the same that a nation's cultural point of reference be Dante's *Divine Comedy*, the works of Shakespeare, or Cervantes' *Don Quixote*. The fact that students from those nations familiarize themselves and identify themselves with each one of those literary referents marks their way of understanding the world, of evaluating it and of positioning themselves before it.

Indeed, *determinism*, based on these facts, affirms that linguistic structures determine thought mechanisms, that is, language has primacy over thought; and *relativism* draws as a consequence that, since there are different languages, people's mental structure is different and depends on the linguistic world in which one dwells.

b) Identification between Thought and Language: J. B. Watson

J. B. Watson has maintained the most extravagant thesis in this complex problem, sustaining the identification between language and thought, and defining the latter as a language which we address to ourselves. It is an extreme position, elaborated in the context of early 20th century behaviorism, and motivated by the desire to make of psychology an exact science like the experimental sciences, which led the behaviorists to eliminate from psychology all the non-controllable, internal psychical aspects. Within this line of thought, Watson identified thought and language, and ended up reducing language to a series of controllable motor and physiological behaviors.

This thesis, while it may have contributed some interesting element to the question which we are studying, is evidently erroneous, since it is obvious that there is a dissociation between language and thought. It occurs, for example, with relative ease, that we have difficulty verbally expressing an idea about which we, however, have no doubts, which clearly indicates that we are before different realities. In addition, according to this theory one would come to the absurdity that someone who was incapable of speaking due to physiological causes (deafmutes, for example) could not think.

c) Language Depends on Thought

The most essential representative of this position is Piaget, whose investigations of evolutionary psychology led him to the conclusion that intellectual structures are previous to and more radical than linguistic ones. This can be noted, for example, in the child, who first develops his intellectual abilities and subsequently adapts his linguistic level to his intellectual level. The same may also be observed in expressive processes. First we think, we have the idea, and afterwards we attempt to express it with more or less success. In addition, for Piaget, the structure of our mental and linguistic processes is different, and the primacy belongs to the former. Our mind can simultaneously contain numerous thoughts with a comprehensive and multiform structure composed of numerous interconnected ideas. But only one of them, and in a progressive way, can be verbally transmitted. We cannot say more than one thing, and only progressively, while the intelligence is much faster and more multiform. Thus, sometimes some particularly intelligent people have difficulties with expression because they do not manage to make the powerful flux of their thought flow with a verbally adequate cadence.

In the end, for Piaget, intelligence is a much more profound structure than language. A deafmute who has never spoken does not for that reason cease to have intelligence or the capacity to reason, while a coherent language without intelligence is unthinkable.

d) Relative Primacy of Thought

Which of these three positions responds to the reality of things? From our perspective, we think that the adequate position is constituted by a synthesis of the third and the first positions, but maintaining the primacy of the intellect. In other words, Piaget was right in the most essential aspects, but undervalued the influence of language on cognitive processes.

Intelligence, for the reasons already mentioned, is superior and primary with respect to language, but the latter influences notably the intellectual structure of persons. It influences from birth itself, marking the intellectual orientation of the subject because, while cultural relativism in its extreme version is incorrect, it is correct in its moderate version. We are introduced into the world through a language which acts as an *access filter to reality*. A cultivated and rich language obliges the intelligence toward a sophisticated development; an essential and archaic language blocks to some extent its resources. Words are like the machinery of our thought and, if that machinery is defective or clumsy, thought will be limited, although it will continue to have its own existence. If I am not able to objectify my knowledge in words, my mind will be stunted or delayed because, while concepts initially proceed from things and are formed in words, the inverse process also occurs: words help me to establish concepts, to delimit their contours and establish their physiognomy, and phrases and language oblige me to determine the relations which exist between them.[14]

---

[14] "Philosophy's results are the discovery of one or the other piece of gibberish and the bumps which the understanding has caused itself when it has hit the limits of language. These, the bumps, make us recognize the value of that discovery." (L. Wittgenstein, *Investigaciones filosóficas*, n. 119).

In addition, *words* designate reality and, in this sense, *are a way of knowledge distinct from experience.* They are verbal experiences, accumulated by previous generations to which I make access through language. If, for example, I read the word "swarm" and, not knowing its meaning, I look it up in the dictionary, I will discover that the world of bees and of swarms contains possibilities that I had not thought about nor imagined and which open before me a new space of reality. A space which I have not personally lived, but into which I can introduce myself thanks to the experience of my ancestors who have determined it linguistically. In addition, these spaces of reality are not intermittent, because the dictionary is a self-referential system. It not only offers me isolated connections with reality, but also a linguistically structured conception of life, "the" conception of life of the society which I inhabit, which I have assimilated in its most elemental forms in childhood and in its more sophisticated forms throughout my process of socialization (cf. Ch. 13.2).

All this becomes manifest with special clarity when we learn to speak a new language fluently. A new world – also self-referential – then appears before us, one which is subtler or more rugged, with another order of priorities, with another sensibility for reality, poetic or rigid, urban or country, with a different literary and cultural tradition and with different syntactical structures, although not necessarily of a semantic character. Thus the difficulties with translation.

The key question, and here is where determinists and linguistic relativists err, is that, while all this is very important, it is not essential. What is most important is the intelligence of the person. Without it, the process of mediation with reality which language causes would not have any meaning. And intelligence is essentially identical among all humans. Therefore, although languages may be very different among themselves, persons can, in fact, communicate, transmit experiences and knowledge, translate literary works from one language to another.[15]

---

[15] There are two basic ways to explain this phenomenon. Formalist theories, like Chomskyan generativism, defend the existence of an innate ability, understood as a Universal Grammar, which allows the person to acquire language in a limited way, similar in all languages, but with a different superficial execution. Functionalist models (like Greenberg's) have as their starting point the fact that language is an act of communication and, since the communication needs are basically the same for all human beings, they all have to coincide in some essential features. The variations proceed from different experiences of a physical, cultural or social type, and not so much from innate, *a priori* factors. Cf. J. J. Acero, *Filosofía del Lenguaje I. Semántica* (Madrid: Trotta-CSIC, 2007) and V. J. Cook & M. Newson, *Chomsky's Universal Grammar* (Oxford: Blackwell, 1996).

In conclusion: there is an essential and temporal primacy of intelligence in relation to language, but the latter, in turn, influences the formation of the mind and the development of intelligence in many and important ways.

9.3 Language as Action

a) Doing Things with Words

To consider language as action is not obvious, and in fact it is a very recent perspective, even for philosophy of language which, in its relatively short life, has centered on other questions like meaning (the relationship of words with things) or the relation between thought and language. But language is, fundamentally, *a mode of interpersonal relationship*; languages are systems of communication, linguistic modes of interrelation which allow the subjects to exchange their experiences, their feelings and their knowledge. Only within this precise framework is it possible to deeply comprehend what language means and how and why is has determined rules and structures.[16]

This neglect has fortunately been giving way in recent years to a suggestive and rich philosophical consideration of language as action, thanks, above all, to a profound change of mentality of analytic philosophy, which some have described as a "revolution".[17] It is well-known that this change of mentality has a remote antecedent in the so-called second Wittgenstein. The first Wittgenstein was trapped by the siren songs of logical formalism, and in the *Tractatus* he contributed to the unfruitful search for the linguistic Holy Grail: a precise and formal language in which everything would be rigorous and precise and each word would have only one meaning. However, in his second period, that of the *Philosophical Investigations*, he broke with that path which had been shown to be decidedly false and sterile because it did not recognize an essential fact: language is a system of communication *between persons*, not a logical procedure to define concepts or meanings univocally. Wittgenstein had the merit of admitting errors in his first perspective[18], thus discrediting the path of scientism applied to linguistics; but the great importance of this text is rooted in the fact that it was the starting gun for the philosophical

---

[16] "If one considers that the human being is a communitarian dialogic being, not a being closed in on himself, one realizes that language appears among the moments which form the process of constitution of the reality which is the human person." A. López Quintás, *Estrategia del lenguaje y manipulación del hombre* (3ª ed.) (Madrid: Narcea, 1984)140.

[17] Cf. J. Nubiola, *La revolución pragmatista de la filosofía analítica* (Pamplona: Eunsa, 1996).

[18] Cf. L. Wittgenstein, *Investigaciones filosóficas*, introduction.

reflection on real – that is, conversational – language, basically through two realities: the realization that language is a collective phenomenon, not a private one, and that it works through systems of shared rules which can be compared to games or sports, and which he called language rules.

Wittgenstein, in any case, only initiated the path. The fundamental developments are due to other authors who have elaborated what is considered to be modern linguistic pragmatics. *Pragmatics is characterized, fundamentally, by the fact that it is interested in the use of language* and not by its meaning, as in semantics. What is important to pragmatics is how words are *employed*. And although this evidently depends on what they mean, the principal contribution of modern pragmatics consists of indicating that this relation is not one-directional (from meaning to use) nor trivial. What it affirms, in other words, is that a strict separation does not exist between pragmatics and semantics, since the meaning of the words depends, in great measure, on their *use*. This affirmation may initially seem surprising and even anti-realistic, but it is not, and one example will suffice to indicate what we wish to express. The phrase: "You're so dumb" inserted into the flow of a conversation does not at all have only one meaning. If, for example, it is said with anger it may imply a grave offense, but if a girl says it to a boy who has played a joke on her, it is probable that it is, on the contrary, a show of fun and affection. Does this mean that the word "dumb" does not have any precise meaning? Of course not. It does have a meaning. But is only acquires its ultimate determination in the conversational or dialogic context which is where language truly lives and has meaning.[19] For the topic which occupies us, this means that, without prescinding from semantics and without confusing it with pragmatics, the study of language can only be complete and comprehensible if it is performed in the framework of *communicative action.*

b) The Principal Representatives of Linguistic Pragmatism: Austin, Searle, Grice

J. L. Austin was the first philosopher of language to seriously confront the question of action. His principal intuition was that language is not merely descriptive, but also performative, that is, when we speak, we do not only describe things, but we also *do things*.[20] For example, in phrases like "I ask your forgiveness" or "I baptize you in the name of the Father and of the Son

---

[19] "When someone says the word 'bucket' to me, for example, I know what it means. But, can the complete *use* of the word come to my mind when I understand it in that way? Yes, but on the other hand, isn't the meaning of the word also determined by this use?" (L. Wittgenstein, *Investigaciones filosóficas*, n. 139).

[20] Cf. J. L. Austin, *How to do things with words.*

and of the Holy Spirit", one is not describing a real situation, what one is doing is modifying the situation. We are before linguistic actions in which "I do things" through language. Based on this discovery, and as its development, Austin elaborated his classification of the elements of the linguistic act. The *locutionary* act is the one that we perform by saying something (we emit sounds and sequences of words with a meaning). The *illocutionary* act is what we do by saying something; with a determined sequence of words, for example, I can forgive, advise, suggest, order, etc. Finally, the *perlocutionary* act is the one which is performed because one has said something and refers, fundamentally, to the consequences. Ordering, for example, would be an illocutionary act, while persuading would be perlocutionary because it refers to the effects over the subject.

John Searle, a disciple of Austin, continued the path traced by his teacher, developing the theory of speech acts. "To speak a language," he explains, "consists of performing speech acts, acts such as making statements, giving orders, asking questions, making promises, etc., and, more abstractly, acts such as referring or preaching, and, in the second place, these acts are possible, in general, thanks to, and are performed with, certain rules for the use of the linguistic elements."[21] One of Searle's principal contributions has been his classification of speech acts, which implies an important contribution to the question of *language functions*. His classification is as follows:

- assertive acts: convincing the listener that something is in a determined way,

- directive acts: attempt to make the listener do something: ordering, suggesting,

- commisive acts: committing the speaker to a future behavior,

- expressive acts: expressing the psychological state of the speaker: thanking, forgiving, congratulating,

- declarative acts: modifying a situation, creating a new one: "ceasing", "resigning", "marrying", etc.

---

[21] J. R. Searle, *Actos de habla. Ensayo de filosofía del lenguaje* (Madrid: Cátedra, 1980) 31. English version: *Speech Acts: An Essay in the Philosophy of Language* (Cambridge: Cambridge University Press 1989).

Finally, one must mention H. P. Grice's studies, which imply a further step in this line of investigation and lead toward what one could call *conversation philosophy*.[22] Grice has studied in detail the influence of the speaker's intention on the content and meaning of language and, in addition, has analyzed in an especially profound and new way the rules which speakers implicitly or explicitly maintain in any conversation and which are essential in order for language to be able to function as such and to be meaningful. On this point, his investigations on the principle of cooperation, the implicit presuppositions in conversation, conversational implicatures, etc., are especially interesting.

---

[22] His principal work is collected in H.P. Grice, *Studies in the Way of Words* (Cambridge: Harvard Univ. Press, 1989).

Chapter 10

Work

Work in our society is so obvious that it can be difficult to go deeper into its content and unravel the anthropological resonances that it possesses. For that reason, we are going to begin the study of this topic with a historical outlook which, in addition to offering us interesting information, will allow us to introduce ourselves into the anthropological density which is hidden beneath this word. Once this historical outlook has concluded, it will be much easier to analyze the concept of work philosophically.

10.1 Historical Outlook on the Idea of Work

a) The Ancient World

The Ancient World (Mesopotamia, India, Egypt, Greece, Rome) had a vision of work radically distinct from the one we currently possess. First of all, the concept of work as such did not exist, and the closest concept, manual activity, was undervalued and scorned. It was fundamentally considered an ignominious burden, a necessity which nature imposed and, therefore, proper to inferior social classes, when not to slaves. A text from ancient Egypt in which the activity of the potter is described seems, in this sense, quite revealing. "The potter baths himself in clay and lives like a beast, walks around dirtier with mud than a pig. His clothes are hardened by the clay and his belt is no more than a dirty rag. The torrid air that leaves the oven burns his face. He shapes the clay with his hands and feet, and becomes extenuated with this labor. His entire house is stained with earth and its floor is deformed."[1] This vision of manual work led in practice to a telling identification between work and slavery, on the one hand, and contemplative or leisure activities and free men, on the other. Working was proper to slaves, to such a point that it has been affirmed that, in

---

[1] Quoted in A. J. Carro, *Historia social del trabajo* (8ª ed.) (Barcelona: Bosch, 1992) 85. The description of work in the different ancient cultures is collected on 75-121. As a curious note, one may indicate that already in Ancient Egypt, it was common to recommend to one's children that they become civil servants (cf. ibid., 84-85).

ancient times, "the great nucleus of labor relations was verified through the juridical institution of slavery"[2].

As could be expected, the theoretical formalization of this vision is found principally in the Greeks: Hesiod, Plato and, above all, Aristotle. It was the latter of these who, as we have seen in the chapter on action, elaborated the classical tripartition of human action: contemplation, action and making or production. Work forms part of the third category, which means that it is a transitive and imperfect activity; that is, it has its end outside itself and, thus, has an instrumental value. It only has value in the measure that it serves the consecution of a determined objective. And thus it is naturally associated with slavery. The slave is a mere instrument of the owner, so it is logical that he would do instrumental tasks, leaving the owner (the free man) free for specifically human activities: intellectual contemplation and politics.[3]

Aristotle is very clear in this sense and affirms unequivocally, for example, that if nature had not wanted there to be slaves, it would have made the weaving shuttle function on its own. Since that is not the case, certain beings, slaves, should exist who are destined by nature to make the shuttles function, so that free men (freed from work) may dedicate themselves to occupations that are truly worthy and natural for them.

b) The Middle Ages and the First Centuries of Christianity

Christianity caused a revolution for this perspective for many reasons. First of all, and most of all, because Jesus Christ was a manual laborer, which added one more contradiction to the many which Christianity implied for the ancient mentality. He who presented himself as the Savior of the world had done precisely those jobs which the great of the world deprecated. And, logically, as Christianity imposed itself, a very different conception of work began to arise. First of all, it ceased to be considered as something inferior or despicable, becoming, on the contrary, something which everyone should do. St. Paul's admonition in this sense is paradigmatic: "If any would not work, neither should he eat."[4]

But, in addition, work receives a new meaning and value by being integrated into the religious dimension proper to Christianity. By means of the effort and sacrifices which any work imposes, a human being can be purified, liberated

---

[2] Ibid., 19.

[3] Cf. Aristotle, *Politics* 1331 b12, but the same idea can be found in many other places.

[4] Saint Paul, *Second Letter to the Thessalonians*, 3:10; cf. also *First Letter to the Thessalonians*, 4:9-12.

from his or her faults, and united to the sufferings of Christ, thus collaborating in a redeeming and liberating activity, in the Christian saga of the salvation of humanity. Work, it is true, oppresses and is a heavy burden, but that burden can turn into liberation if an adequate ascetical attitude is adopted, which integrates it into the mysteries of Christianity.

This set of factors constitutes the key points of the Christian "revolution" regarding work. In the words of E. Borne, work, "by acquiring a religious value, enters into human life, serves to place in a person's life the values of sacrifice and detachment; the farmer, the worker has their personal ends and they are no longer mere animated instruments; work no longer exists exclusively to dispense a few who are predestined to the speculative or heroic life from the concerns of existence; it has an inner meaning and it rests on the interior life."[5] But, together with these positive aspects, it is inevitable to observe that Christianity in the Middles Ages did not come to fully value work. The principal limitation consisted of not realizing "the value of work as action,"[6] that is, in *not realizing the value of work in itself,* but only as a means to achieve other objectives; in other words, in not radically overcoming the Greek conception of work as an instrumental, and thus secondary, reality.

The Middle Ages, therefore, maintained – although slightly modified – the Aristotelian tripartition regarding human action, and herein lies its principal limitation in relation to work. In the medieval tripartition, the first place still belongs to contemplation, although now, in contrast to Greek contemplation, it is no longer merely intellectual, but loving contemplation[7]; it is a religious contemplation of God who, in principle, is within the reach of any Christian, although members of the religious life can more easily gain access to it. Then follows moral action, and finally manual or technical activity, work which no longer drags with it the stigma of antiquity, but whose value continues to be merely instrumental. St. Thomas' posture, in this sense, is paradigmatic. When he considers whether manual activity has value, Thomas responds very positively and gives these four reasons. It serves to (1) eliminate vices; (2) acquire virtues; (3) avoid idleness, and (4) give alms.[8] These are evidently positive elements, but the absence of any mention of the value of work in itself is telling.

Why did the Middle Ages not come to understand all the possibilities of work? Above all, there was a deficient interpretation of Christianity. The

---

[5] E. Borne, *El trabajo y el hombre* (Buenos Aires, 1945), 38.
[6] Ibid., 39.
[7] Cf. Thomas Aquinas, *S. Th.,* II-II, q. 180.
[8] Ibid., II-II, q. 187, a. 2.

Middle Ages centered on the curse regarding work found in Genesis: "cursed be the soil because of you: with fatigue will you bring from it your sustenance all the days of your life. It will produce thorns and thistles for you and you will eat the plants of the field. With the sweat of your brow you will eat your bread, until you return to the soil, for from it were you taken."[9] But the Middle Ages did not take account with sufficient clarity of the fact that *it was not a curse on work as such*. The curse consisted of the effort and sweat which, from that moment on, work would include; because, as a matter of fact, in the earthly paradise, and thus before the fall, man had been called to work: he had to cultivate and guard the garden of Eden[10] and he had been entrusted with the task of naming all the living beings.[11]

Why did the deficient interpretation of the Bible prevail instead of the integral interpretation? It is not easy to make strict affirmations, but at least two reasons may be noted. On one hand, the excessive intellectual and social weight of the ecclesiastical and religious class, to which it was difficult, for obvious reasons, to have a profound comprehension of the value of work as action. In addition, one must take into account the social and cultural conditions specific to the era. In the Middle Ages, jobs linked to what we now call the middle class were practically nonexistent, and only some artisans and merchants could be found (apart from peasants and farmers) with a very limited activity with little social recognition in comparison, for example, to the nobility and warriors. In this context, it was very difficult to recognize the intrinsic value of work which may now seem clear to us.[12]

c) The Modern "Invention" of Work

This way of thinking about work changes with the arrival of Modernity, and it changes in such a radical way that some have come to speak of the "invention" of work or, more moderately, of the appearance of the modern idea of work[13]. The deepest reasons for this change may be framed within the general transformation which occurs in the West during these centuries; but,

---

[9] Genesis 3:17-19.

[10] Genesis 2:15.

[11] Genesis 2:19-20.

[12] In the same way, a certain comprehension of the ancient attitude toward manual work is possible if one becomes conscious of the roughness and harshness of manual labor in those eras.

[13] Cfr. D. Mèda, *El trabajo. Un valor en peligro de extinción* (Barcelona: Gedisa, 1998), 50-75 y F. Díez, *Utilidad, deseo y virtud. La formación de la idea moderna del trabajo* (Barcelona: Península, 2001).

if we center specifically on work, we may indicate at least the following reasons, following Unzueta. "The great overseas discoveries transformed everything: immense fortunes were collected, commerce was developed at a large scale, modifications were produced in the nature of the State, the economy, and society, and the bases we set for modern science. A new relation between humanity and the cosmos was also established, a relation which was not closed, with the consequence that, from then on, nature would be a sphere of study and dominion, exploration and exploitation. This change of mentality notably prompted the scientific and technological discoveries and inventions, as well as a concept of work sustained by that idea of dominion, control, and victory over nature. In these circumstances, the Aristotelian primacy of action over work is disrupted, in such a way that human work (*opera*) on nature imposes, from this point on, its superiority over action."[14]

This change of mentality can be detected in many authors, but probably the most significant are Bacon and Descartes. Francis Bacon is the paradigmatic representative of the change of mentality in relation to science. Science is no longer sought in order to contemplate the essences, but to dominate the world; science is power. And the same idea appears in Descartes. "But as soon as I acquired some general notions of physics (...), those notions have taught me that it is possible to come to a very useful knowledge for life and that, instead of the speculative philosophy taught in the schools, it is possible to find a praxis by which, knowing the force and the actions of fire, of water, of air, of the stars, of the heavens and of all the other bodies around us as distinctly as we know the various trades of our artisans, we could take advantage of them in the same way in all the appropriate uses, and in that way become owners and possessors of nature."[15]

These new ideas had in the background the new conception of the individual proper to Humanism, *the anthropocentric turn* characteristic of the Renaissance. The human being is constantly more conscious of his power, of his force and of his creativity, and is determined to explore those capabilities and takes them to their final consequences. And this is going to end in a radical change of mentality in relation to work, because there is already an intuition of all the force of the immense power of the "work", exactly what the Middle Ages had not been able to understand.

---

[14] I. Unzueta, *La crisis de la «sociedad del trabajo» (De Marx a la escuela de Francfort)*, (Bilbao: Servicio editorial de la Universidad del País Vasco, 2002) 33.
[15] R. Descartes, *Discurso del método* (Madrid: Alianza, 1979) 117-118. English version: *Discourse on the Method of Rightly Conducting One's Reason and of Seeking Truth.*

For its part, the Protestant Reformation, under the impulse of Luther and Calvin, meant a relative introduction of worldliness for the Church, and this secularization had a similar effect to that of the "discovery" of the individual: to direct the attention to work in itself, to what it is as a reality as such, not as an instrument to obtain other goods. Max Weber, in his famous work *The Protestant Ethic and the Spirit of Capitalism*, studied this question in depth, placing in relief the contribution of Protestantism to a positive, intrinsic consideration of work. "What was absolutely new was to consider that the most noble content of one's own moral conduct consisted precisely of feeling as a duty the fulfillment of the professional task in the world. Such was the inevitable consequence of the, so to speak, sacred meaning of work, and what engendered the ethical-religious concept of profession (*Beruf*): a concept which translates the dogma common to all Protestant confessions, opposed to the distinction of the gospel norms which Catholic ethics made between *praecepta* and *consilia* and which, as the only way of life agreeable to God, recognizes, not the overcoming of earthly morality through monastic ascesis, but precisely the fulfillment in the world of the duties which are imposed on each person by the position he occupies in life, and which becomes for him, for that very reason, 'profession'."[16]

It is, thus, this complex set of factors that initiates the modern conception of work. The human being, through his work and, thanks to technology and science, continually more powerful and effective, begins to be able to transform the world, to create wealth and modify reality. Work thus starts to be something important and valuable, a basic element of the social structure, a value which societies should care for, foment and preserve. Adam Smith is generally considered the reference point for this transformation, and his work *An Inquiry into the Nature and Causes of the Wealth of Nations* (1776), the first explicit and conscious formulation of this new reality. Work has ceased to be a heavy curse, a mere means to achieve virtues or eliminate vices, and begins to show its potentialities: it is a factor of enrichment, a means to gain time, a social bond and also a commodity that can be sold and bought.

---

[16] M. Weber, *La ética protestante y el espíritu del capitalismo* (Barcelona: Península, 1993) 88-90. English version: *The Protestant Ethic and the Spirit of Capitalism* (New York: Routledge, 2013). The concept of *Beruf* is difficult to translate because in German it means both profession and vocation, a problem which Weber himself indicates explicitly (cf. ibid., 81 and ff.). For a general evaluation of Weber's thesis see J. M. Burgos, *Max Weber e l'etica del capitalismo. Storia di una controversia e nuove prospettive*, «Acta Philosophica», 5 (1996), 197-220.

d) The Society of Work

The new vision of work, however, took time to be implanted, to such a point that, in the *Encyclopédie* of Diderot and D'Alambert, work is still defined as "the daily occupation to which man is by necessity condemned and to which he owes his health, his subsistence, his serenity, his good judgment and, perhaps, his virtue."[17] In fact, only in the 19th century would a conception of work similar to the current one be elaborated. This definitive modern vision arises, on one hand, from the unstoppable development of science and technology which, if in the 17th and 18th centuries showed signs of what it could mean for human activity and the transformation of the world, in the 19th century became present already as a palpable, evident, and amazing reality. The new and numerous inventions allowed for the performance of actions unthinkable until then, the human ability to transform reality was elevated to unsuspected heights, the levels of production of goods and wealth multiplied, etc. Those immense possibilities become configured, in addition, as the fundamental medium for the individual to unfold his possibilities, in such a way that work acquires new values that go beyond what Smith had indicated and formulated. Work becomes a creative personal activity, a means for the development of individual freedom and the key activity for the self-realization of the person. It thus reaches its moment of greatest splendor. It is publicly glorified and becomes configured as the *essential social structure* leading to what has been called the *societies of work*.

The concept of glorification is clear. Work is extolled and valued as one, if not the greatest, of the fundamental goods by all the social classes and from the most disparate ideological postures (liberals, utopic socialists, Marxists, Hegel, etc.).[18] The term "societies of work" is used because this activity has become so important that it constitutes the essential nucleus around which the collective storyline is articulated and constituted. More concretely, this implies at least the following: "1) work permits the learning of social life and the constitution of identities (it teaches us the obligations proper to life in community); 2) it is the measure of social exchange (it is the social norm and the basic principle of the mechanism of contribution/retribution on which

---

[17] *Encyclopédie*, articule «Travail», volume XVII, col. 567b, 1765; quoted by D. Mèda, *El trabajo*, 75.

[18] "Work is the practical art of happiness, while philosophy is its speculative science. It is the remedy of the passions, or better, it is itself a passion which takes the place of all the others; it includes the most precious interests of life, family, city, homeland." (A. De Laborde, *De l'esprit d'association dans tous les intérêts de la communauté*, Paris 1818, 3-4; quoted by D. Mèda, *El trabajo*, 93).

the social bond rests); 3) it permits everyone to have a social usefulness (each person contributes to social life adapting their abilities to social needs) and 4) it is a context for encounters and cooperation different from non-public contexts like the family or the couple."[19]

Currently, and to conclude this panorama, social observers indicate that the society-work relation seems to be in a process of inversion or modification in the direction of a loss of the importance of work. There is talk of a crisis of the societies of work and some authors have spoken of the end of work.[20] Although such an attitude seems clearly disproportionate, that does not mean that problems are not in fact appearing which may acquire continually greater entity if adequate means are not adopted. One of them, indicated by Mèda, proceeds from the disproportionate growth of work within the whole of human activity, which makes other activities (esthetic activities, solidarity, etc.), which are also very important, disappear or become drastically reduced. The solution which this author proposes consists of not "extending the form of work to as many activities as possible, but, on the contrary, reducing the weight of work and allowing those activities which are radically extraneous to the logic of work to be developed."[21] Sennett has described brilliantly a second problem linked to the *form* which work adopts in new capitalism.[22] In today's world, flexible and globalized, a distinctive type of work is constantly being more asserted: short-term work, subject to a great mobility, without clear organizational references, extremely flexible, etc., which, while it may be the adequate response to the economic challenges, has a grave repercussion on the worker, because it imposes on him a degree of inner ductility and uprootedness which only few people can adopt without it affecting their character, their inner stability and their family life. It seems that these serious problems could be solved, at least in part, by the increasing weight of

---

[19] Cf. D. Mèda, *El trabajo*, 135. Although Mèda makes reference to this synthesis, she does not identify with it.

[20] Some references in F. Díez, *Utilidad, deseo y virtud*, 9 and ff.

[21] D. Mèda, *El trabajo*, 238 and in a similar sense S. Zamagni, *Organizzazione del lavoro, uso del tempo e prospettive*, in F. Alacevich, S. Zamagni, A. Grillo, *Tempo del lavoro e senso della festa* (Milano: San Paolo, 1999). In any case, although Mèda is right on this point, her criticism of the current concept of work (above all in chapters 6 and 7) is excessively negative. The return to the contemplative values of antiquity with respect to the supposed exclusively commercial and productive dynamic of current work is, in addition to partial, utopic in the negative sense of the term, in that we have already seen what it implied: the slavery of many for the contemplation of a few.

[22] Cf. R. Sennett, *The Corrosion of Character: Personal Consequences of Work in the New Capitalism* (WW Norton and Co, 1998).

teleworking, which is showing itself capable of increasing the reconciliation between family life and the demanding obligations of professional work.

10.2 Work as Action

The historical analysis we have just made has allowed us to introduce ourselves into the polyhedral reality of work and it has also proportioned us with some keys for elaborating a detailed philosophical analysis. Here, logically, we can only briefly take note of a few questions and we have decided to center on the consideration of work as action.

From this perspective, work fundamentally appears as a *specific type* of action, which cannot be cataloged according to the classical tripartition because it would automatically be included in the category of doing and hence be reduced to a merely transitive and instrumental activity. But, as the history of the concept of work has shown us, this way of looking at things is insufficient and erroneous. It is thus necessary to opt for a personalist analysis of action which may allow us to contemplate it in all its richness and profundity and without reductionism.

This means, first of all, that we must consider *work as an activity which the entire person performs, and which affects the entire person*, not just one or another of his faculties or dimensions. In work, the human being becomes fully implicated; he does not just look outward, toward the job or the product, but he also looks inward, toward himself. Work leaves a very profound mark on the world, but it also leaves a profound mark on the human being. And the adequate way to be able to analyze this phenomenon is to distinguish between a subjective dimension and an objective one, or, in other words, to apply the distinction between the subjective and the objective aspect of action to the concrete case of work.[23]

---

[23] While Christianity was present in the first two phases of the evolution of the concept of work, it has not been so in the last two centuries, in such a way that there does exist a philosophy of praxis and of work from a Christian perspective, which has contributed to the current dissociation between work and religion. In the last decades, the Church has sought to invert this tendency from different areas (doctrines of conciliation between work and religion like that of Escrivá de Balaguer, the Second Vatican Council, etc.). In this sense, the contribution of John Paul II has been particularly important, through the encyclical *Laborem exercens* in which may be found, among other ideas, a systematic presentation of work in terms of subjective and objective work.

a) The Objective Dimension

The objective dimension of work basically reflects its productive and transitive character, which includes not just the possible material results (products, goods), but also the cultural ones. The objective dimension includes all that which work creates and objectifies outside the interior of the person.

In the historical review we have performed we have already had the occasion to observe some of these objectifications, so we will now limit ourselves to taking note of them. Work, in the first place, *transforms the world* thanks especially to the technical realm and, more recently, to its more modern form, technology. The human being unfolds, in a continually more fascinating and powerful way, an immense capacity for humanization, transformation and dominion of the world which implies, in turn, a similar capacity for destruction and annihilation that can now reach even the planet earth as a whole. A second objective dimension of work is its capacity for *production of wealth and wellbeing* which has multiplied (thanks also to technology) with the passage of the centuries and which currently reaches limits previously unsuspected. And, finally, there is its *capacity for social configuration.* Work is not just important for the society due to the goods it produces, rather, it is also the principal element around which society is constituted, and persons position themselves in relation to one another (cf. Ch. 13.3).

b) The Subjective Dimension

The subjective dimension of work arises from the self-referential character which all actions have. As we know, all action, due to its being free, necessarily reverts over the subject who performs it and, thus, this also occurs in work. When he works, the human being not only modifies nature or society, but he modifies himself. "Work is a good of the human being – it is a good of his humanity – because through work, the human being *does not just transform nature* adapting it to his own needs, but he *realizes himself as a human being* and, in a certain sense, 'makes himself more human.'"[24]

In what specific ways does the human being realize himself through work? The historical analysis also gives us some information in this regard. On one hand, there is the discovery of the 19th and 20th centuries: work as an *exercise of freedom and creativity*, as a means of self-realization. By producing and creating, the human being realizes himself because he unfolds and executes his possibilities and abilities, that is, he brings to term in a satisfactory way what we have called existential self-realization (cf. Ch. 6.3). In addition, work

---

[24] John Paul II, *Laborem exercens*, n. 9.

presents *moral* dimensions and it forges his personality. In the complex dynamisms which it presupposes and implies, the human being forges his character, develops specific virtues and aptitudes, learns to live and cooperate with others, contributes to the wellbeing of society, etc. A job well done contributes, therefore, to a second dimension by which the person realizes himself through freedom: ethics.

Josemaría Escrivá has brilliantly synthesized the subjective and objective dimensions of work in an important text in which are included, in addition, other dimensions which can be activated from a religious perspective. "Work," this author indicated, "all work, is a testimony to the dignity of the human being, of his dominion over creation. It is an occasion for the development of one's own personality. It is a bond of union with other beings, a font of resources for the sustenance of one's own family; a means to contribute to the bettering of the society in which one lives, and to the progress of all Humanity. For a Christian, these perspectives expand and widen. Because work appears as a participation in the creating work of God (...) and, having been taken on by Christ, work is presented to us as a redeemed and redeeming reality; it is not just the area in which the human being lives, but also the means and path of holiness, a reality which is sanctifiable and sanctifying."[25]

Finally, and to conclude, we will give two indications about the relation between the subjective and the objective dimensions of work. The first consists of affirming *the primacy of the subjective dimension over the objective one,* which is fundamentally a corollary of the primacy of the human being over his works. As important and amazing as the objectifications which work adopts may be, the subject from which they arise and which has performed them is always more important. Karol Wojtyła has reflected this priority beautifully in a poem entitled *The Quarry.*

"Listen to the constant rhythm of the hammers, so well known,
I project it into humans, to test the force of each strike.
Listen. An electrical discharge cuts the river of rock,
and in me grows the thought day by day,
that all the greatness of work is within the human being."[26]

But that does not mean, and this is the second question, that the objective dimension is not important, nor that it is merely material. In the task performed, in the fruit of work, the human being is present: the effort of his

---

[25] J. Escrivá, *Christ is passing by* (New York: Scepter Publishers, 2010) n. 47.
[26] K. Wojtyła, *Opere letterarie. Poesie e drammi* (Roma: Libreria Editrice Vaticana, 1993), 128

mind and his arms, his dreams, his beliefs and his hopes. Thus, it is very important to establish an adequate and harmonious relation between the human being and the objective aspects of his work, since, if this relation is not achieved, the consequences for the person will be disastrous. Marx understood clearly the existence of this problem in the terrible situation of the proletariat in the era of the industrial revolution and he called it *alienation*. But this same problem, from different perspectives, such as those that Sennett mentions in his study on modern capitalism, is always a threat and should be adequately resolved.[27]

---

[27] We will not treat here the existence of different types of work or, expressed negatively, the difficulty implied in the fact that today work is identified only with "tasks performed within the current juridical and economic framework and remunerated by society" (D. Mèda, *El trabajo*, cit., 114), a conception which leaves out activities as important as some tasks related to solidarity or work in the home. Regarding the meaning of the holiday and free time both in themselves and in their relation to work, see J. Pieper, *Leisure. The basis of culture* (San Francisco: Ignatius Press, 2014).

Part IV. Others

The realms of human acting have shown us the human being in interaction with the world: attempting to understand it or transform it, modify it or dominate it. And it has also shown us the human being dominated, molded or modified by the world. But in those considerations, we have not directly faced a radical question: the existence of other persons and the relation with them. Because the human being does not exist alone, he does not even exist only surrounded by things. He exists, we exist, surrounded by persons, by "others," in an incredible universe of personal beings with whom we establish an inexhaustible multiplicity of relations: relations of love and of hate, of indifference or of self-giving, of understanding or of rejection, of acceptance, of help, of admiration or of astonishment.

In addition, and it is fundamental to emphasize it, the existence of other persons and my relationship with them is not a mere accessory or something optional, it is not even simply something that perfects me, rather it forms an intrinsic part of our being. *As persons we are beings in relation.* We have no meaning, nor are we comprehensible outside the framework of personal relationships. Biologically, we are the product of an interpersonal relationship, that of our parents, and also, from the point of view of our psychological constitution, we are the result of an innumerable flux of personal interactions. Our mode of being, what we in fact are today and what we will be tomorrow, is inseparable from the framework of interpersonal relationships – family, friends, society[1] – in which we have been formed and in which we continue to live.

This is the world we must now explore in its multiple facets, and we will begin with the most elemental structure: the person-to-person relationship.

---

[1] The family and society have a personal aspect and a collective aspect: the family or society as such; or the State as such. In this anthropological study we will focus not on that collective aspect but mainly on the role of the individual person in the family, in society and in the State.

Chapter 11

Interpersonal Relationships

11.1 Person and persons

a) "It is not good that man be alone."

The text which probably shows in the most patent, beautiful and precise way the human need for relationship is found in the first pages of Genesis:

"Then the Lord God said, 'It is not good that the man should be alone; I will make him a helper as his partner.' So out of the ground the Lord God formed every animal of the field and every bird of the air, and brought them to the man to see what he would call them; and whatever the man called every living creature, that was its name. The man gave names to all cattle, and to the birds of the air, and to every animal of the field; but for the man there was not found a helper as his partner. So the Lord God caused a deep sleep to fall upon the man, and he slept; then he took one of his ribs and closed up its place with flesh. And the rib that the Lord God had taken from the man he made into a woman and brought her to the man.

> Then the man said,
> 'This at last is bone of my bones
> and flesh of my flesh;
> this one shall be called Woman,
> for out of Man this one was taken.'

Therefore a man leaves his father and his mother and clings to his wife, and they become one flesh" [1].

This text, full of anthropological significance, shows at least the following realities:

---

[1] Genesis 2:18-24. A very profound analysis of the anthropological and theological message of the initial chapters of Genesis is performed by Karol Wojtyła/John Paul II, *Man and Woman He Created Them: A Theology of the Body*. Translated by Michael Waldstein. (Boston: Pauline Books & Media, 2006). Wojtyła's general vision of interpersonality is offered by Sergio Lozano, *La interpersonalidad en K. Wojtyła* (Valencia: Edicep, 2016).

a.1) The Insufficiency of Acting

Adam (the human being) finds himself surrounded by things and animals and even has an important task to perform: to give a name to created things, that is, to know and to possess all that exists, since, as we know, "the name is placed on things as a veil or as a chain"[2]. But that task, as exciting as it may appear, ends up being insufficient, unsatisfying. Adam-the human being performs it, but it does not satisfy him, because there is something essential which he does not find in that world so diverse ("he did not find an adequate help for him") and whose lack implies loneliness.

Here we find one of the constants of human existence: the tension between activity, with the personal fulfillment and the domination which it brings with it, and its insufficiency as a radical goal of human aspirations. Things never fully satisfy the human being because they do not respond to the most elevated needs of his interiority. And that dissatisfaction or unrest is perhaps something that comes especially into relief in our urban and technological era, in which an exorbitant capacity for possession becomes confronted with an impoverishment of personal relationships.

a.2) The Need for the Other

Loneliness only disappears with the appearance of the other. Eve appears before Adam as something radically distinct from all that he had previously contemplated; she is not a thing or an animal, but *another person*, another self: "bone of my bone and flesh of my flesh". She is similar to him and that implies that Adam can share with her his life. He is not, we are not alone. There exists an interlocutor, another self with whom to establish a dialogue, with whom to articulate the "I-thou" relationship which liberates the human being from the ontological monologue and places him in an existential relationship.[3]

The second topic which this text of the Bible offers us has only been treated by philosophy in recent times. It appears initially with Kierkegaard but is strengthened and developed with the philosophers of dialogue. "Until then," Lorda explains, "the human spirit had been defined especially by its relationship with objects: relations of knowledge (the object before consciousness) and of will (the object as a wanted good). Kierkegaard's contribution puts in first place the relation with a personal being, God. The

---

[2] Cf. Jaspers, *Lo trágico. El lenguaje*, 158.
[3] Cf. Martin Buber. *I and Thou*. Translated by Walter Kaufmann. (New York: Scribner's Sons, 1970) and Juan José Pérez-Soba, *La pregunta por la persona. La respuesta de la interpersonalidad* (Madrid: Facultad de Teología San Dámaso, 2004).

the benevolent attitude; 3) friendship and 4) love[7]. In the last of these, in turn, we will distinguish four types: 1) love as a generic act; 2) love of self; 3) love of neighbor and 4) the type of love expressed in the expression "I love you". We will now treat very briefly the first two interpersonal relationships and we will then spend more time, under the following headings, on friendship and love[8].

1)   The Service Relationship: This type of relationship occurs when the other person is fundamentally for the consecution of a service or the achievement of an objective. For example, if I am going to a pharmacy to buy medicines, my relationship with the pharmacist will be indirect, so to speak, because the person as such does not interest me, but rather what I can get in the pharmacy. This type of relationship is frequent, necessary and possible, although it is evidently the most superficial. In any case, it is convenient to indicate that, although my interest in these cases resides, fundamentally, in the objective that I want to achieve, this does not, however, authorize me to treat the other person in a merely instrumental way. I have to respect him and value him. Social norms of etiquette have, in part, this function. They oblige me to realize that the service is not performed by a faceless being, but by "another someone" whom I should respect.

2)   The Benevolent Attitude: It is a higher level of personal relationship that can be described as a positive attitude, but not excessively committed, with a group of persons with whom we have a more habitual relationship, but without attaching us in an especially strong way. It is, for example, the type of relationship that we may have with workmates, acquaintances, people we see habitually in a café, in a store, etc. The frequency of the contact in this case inhibits the service relationship, which is only possible in the strict sense with strangers; however, the benevolent attitude does not reach the point of implying a relevant attachment. In fact, if

[7] Another classification of interpersonal relationships quite similar to ours in Pedro Laín Entralgo, *Sobre la amistad* (Madrid: Espasa-Calpe, 1986), 156.

[8] This classification describes the types of interpersonal relationships that *positively build up the person*. All those who destroy the person are, for brevity, left out: instrumental use, alienation, hatred, etc.

these people disappear from our lived environment, the latter will only be very superficially affected.

11.2 Friendship

a) General Description

Friendship is one of the most important interpersonal relationships. We need to have friends, people with whom to share our life, who are concerned for us and love us. And this need, and the beauty and value it conceals, is something that humans, and philosophers as well, have always valued. Aristotle is one of the philosophers who has most valued friendship to the point that he states that is "is "one of the most pressing needs of life; no one would accept being without friends, even if he possessed all other goods. The richer one is and the more power and authority he exercises, the more he experiences the need for friends around him."[9] And Cicero, in *On Friendship*, comments: "I do not know if, with the exception of wisdom, the immortal gods have given the human being something better than it."[10]

But what exactly is friendship? What are the characteristics of this interpersonal relationship which makes it so valuable? In a first attempt at an answer, it can be described as an especially deep relationship between two persons which implies the following characteristics:

- A fluid *communication* of projects, interests, feelings, etc., that is, of life.

- Wanting the *good of the other because of the other*, not because his friendship proportions me with services, company or any other type of utility, but for his good. This means, in other words, that friendship is a *good in itself* (a *bonum honestum*), something that is valuable by itself and which should not be sought for another end or instrumentalized in view of another objective. This attitude would imply degrading and devaluing it.

---

[9] Aristotle, *Nicomachean Ethics*, Book VIII, 1. Aristotle dedicates enormous attention to the topic of friendship. In the *Nicomachean Ethics* in particular, two entire books: VIII and IX.

[10] Cicero, *On Friendship*, VI. An elaborate historical look at friendship, in which the specific contribution of Christianity and the position of the principal philosophers are detailed, is proportioned by Laín Entralgo, *Sobre la amistad*, 29-153.

. demands *reciprocity*. One cannot be a friend of someone who does not desire it, because then it would be impossible to share. In this, friendship differs from *love*, which, although it may be deeper, does not need correspondence, as is placed in relief in the cases of unrequited love.

Finally, it is important to note that *friendship is not an entirely univocal term*. Many levels and modalities exist, and it is especially important to distinguish two:

1) On one hand there is the *friendly attitude*. It unites the features we have just indicated, but only on a superficial level, in such a way that it is similar to what we have previously denominated the benevolent attitude. It is possible to maintain this type of relationship with a number of people who are, in reality, acquaintances or comrades, more than authentic friends, since we do not share our intimacy with them.

2) This sharing of intimacy only occurs in *friendship in the strict sense* in which we put into play our subjectivity and our intimacy in a profound way and which, for that very reason, is only possible to maintain with a few people. Let us look at its characteristics in a little more detail.

b) Conditions and Characteristics of True Friendship

Some of the features which define a deep and authentic friendship are the following.

True friendship implies *loving the friend as he is*, that is, with his defects and limits. This is an important criterion for identifying the existence of true friendship, since, if we are disinterested in a person when we discover his or her limitations (or the other person is disinterested in us), it is a clear proof that what really existed was a certain type of sympathy or relational compatibility, but nothing more.

Friendship, in contrast to benevolence, implies *responsibility* for the other. The life of the friend is an important part of our life and, thus, we are responsible for what happens, be it good or bad. If he rejoices, we should rejoice with him; if he suffers, we should suffer with him; and, in any case, we should be available to help him, even if it requires effort and sacrifice.

A true friendship arises from *companionship* and, thus, "it does not exist without cultivating the attention towards the friend and without lending him our time. One of the reasons why this is such is that *friendship does not begin to grow until be open our inner world* to the person who begins to be our friend. This is an act which is perfectly localized in time, above all if it involves an introverted person who holds in high consideration the meaning of allowing someone else to enter one's own intimacy, or one's house, and share inner experiences. If this openness does not occur, because of a lack of will or of knowledge, the friendship will never cease to be superficial and one thus ceases to believe in it."[11]

Friendship also has its *conditions* and among them is *affinity*, that is, a certain similitude and community of interests and likes. In order to share life, a certain similarity of interests, character, social and cultural level, intelligence is needed. In any case, affinity does not mean equality (the idea of twin souls is something of a myth) because, not only can the difference be loved, it can be enriching and complementary: leader and follower, quiet and talkative, restless and tranquil, etc. In addition, friendship can go above any difference because what counts above all is the person as such, independent of his conditions.

The *man-woman* relationship introduces a differentiating and perhaps perturbing element in friendship.[12] On the one hand, friendship diversifies on the basis of whether it is between men or between women. "The central factors of feminine friendship are mutual help and emotional support (...) while men place more attention on the common participation in a determined experience. The similarity in values is also important as a prior requirement for friendship between women; in men, on the contrary, common interests are more important. Non-verbal experiences of affection are, finally, more frequent between female friends than between male friends."[13]

On the other hand, there is *intersexual friendship*, friendship between a man and a woman. According to Marías, this type of friendship centers especially on the persons, because the other takes on special relief by being an incarnation of the mystery of masculinity or femininity. In this relationship, it is less necessary to "do something," since there is a special pleasure in the closeness and the mere presence. Man and woman do not need to look in any direction, it is enough for them to look at each other. Thus, this friendship can possess a special force which, however, is also affected frequently by a greater instability. On one hand, the communication codes become complicated. We

---

[11] Yepes, *Fundamentos de antropología*, 208.
[12] Cf. Marías, *La mujer y su sombra*, 129-155.
[13] Félix Requena, *Amigos y redes sociales. Elementos para una sociología de la amistad* (Madrid: CIS, 1994), 64.

understand the motives behind the attitudes of the opposite ...ation, certain phenomena: a broken engagement, a lack of ...erness or of attention do not have the same meaning if they are done by a friend of the same or of the opposite sex. Finally, and above all, in a deep intersexual friendship, the possibility of love is always on the prowl.

Friendship, on the other hand, like any other human reality, also has cycles. Just as it is born, it can disappear if time, attention, and care are not dedicated to it. Sometimes even external material phenomena like moving to a different home or city or changing jobs can confound a friendship if the effort is not made to nourish and renew it.

11.3 Love

The first fact that imposes itself, on speaking of love, is *a discrimination of its meanings*. This word has always meant many things because of the richness of relations that it contains[14], but especially today we may have reached an extreme degree of confusion due to the inflation of the derivatives of love to which we are exposed. To prove it, let us consider, for example, these four phrases: to love ice cream, to have self-love, to make love, to be in love. All of them use the word love, but each one of them has very different anthropological implications. To attempt to avoid this difficulty, we are going to distinguish *four fundamental meanings* which we will study separately: 1) love as a generic act of the will which desires the good; 2) self-love; 3) love of neighbor; 4) the experience that we can summarize in the words "I love you".

a) Love as a Generic Act of the Will

A first way of understanding love is to conceive of it as a generic act of the will which is directed toward any type of good. Thomas Aquinas has a very clear text in this sense: "Everyone who acts, acts for an end. The end is the good which each one loves and desires, in such a way that it is manifest that *every agent performs any action because of some type of love.*"[15] This definition has

---

[14] A good sample of the numerous meanings and nuances that the word love can have and of the variations it adopts in different languages is offered by Joseph Pieper, *El amor en Las virtudes fundamentals* (Madrid: Rialp, 1990) 417-434. English version: *Faith, Hope, Love* (San Francisco: Ignatius Press, 2015).

[15] Thomas Aquinas, *S. Th.*, I-II, q. 28, a. 6 (emphasis ours) and also I-II, q. 26, a. 2: "The first movement of the appetite toward what is appealing is called love." Also classical is the distinction between love of concupiscence and love of friendship or benevolence: the first is sought because of something distinct from itself and the second is sought for itself. Cf. I-II, q. 26, a. 4.

the great advantage of precision, in addition to its connection with experience, since it coincides with the generic use of the word "love". However, it has an important inconvenience: its excessive generality. According to this definition, wanting to buy a car or being in love would simply be two distinct modalities of love; but we are all fully conscious that we are talking about radically distinct human experiences. Perhaps the key to the problem is in the fact that this definition does not adequately distinguish between the person-object relation and the person-person relation. Now, only in the latter can the word love be adequately and fully employed. Thus, from this definition we retain the relation of love with the will and its tendency toward the good but, in what follows, we will restrict the use of this word to interpersonal relationships. Love, therefore, in an initial approach, can be defined as wanting the good for another person.[16]

b) Self-love

The first person with whom we relate is, evidently, with ourselves, and this relation gives occasion for the first type of love that we are going to consider: love of oneself or self-love. What are its characteristics?

The first thing one must say is that, contrary to the traditional image, self-love is *essentially good* for many reasons. First of all, each one of us is a being with dignity and value, since we are persons. Others are not the only persons, we are as well, and in consequence we are worthy of being loved. It would clearly be absurd to love others and not love oneself, as if we were radically different and some other thing. We thus have to care for ourselves and be concerned for ourselves. In addition, although we are responsible for others, we are mainly responsible for ourselves, because our capacity for self-determination is limited to our own being. We can decide what we want to be, not what others want to be. Thus, we are obliged to lend special attention to *ourselves*, since we are the person in whom we can have the greatest influence and whom we can help the most.

In addition, self-love is not only good, but totally *necessary*, because it is the *motor* of all our activity. In any type of activity (playing sports, studying, putting on make-up) we seek, in one way or another, our good, to the point that, if we did not love ourselves, we would not act. We would not do anything. This is what happens, in part, in cases of depression. The person becomes

---

[16] St. Thomas was also conscious of this fact and in another text offers us a more adequate definition of what love really means: "To love is to desire the good for someone." (*S. Th.* I-II, q. 26, a. 4). He does not, however, use this definition in a systematic way.

∧,

ₓ himself (or even deprecates himself due to an important ₋elf-esteem) and ceases to act, because nothing interests him, and ₋ₙg is worth the effort. On the contrary, self-love understood as self-esteem or valuing oneself is action's necessary spring. The stronger the spring, the greater the force with which it propels the person toward the conquering of important goals on the personal or professional level. This is something so certain that, even when I am making the effort to help others, the love of myself, the search for my good, is always present. When someone sacrifices himself for another, he cannot prescind from the search for his personal good, because it would be illogical to make an effort for others and be a traitor against oneself. "He who loves," say St. Thomas, "goes out of himself in the measure in which he wants the good of his friend and acts. But he does not want the good of the friend more than his own, in such a way that it does not follow that he loves others more than himself."[17] And Christ, it is known, places self-love as the criterion for love of others: "You will love your neighbor as yourself."[18]

Why, then, does self-love have such a bad reputation or, in other words, why is it normally identified with egoism? Because it is especially easy for the human being to center on himself, on his own world and on his own activities, isolating himself and forgetting the people who surround him. In other words, *loving oneself too much is too easy*, and it is thus that, for example, in ascetical terminology, expressions like "forgetting oneself" and "denying oneself" are habitually employed, expressions whose authentic meaning is to induce people to go out of their egoistical concentration on their own interests. We thus arrive at the nucleus of another of the deepest and, in a certain sense, paradoxical anthropological structures. In order to find its full realization, love of self needs forgetfulness of self, because only if we love others deeply and sacrificially, do we really love ourselves.[19] In other words, *loving oneself too much in the sense of being centered on one's own life is loving oneself little*, because, in the brilliant phrase of the Second Vatican Council, "the human

---

[17] Thomas Aquinas, *S. Th.*, I-II, q. 28, a. 3, ad 3.

[18] Matthew 22, 39.

[19] This is the adequate perspective for understanding St. Augustine's famous text: "Two loves founded two cities: self-love to the deprecation of God, the earthly city; and love of God to the deprecation of self, the heavenly city. The first glories in itself, and the second in God" (St. Augustine, *The City of God*, XIV, 28). Self-love and love of God are not counterposed realities, but on an ascetical level, it is always convenient to insist on the so-called "forgetfulness of self".

being cannot find his own fulness except in a sincere gift of self to others"[20], or in the verse of Machado:

> "The coin in the hand
> perhaps should be kept,
> the soul's little coin
> is lost if not given."[21]

We can only fully affirm ourselves, affirming the other at the same time, while closing ourselves off from our neighbor leads to belittling and infidelity. We end up, as Altolaguirre says, being "owners of self, owners of nothing".[22]

c) Love of Neighbor (of the Other)

Love of self takes us by the hand to love of the other, but the latter can acquire very different modalities. The first that we can consider is what we have called "love of neighbor" and which we can define as the will to want the good for the people who surround us. By neighbor, we mean here the set of people with whom we come into contact without the mediation of a special attachment. Neighbor is the person who is close to me. This is enough. And by love for the other we mean a will of transcendence on the part of the subject. The person goes out, leaves the self in order to enter into relation with others, with the objective of reaching *his* good, although this means that he will also reach his own.

What does this love imply more exactly?

Love of other implies, above all, his *affirmation*, assent before his existence. Loving, according to Pieper, is equivalent to saying: "It is good that you exist!"[23] But it is not a merely verbal affirmation, the affirmation of love is existential and thus implies *care* and *commitment* for the person who is loved. The other is to be protected, valued, attended to, guarded in the measure that he needs it. Which means, in turn, commitment and sacrifice. The parable of the Good Samaritan, the example *par excellence* of love of neighbor, is very

---

[20] Pastoral Constitution *Gaudium et spes*, n. 24. This idea is rooted in the experience of each human being, but it has been underscored especially by the message and life of Christ: "No one has a greater love than he who give his life for his friends."

[21] Antonio Machado, *Poesías completas* (Madrid: Espasa-Calpe, 1963), 59.

[22] "He was owner of self, owner of nothing. / Since he wasn't of God, nor was he of men, / Never once a rider was he of whiteness / nor a swimmer nor an eagle" (Manuel Altolaguirre, *El egoísta*, in *Antología de los poetas del 27* (Madrid: Espasa-Calpe, 1983), 397.

[23] Pieper, *El amor*, 436.

clear in this sense.[24] Among those who have manifested their love of neighbor theoretically (the priest, the Levite) there is only one who really manifests it: the Samaritan, who sacrifices himself and in fact renounces his plans, his time and his money for the good of the other needy person whom he does not know. In this way, the parable also shows that love is impossible without gift, without detaching oneself from something which our own, which we may perhaps recover later, transformed, but which initially means a renunciation and a dispossession.

But love is not just sacrifice, it is also *union*. Love of neighbor implies *admitting him* into our surroundings and accepting him, taking responsibility for who he is, what he is and, thus, what he needs. One also loves when one receives another: physically, offering a place to live, or morally, making the other a participant in our world, without excluding him or relegating him. And loving the other is also celebrating his existence with a party and a present: that material object which we give as a pledge of our friendship, of our joy for his existence. But, since what is material only has meaning in the context of what is personal, as a result, St. Thomas indicates that, "love is the essential present. Everything else that is given to us without meriting it becomes a present in virtue of love."[25]

Love for the other as we are considering it here is *close to friendship and benevolence but is not identical* to them. It coincides with friendship in the search for the wellbeing of the other, but it is distinct in that, generally, friends are loved more profoundly and, above all, in that love of neighbor is not directed toward people with whom we have a special relationship. We can love the sick, the needy, our workmates, but they are not people who are essential in our life. They can disappear from our existence and our inner world does not enter into commotion. Friendship, on the contrary, has no meaning without intimacy and knowledge. Love of neighbor is separate from benevolence above all in the degree of implication. Love implies great sacrifices if necessary, while benevolence does not go beyond a generally positive attitude.

d) "I love you."

Love of neighbor is directed to others, but not in a specific way. There is, however, a group of people, generally very reduced in number, with which we establish a *very special and unique* relationship which allows us to say: "I love

---

[24] Cf. Luke 10, 25-37.
[25] Thomas Aquinas, *S. Th.*, I, q. 38, a. 2.

you," with all that that means and brings with it. It is the most elevated level of love and generally is limited to: 1) a particularly deep friendship; 2) family relationships, above all between parents, children and siblings; 3) love between a man and a woman. This modality of love unites all the qualities of love of neighbor in an especially elevated degree, but in addition, it possesses some exclusive and peculiar features. Let us see what they are.

It is *tremendously detached from self.* For the person who is loved, one is ready to give anything, even one's own life: either all at once or little by little, in daily self-giving, like the mother who thinks about her children day and night, or the husband who constantly cares for his sick wife. But, paradoxically and simultaneously, it is a *tremendously needy* love. People who love each other want to be together because they need each other. Presence is necessary: to see, hear, touch and caress each other. And the absence implies the greatest pain, although it does not eliminate the love, but rather reinforces it, if it is true.

In addition, the people we love really are *irreplaceable*; it is as if there were an emptiness in one's heart which only the beloved and no one else can fill. Thus, the disappearance of the beloved constitutes a *tragedy* in the strict sense of the term, that is, a misfortune with no solution. The death of a mother, of a father is irreparable. No one can substitute them. No one will love us with the love with which they loved us: therefore, the only option is to weep their loss, with admiration, as St. Augustine says in *The Confessions*, about the world's indifference to their disappearance. "I marveled at the fact that people continued living, while my friend was dead, as if he had never had to die; and I marveled still more that, having died he whom I had loved so much, I should continue living. Well said the poet Horatius of his friend that he was half of his soul, because I felt too, like Ovid, that my soul and his were no more than one in two bodies, and thus living produced in me tediousness, because I did not want to live partially, and at the same time I feared perhaps my own death, that he whom I loved so much would not die completely." Only time, sometimes more tenacious than love, returns us to life, but the people we have truly loved are never forgotten.

Those we love are, in addition, part of our *identity*, they are inside of us, we are they in some measure. Thus, one is so happy in their presence, and rupture or disappearance can be so painful, since it means breaking with part of oneself. Our parents are in our genes and in our soul, our friends are in our life, and conjugal love is the nucleus of existence. Love, on the other hand, is an *essential part of happiness*. No one can be happy without loving and being loved, as an infinity of poems and songs remind us. But, curiously, *love is a gift*, since no one can be asked, and much less demanded, to love us that way.

Love also brings with it *suffering*. We must in part renounce our own personal things in order to be able to enter into the lives of others and, when we have already been introduced in this path, the separation, illness or misfortune of the person we love, or their lack of love, hurts, because love also makes us *vulnerable*. If we love, we do not manage life in a solitary way, but rather in company and renouncing the barriers, separation and isolation. We depend on others and thus be attacked and injured, since we do not control all the gateways of our existence. The only valid alternative is enclosing oneself and not loving, in order to avoid being weak. But this implies opting also for dryness and sadness, for a type of sentimental suicide. It is for that reason that the poets of all times have always opted for the pain of love instead of the tranquility of routine existence. "It is better to trade pleasure for pain, than to be without love," Juan de Encina tells us in his famous verses.

The Song of Songs is probably one of the texts in which the *force of love* has been most exalted. "Love is strong like death (...) Its darts are burning arrows, they are the flames of the Lord. Copious waters could not extinguish it, nor rivers wipe it away. If some offered for love all his estate, he would be deprecated."[26] Love is terribly forceful because the essence of the person is rooted in it, it is the force of his existential nucleus: the heart. Thus, it can overcome barriers which, for he who does not love, are impenetrable and it can take on enterprises which only have meaning under its impulse. But, at the same time, it also has its *limits*. It requires care and attention, and if it does not receive it, it may die, consumed perhaps not by huge evils, but by the routine of the quotidian, by becoming accustomed to the marvelous.

11.4 Falling in Love

We are finally going to consider love between a man and a woman, "love" *par excellence*, the indisputable reference point for the words "I love you". In the first place, and in this chapter, we are going to consider the process of falling in love, that strange and fascinating mechanism which links in an extraordinary way a man and a woman. In the next chapter, we will take another step, looking at how that love can become stable in marriage and how it bears fruit and becomes social through the constitution of a family.[27]

---

[26] Song of Songs 8, 6-7.

[27] Regarding this question, cf. Wojtyła, *Amor y responsabilidad*, 92-171 and Juan José Pérez-Soba, *El amor: introducción a un misterio* (Madrid: BAC, 2011). Viktor Frankl, *Psicoanálisis y existencialismo*, also has some luminous considerations.

a) The Process of Falling in Love

The love between a man and a woman arises from a primary phenomenon: *attraction and complementarity.* Man and woman are attracted to each other, like each other, need each other and complement each other, not just from the biological-sexual point of view, but much more deeply as persons, that is, emotionally, psychologically and spiritually. This makes the relations between the two sexes constantly tinged with a different coloration than that which marks the relations between men and women separately. This peculiar nuance does not habitually have a very significant relevance. However, there are occasions, few, in which a special spark jumps up between a man and a woman, in a glimmer which seems to indicate that that person is someone transcendental in our life. That glimmer, that chemistry, if it is developed in a specific way, drives falling in love, the process by which a man and a woman become decisive and irreplaceable beings for the rest of their lives. Let us see what the characteristics of this process are.[28]

Above all, falling in love is something that *happens*, which means that it is fundamentally linked *to the heart* and not to the will. Falling in love is not a decision or an election, but a process, something that occurs, sometimes even against one's own will. One does not decide to fall in love with a person, but rather a man or a woman clearly stands out in the middle of the world's crossroads and love arises. That does not mean that the will has no role in this process, but it is always secondary. We can, for example, foresee that we are going to fall in love and avoid the relationship; we can also attempt to conquer another person and make them fall in love, but the nucleus of the process, the essence of falling in love is not in the will or in the intellect, but in the heart, it is an *affective-emotional* question, it is one of the types of spiritual feeling that we have considered (cf. Ch. 4).

In the process of falling in love, the other person attracts as a man or as a woman, but in his or her *totality*, not only in the sexual aspect. Julián Marías has correctly made the distinction in Spanish between *lo sexuado* (masculine or feminine in all their aspects) and *lo sexual* (what is specifically physical and genital).[29]

So, real falling in love is only possible when the man or the woman, together with the properly sexual attraction, which is necessary, feels attracted by the other in his or her totality, that is, by his or her personality, laugh, appearance, character, gaze, intelligence, etc., although all of this is nuanced by a

---

[28] Cf. Rocco Buttiglione, *La persona y la familia* (Madrid: Palabra, 1999), 69 and ff.
[29] Cf. Marías, *Antropología metafísica*, 120 ff.

specifically masculine or feminine tonality. The man falls in love with the feminine gaze, her personality and her grace, and the woman, on the contrary, falls in love with the person of the man in his masculinity.

But, falling in love is not equivalent to being attracted. Falling in love goes much further. It implies that, little by little, the person of the other begins to be essential in one's life. Each one of the details of his or her existence, which may even be irrelevant for others, acquires a transcendental value: their way of walking, of gazing, what he or she does at a certain moment, what he or she thinks and desires. And, gradually, the transcendental step is taken: the subject begins to realize that he or she ceases to be one, *in order to be I-with*, that is, us.[30] A new nucleus of life begins to arise which did not exist before, made of symbols, hidden understanding, anniversaries, favorite places. A world for the moment exclusively private, to which only the two lovers have access, but which grows in an absorbent and expansive way. Love erases the features of others and maximizes the face of the beloved, who becomes omnipresent and enormous, to the point of occupying all time and space.

Love thus acquires its central, decisive and rapturing character, its terrible and beautiful, almost divine, force, which models reality and decides the destiny of human beings because, from that moment on, life only has meaning in the presence of and together with the beloved person. Fernando de Rojas in *La Celestina* has memorably recreated this experience. When Calixto, the novel's protagonist, discovers Melibea, his life is forever altered because he realizes that in this woman is his happiness and his destiny, to the point that he affirms before whoever is willing to hear it, that he prefers the beauty of Melibea to the happiness of heaven. And when his servant, alarmed by his affirmations, asks him, "Are you not a Christian?", he responds, "Me? I am Melibeo and I adore Melibea and I believe in Melibea and I love Melibea."[31]

What do these strong expressions mean? For Marías, it means the discovery of personal love in Western literature[32], that is, the discovery of the existence of an experience through which man and woman recognize each other as absolutely unique and irreplaceable for one another and, thus, forever linked. This is the culmination of love, *its tendency toward permanence*: "until death

---

[30] "Reciprocity obliges us to consider the love of man and woman not so much as the love of one *for* the other, rather as something that exists *between* them. (…) It suggests that love is not *in* the woman or *in* the man – because if that were the case, there would be two loves –; instead, the love is one, *something that binds them*." (Wojtyła, *Amor y responsabilidad*, 104-105).

[31] Fernando de Rojas, *La Celestina* (Madrid: Edaf, 1991), 83.

[32] Cf. Marías, *La educación sentimental*, 84 ff.

do us part". If love is real, if it is not a mirage of my senses or of my intellect, if the other really exists and is unique and my life has no meaning except together with him or her, it is logical to desire that person's presence forever, a presence which is similar to eternity, because time passes quickly with the beloved person, because one lives the fullness of happiness. "I will love you always because you are my love," even in old age or illness, since you will always be the same person with whom I have linked my life.

b) A Few Reflections

The process of falling in love that we have just succinctly described is, however, very complicated and rich and allows for very many modalities and situations. We will briefly take note of some of them.

Above all, *it is not always lineal or complete*, which permits very different situations and also multiple phenomena implying instability: unrequited love, broken and abandoned love, betrayal, forgetfulness, emotional confusions, etc. It is the complex, multiform and mysterious world of love which the human being is always attempting to know and dominate, but which he can never definitively achieve.

An especially important type of situation, which today occurs very frequently due to the excess of sentimentalism which impregnates our society, is *false falling in love*, which can happen for multiple reasons. Sometimes, the cause lies in *erroneously identifying the person with one (or several) of his characteristics*. One quality (beauty, intelligence, etc.) can blind the person, incapacitating him or her from objectively seeing the personality of the other person with whom he or she is (believes him or herself to be) in love. If, for example, a woman is beautiful, one may perhaps forgive her for her bad manners, her roughness or her whims, and a man could perhaps think he is in love with her, when in reality he is blinded by her beauty. Now, if that relationship continues and culminates in a life in common, the failure is practically assured, when the man runs into the true personality of the woman.

A false falling in love can also occur due to a *lack of deepness in the relationship*. The man (or the woman) is momentarily "pierced" and (supposedly) falls in love, but a few weeks or months later, that feeling disappears without leaving a trace. What happened? Evidently, we are not before a case of falling in love, but rather a strong attraction which has not reached the deep layers of the subject. That he or she may have experienced the feeling as a falling in love can have its cause in multiple factors: the immaturity proper to the adolescent who neither knows himself nor knows what love is, or simply a devaluation of the word "love" which ends up being used to designate any type of strong attraction between a man and a woman.

This situation has become widespread in our societies due to a strong devaluation of love, turned into a mere attraction and, therefore, easily interchangeable or disposable. Today, supposedly, a person is deeply loved, but tomorrow, love has disappeared and the person, previously so "loved," has been replaced by another who, in turn, will be replaced by another in the future. Although in some cases a true love could end and be replaced by another authentic love, love has been trivialized and this intense word is often used to describe interpersonal relationships governed by mutual selfishness rather than by a true love of gift. Naturally, they are fragile and ephemeral relationships, which break at the slightest disagreement or frustration.

A different phenomenon related to falling in love happens when someone *truly falls in love with the wrong person* because this person does not correspond, is married or otherwise committed, or for other reasons. These situations are inevitably painful (and sometimes tragic), but they cannot always be blamed on immaturity or irresponsibility on anyone's part because, as we have said, love does not depend entirely on the will. Thus, someone can fall in love with another person, even if they do not want to, and it can also be impossible to stop loving someone, even if you know that it is an impossible or inadequate relationship.[33]

Finally, *love allows for degrees and modalities.* We may be more or less in love with a person but without feeling the need to bind ourselves to that person for life because he or she is irreplaceable. In addition, like any other human reality, it is influenced by culture and history.[34] The love relationship between man and woman inevitably depends on the conception that each one has of the other. And, while the personal love that we have described here can probably be found in any culture, it is the love *par excellence* of Western and Christian culture which assigns a very high and equal value to each person, whether man or woman. Only from these premises does it make sense to bind oneself for life and exclusively to a man or a woman in a project of common life.

---

[33] Cervantes offers in *Don Quixote* a wide range of unrequited loves.
[34] Cf. Marías, *La educación sentimental,* where some of the modalities which love has adopted in the West are analyzed: courtly love, institutional love, romantic love, etc.

Chapter 12

The Family

12.1 The Founding of the Family: Engagement and Marriage

a) Engagement

When a man and a woman are conscious of the fact that they are fully and radically in love, the question of their future appears. The internal characteristics of falling in love – sharing a life, the tendency toward permanence, sexual complementarity, the lived need for the other person, the possibility of having children and forming a family, etc.[1] – naturally make a life in common and a life project advisable. But this project does not arise on its own, it is a long and enduring path. In the first place, this project should begin with a *decision* to undertake it: "I do." And then it should be maintained despite the difficulties: "Until death do us part." The time of engagement is precisely the period of time in which a man and a woman evaluate and mature the possibility and convenience of making this decision and transforming love into a joint project of common life; that is, it consists of passing from a phase of knowledge and affectivity to a moment in which through freedom they will be at each other's mutual disposal for the future.

In that period of time, the man and the woman should, above all, verify the reality of their love, because we have already seen that this area is very prone to illusions. It is necessary to assure that the love for the other person is a reality, that is, that one loves the other person as he is, with that person's virtues and positive qualities, but also with his limitations, avoiding the grave error of loving, not a real and concrete person, but a feeling or a non-existent

---

[1] There are many ways of understanding family, love and interpersonal relationships between men and women. When treating them in a very synthetic way in this book, for reasons of space, we will limit ourselves to *directly developing* the one that we consider most appropriate according to the personalist vision that we have presented in the previous pages More specifically, we are going to present the interpersonal and social features of what we have called the *contemporary western family* according to the classification we have made in J. M. Burgos *Diagnóstico sobre la familia* (Madrid: Palabra, 2004). Similar views can be found regarding the interpersonal dimension in Wojtyla and Xosé Manuel Domínguez Prieto, *Antropología de la familia. Persona, matrimonio y familia* (Madrid: BAC, 2007) and, in the sociological part, in Donati and De Nicola.

person, a product of an immature imagination. And this verification requires time and mutual knowledge, because the couple is not going to share a few hours together, but an entire life. Thus, a deep knowledge of the other person is necessary, a knowledge of his character, interests, life history, moral and religious convictions, family, aspirations, etc., which may permit one to be reasonably sure that it will be possible to share a life together.[2] The knowledge should also include the conviction that the other person is capable of taking on the commitment which a life in common implies: having children and educating them, moral height, deep convictions, etc. Because, even if two people are in love, one of them may be incapable – due to his character, mentality, or for other reasons – of taking on the commitment and obligations which marriage implies. Taking the step toward a conjugal relationship in these conditions would mean, with a good probability, the beginning of a small or large tragedy.

b) Marriage

When love's process of maturation is considered complete, the transcendental moment of the decision to marry arrives, a decision full of anthropological content and which encompasses at least the following dimensions:

b.1) The Interpersonal Dimension

Marriage is *above all the personal commitment of a man and a woman to form a community of life* which gathers together the following characteristics. It is a *life-long commitment* since what is sought is precisely to share one's existence with a concrete person. Thus, while that person lives, our existence will be linked to him. In addition, it is a commitment which is founded on the idea of a *full self-giving*. The spouses mutually give their life to one another as man and as woman and from here do the other characteristics of marriage arise.[3]

---

[2] Since the engagement does not yet imply a decision to share a life together, it excludes a total corporeal (sexual) self-giving. "*It is nefarious in human life to perform gestures which do not express that of which they are a sign.* Sexual relations move the spirit precisely because they remit to an occurrence of the greatest importance: *the committed intermixture of two persons.* If such a commitment and such an intermixture does not exist, the sexual gesture is reduced to a mere corporeal joining which, seen alone, lacks meaning, and thus appears literally 'senseless,' absurd." Alfonso López Quintás, *El amor humano* (Valencia: Edibesa 2017), 212.

[3] Full self-giving does not mean absolute self-giving. The spouses give themselves to one another completely only in the conjugal dimension, since otherwise marriage would smother the person.

Above all, it is exclusive from the personal point of view, that is, *it is only possible to marry one person* since one cannot share one's life fully with various men or women at a time. But it also *demands the exclusivity of sexual intercourse* for various reasons.[4] First, because the spouses give their sexuality to one another in view of the configuration of a family. The man makes a commitment with the woman in such a way that she may be able to develop her potentiality as a mother and, in a similar way, the woman gives the man her femininity so that he may also develop his paternal potential. This relationship cannot be generalized without breaking the personal intimacy on which it is founded. But, in addition, the sexual exclusivity is demanded because the sexual act only has meaning within the framework of the full personal union, since, as we have seen, the body is not an instrument of the person, but rather the person himself in his corporeal dimension. Bodies that unite fully can only be a reflection and confirmation of persons fully united. Thus, separating sexuality from the marriage relationship and performing it with other persons implies a betrayal of the personal relationship which is lived out between the man and the woman, and it is subjectively experienced as such when this actually happens to a couple[5].

b.2) Social Dimension

Although marriage is essentially an interpersonal relationship, it also has a social dimension. Our culture, perhaps especially from Romanticism on, has insisted a lot on the personal aspect in comparison to the institutional-social aspect, which has served to revalorize all of its affective and interpersonal aspects. But it is important not to fall into the opposite extreme and emphasize this aspect so much that the social dimension is annulled or becomes publicly invisible, because this in the long run would end up doing damage to marriage, which would then become a private institution, without social relevance.[6]

Marriage, as an act in which two persons marry and as the life community which arises from that act, is a social reality fundamentally for two reasons.

---

[4] Cf. K. Wojtyła, *Amor y responsabilidad,* 255ff.

[5] This type of behavior suffers a strong erosion in our days but both people and society pay a high price for it in terms of personal suffering and social disruption.

[6] Domestic partnerships constitute one of the most recent attempts to annul or limit as much as possible the social dimension of marriage, reducing it to its interpersonal aspect. But the intrinsic instability and difficulty of this relationship becomes manifest in the fact that the society ends up regulating (through domestic partnership laws) what was initially characterized precisely by its essential rejection of all legal regulation.

First, due to the elemental fact that the bride and groom, as much as love may for a period of time isolate them from the rest of the world, *come from a determined social setting and will later live in another social setting* which will influence their life in an important way. In Hitchcock's *Rebecca* this problem is posed directly and dramatically. A man and a woman fall in love in a hotel in which they live (momentarily) as subjects independent and isolated from their social environment and their past. But, when that process of falling in love is transformed into a wedding, that is, into a common life, the confrontation with the social context from which they come and in which they must live inevitably occurs. And, in the concrete case which Hitchcock proposes to us, this means that, if the young Rebecca, American and pretty, but not very cultured and refined, does not want her marriage with her noble Englishman to fail, she will have to be able to assume her social role as an English lady and overcome, as well, the profound influence which her husband's previous marriage left on this personal environment.

But marriage does not have a social dimension just because it occurs in the context of a society, but also for a much deeper reason: it implies *the creation of the key element of society:* the family. Marriage is the seed of the family and the family is the essential structure of the society. Therefore, marriage, although it is a fundamentally personal act, is at the same time essentially social, in such a way that, under normal conditions, the wedding always occurs in that context. It does not make sense to get married alone. The wedding occurs in the presence of parents, friends, and the totality of the society in which the bride and groom live; it is public and known and is legally regulated, because both those who get married and society want to place into relief (and regulate) the formation of a new social nucleus which will later develop as a family with the appearance of children, who are the new members of the society.

b.3) The Religious Dimension

Finally, marriage has a religious dimension.[7] In this case, it is not an essential dimension, since this aspect is not placed directly in play in the relationship between the man and the woman; but it will necessarily be present if the bride and groom are believers, since they are probably making the most transcendental decision of their lives. For this reason, and thus does it in fact habitually occur in the majority of societies, this dimension cannot be lacking at

---

[7] Cf. Aristotle, *Economy*, III, 2.

human spirit is defined much more by its personal relations than by its relations to objects. After the immense Hegelian monologue of the Absolute Spirit, the philosophies of dialogue were going to arise."[4] Later, through works like those of Nédoncelle and Levinas, there has been a great deepening in the importance and transcendence of intersubjective relations, to the point that Levinas, in *Totality and Infinity*, and perhaps in an excessively unilateral way, has even attempted to rethink philosophy in its entirety from the starting point of the relationship with the other.

a.3) The "Other" as Man and as Woman

But Eve is not just a person, *she is a woman*. Adam's admiration is also admiration before someone equal to him and at the same time profoundly distinct. It is the eternal admiration of man for woman in its first manifestation and it is also a primordial ascertainment of the fact that, in reality, the "human person" does not exist in abstract, but rather two distinct types of human persons exist: man and woman[5], who, in addition, are marked from their origin by a common corporeal and existential destiny: "Therefore, man will leave his father and his mother and will be united with his wife and they will be one flesh."

This fact, evident in itself, is however also *relatively new from the philosophical point of view*. Philosophical anthropology has for centuries centered on the exclusive study of "the human being" as such, forgetting the difference between the two types of "human persons". Only with romanticism has this richness of diversity with its multiple implications begun to be faced.[6]

b) Levels and Types of Interpersonal Relationship

The "I-thou" relationship is especially rich and difficult to classify because persons can activate within it a practically infinite gamma of types. Thus, its study makes a selection necessary. In this text, we are going to center on four types which seem especially significant to us: 1) the service relationship; 2)

---

[4] Juan Luis Lorda, *Antropología. Del Concilio Vaticano II a Juan Pablo II* (Madrid: Palabra, 1996) 30. Regarding dialogic philosophy see Pedro Laín Entralgo, *Teoría y realidad del otro* (Madrid: Alianza, 1983).

[5] See G. P. Di Nicola, *Uguaglianza e differenza. La reciprocità uomo donna* (Rome: Città Nuova, 1989).

[6] Personalism is one of the philosophies which has most developed this point. For example, Julián Marías' *Metaphysical Anthropology* is one of the first systematic texts of "dual anthropology", that is, in which the man-woman difference is treated directly and extensively.

the moment in which the society attends the birth of a new nucleus of life and the bride and groom consolidate their future together as man and woman.

The wedding unites, from the starting point of a *festive gathering,* these three dimensions in almost all cultures. It is, above all, the feast of love and joy between a man and a woman, the mystery of masculinity and femininity which intertwine once again in a unique couple among the millions of couples which have populated and will populate history. It is also society's feast because the wheel of life continues. From the love which is sealed between the man and the woman will arise the new children who will farm the fields, build the houses, work in and direct the businesses, and take care of their elders when they begin to get old. And, for such a transcendental phenomenon, the blessing of God is required, because it does not make sense to undertake such an important enterprise in the absence of his blessing or against it. The Christian wedding, for example, is a magnificent show of the conjunction of these three realities in the framework of an eminently festive celebration.

c) The Failure of the Marital Project

The marital project does not always consolidate itself. On occasions, the conjugal relationship deteriorates to the point of making very difficult and sometimes impossible not only the achievement of common objectives, but even the common life itself. Authentic tragedies then occur, because the collapse of the existential project of the subject affects him in its very roots. Marriage and family can be the most important source of happiness, but for that very reason, its disappearance or fracturing implies terrible suffering.

What are the possible ways out of this situation? The simplest is separation, which should normally be temporary, but if it is not effective, then definitive. Man and woman separate from each other temporarily so that the distance may calm the tensions and positions and assist in reflecting on and rebuilding the relationship. But if that measure is not adequately effective, then the only option is definitive separation. Separation, as such, implies the decision not to build a similar life project with another man or another woman, because an irrevocable decision was made, which should remain while the person with whom that decision was established continues to exist. It is a decision which is coherent with the reality of marriage, but it is hard, which means that it can be very difficult to maintain without the support of strong moral and religious motivations.

Another possible way out, which has for some time been admitted by legislation in many countries, is divorce, which means the total rupture of the previous attachment and which implies, thus, the explicit possibility of building a new attachment. This possibility might seem to be the most reasonable and logical, but it is very important to realize that the acceptance of divorce profoundly changes the intrinsic reality of marriage. Building a life project in which the man and the woman give themselves to each other fully for their entire life in order to form a family is one type of personal relationship. Building a life project in which a man and a woman decide to live together as long as their relationship is correct and during the timeframe in which it is, is a different type of relationship, because the implication of each member of the marriage is lesser, and thus the stability of the relationship is much more fragile. In the first case, there is a total self-giving; in the second, there is a partial self-giving, since the person always leaves open the door out, if difficulties arise. And the problem is that that door, much more easily than it should, can end up becoming an authentic hole which is used with incredible frivolity, as the statistics of so many countries show.

But one must insist that, although divorce is a way out of a grave problem, in itself it is something bad: the recognition of a failure and, habitually, the beginning of a tragedy, especially if that couple has had children.[8] The child is the fruit of the corporeal fusion of the father and the mother, in such a way that the rupture radically affects the child. In the child, two worlds which separate and take different and normally incompatible paths will remain vitally united, in such a way that the tension is permanently assured. On the other hand, the rupture is also profoundly traumatic for the couple, since the fabric that has been weaved through years of common life cannot be separated painlessly. Friendly separations are possible but occur much more frequently in movies than in reality. This whole set of evils implies that the society (and governments) should make an effort to promote familial stability.

12.2 The Essential Human Community

The family is born in marriage as a project, as a foundation, but it is fully constituted with the appearance of *the child*. The child marks the passage from "couple" to family, creating a new reality which modifies forever the previous relationship between man and woman.[9]

---

[8] Regarding the practically unsolvable problems which divorce creates see I. Théry, *Le démariage. Justice et vie privée* (Paris: Odile Jacob, 1993), especially chapter III.

[9] In this section we analyze the family from a structural point of view. Some indications regarding its historical variations and how these should be interpreted may be found in J. M. Burgos, *Diagnóstico sobre la familia* (Madrid: Palabra, 2004), G. Campanini, *Realtà e problemi della famiglia contemporánea. Compendio di sociologia della familia* (Milano: Paoline, 1989) and D. Herlihy, *La famiglia nel medioevo* (Bari: Laterza, 1994).

a) The Family is Fully Constituted with Children

The birth of the child implies the culmination of the project of love of the man and the woman because it is love made life and incarnated forever in a person, as Miguel Hernández has beautifully expressed:

"Melted together forever in the child we have become:
melted together as our voracious yearning desires:
in a bouquet of time, of blood, the two branches
in a bundle of caresses, of hair, you make the two."[10]

And from this culmination and fructification of love, the family is born.

It is born, first of all, through the unfolding, development and transformation of the complete framework of *interpersonal relationships* which constitute it. The man ceases to be simply a husband in order to be, in addition, a father; and, in the same way, the woman ceases to be just a wife, in order to be, in addition, a mother. And logically, they are father and mother in reference to a radically new person who is the child and who will live the relation of sonship or daughterhood. Fatherhood, motherhood, sonship, daughterhood, this is the goal to which the man and the woman confusedly aspired in the phase of falling in love and to which they arrive with the appearance of the child. A goal which implies a radical change in their lives and which becomes manifest, for example, in the fact that within the family the man and the woman will gradually transition from being called by their given name (reflection of their personal identity) to being called dad and mom: their new identity. And not only by the children, but sometimes also by the husband or the wife ("tell your father…"), which is proof that this change implies not just the creation of new relationships (fatherhood, motherhood, sonship, daughterhood), but also a modification of the existing relationships (those of the couple).

In the second place, the family is born as a *social reality*. This framework of relationships is socially constituted as a new social nucleus, as a new community or, as it is also habitual to say, a new essential cell of society.[11]

---

[10] Miguel Hernández, "Hijo de la luz y de la sombra," in *Obra poética completa* (Madrid: Alianza, 1990), 439-440. The child's birth shows, in addition, the superiority of marriage over other human projects, because these can produce things or structures – perhaps spectacular – but only marriage is capable of "producing" persons.

[11] It is common to distinguish between communities of *adscription* (those which persons constitute with their free acts) and those of *belonging* (in which one participates without the mediation of a free decision and even without knowing it, such as the nation). The family is a mixed community which unites elements of both.

b) Essential Characteristics of the Family

Let us now see what the principal characteristics of the family are:

1) It is the place of *origin of life* and, thus, of the perpetuation of society.

2) It is the *first interpersonal community* for the child: every human being establishes his relationship with the world and with society through a family and it is, therefore, the place where each human being forms his *identity*.

3) It is the *first intersexual community*. The two sexes relate to each other in society fundamentally through the family. In the first place, husband and wife, then the children with the father and with the mother, and finally the brothers with the sisters, depending on the situation.

4) It is also the *first intergenerational community*. The parents create the next generation (which constitutes the future) and the grandparents imply the connection with the generation of the past. Here as well, we may turn to some verses by Miguel Hernández to capture this with profundity.

"I do not love you alone, I love you in your ancestry
and in all that, from your womb, will descend tomorrow.
Because the human species they have given to me in inheritance
the family of the child will be the human species.

With love on our shoulders, asleep or awake,
we will keep kissing each other in the profound child.
Kissing each other, you and I, our deceased kiss each other,
the first inhabitants of the world kiss each other."[12]

5) It is the place where the most essential human relationships are established and inhabit: couple love; fatherhood, motherhood, sonship or daughterhood, and siblingship, in such a way that it can correctly be called the *affective center of the person*. These relationships are ends in themselves, in

---

[12] Miguel Hernández, "Hijo de la luz y de la sombra," in *Obra poética completa*, 440.

contrast to what occurs in other communities. These relationships are not sought in order to achieve other objectives, but rather as final ends of existence which do not require anything beyond themselves.

6) The family develops, in addition and finally, other *social functions*: economic, educational, primary and secondary socialization, assistance to persons with disabilities, etc., which vary between cultures and eras, but which are always very important.[13]

For all these reasons, one may clearly affirm that the family is the essential cell or structure of society and that the overall functioning of the social framework depends to a great extent on the good functioning of the family.[14]

12.3 The Formation of the Subject

We have just seen the importance of the family considered structurally. Now, we are going to discuss the family-person relationship which we will analyze from two perspectives: the *initial phase*, in which the subject is born and is forged as a person, and the *family-adult person relationship*. We will begin with the first and we will distinguish several levels, since only in that way is it possible to describe the transcendental importance which the family has in the formation of the subject.

a) Basic Care

The family intervenes, in the first place, proportioning the subject what is necessary to satisfy his life needs. It is certainly a basic, but essential, level. Especially in the first years of life, the child receives, thanks to the very important dedication of time on the part of the parents, such elemental but indispensable things as, above all, life itself, and, later, nourishment, clothing, care in case of illness, a place to inhabit, etc.

The fact that it has to do with biological necessities could lead one to think that, on this level, the human being acts in a way similar to animals, but this is not completely correct. As we have commented, in the person practically nothing is purely biological, in such a way that what the parents offer their children always has a cultural mediation (cf. Ch. 3.4). A child is not nourished

---

[13] Cf. Pier Paolo Donati, *Manuale di Sociologia della Famiglia* (Bari: Laterza, 2006).
[14] Cf. Pier Paolo Donati, *La familia il genoma che fa vivere la società* (Rubettino 2013).

like an animal, nor does he sleep in the same way, nor does he inhabit a similar place. In any of these cases, there is a social, intellectual and cultural mediation, which leads us to the second level of influence of the family on the subject.

b) Primary Socialization

The second dimension through which the family influences the person in a significant way is the so-called process of primary socialization, which consists of proportioning the person with *the basic elements that allow him to integrate into a determined society:* primary abilities (walking, eating, moving around, orienting oneself, etc.); basic knowledge of places, persons, objects, etc.; language; the basic norms of social relations (manners, the importance of sharing, respect for others, thankfulness, etc.).[15]

This process is very important, above all because it has to do with abilities that are so essential that the subject would be practically incapable of living if he did not possess them. In fact, a child without any exterior help would surely perish. But, in addition, primary socialization is crucial because it configures the structure of the person in an almost physical way, since in this stage of life, the person is like moldable plaster which, to a great degree, will take one form or another depending on what he finds in his surroundings. One of the reasons for this malleability is that the newborn child's brain is still in formation, and depending on the stimuli it receives, it will be more or less rich. Although the person's number of neurons does not increase in the first years, what does happen is that the neurons themselves grow and branch out (process of arborization) and the final result depends on the influence of the environment. A greater number of external entrances corresponds to a greater arborization and a great personal richness. Thus, as an example, although all children are born with the ability to discriminate all vocalic sounds (universal phonemic perception), at about age two, they have already lost the capacity to recognize sound they have not heard in the language of their surroundings.[16]

---

[15] Primary socialization has its limit in the formation of the concept of a role, which can only be acquired in society (cf. Ch 13.3). In the family, role and person are inseparable (the mother and the father are specific and irreplaceable persons), while in society this does not occur; a determined social role is in fact exercised by different and interchangeable persons (it does not matter *who* drives the bus, but rather that he knows how to).

[16] Cf. H. I. Kaplan, B. I. Sadock, *Sinopsis de Psiquiatría* (Madrid: Ed. Médica Panamericana, 2000), 20.

In conclusion, although the person has an important capacity for self-disposition and can modify the legacy which constitutes him, there are key elements which already mark a determined path for him from childhood.

c) Identity Formation

By identity, we mean here not just personality (character), but a deeper structure of the subject, which signifies what he is, how he sees himself, and how he sees the world (cf. Ch. 7.2). The family has a profound influence on this dimension from at least two perspectives.

c.1) General Attitude About the World

The child sees the world through the family, because in the first years *world and family are identical* and, later on, he gains access to the exterior through the family environment. Thus, if he finds himself surrounded by love and affection, he will consider the world a positive and accepting place and will adopt before it an open and constructive attitude which will progressively penetrate into his personality and will be very relevant in the future for all of his decisions. This mentality is evidently not transmitted to the child in a notional way, but rather through attitudes, sensations, and experiences which the child perceives around himself: caresses, attention, love, tranquility, affection, order, etc.[17]

The religious sentiment of the parents plays a significant role in this attitude, because through it important notions which reinforce (or weaken) their open attitude before the world are able to reach the child. For example, if the child is taught that there is a God who has created him out of love, protects and cares for him, he will conclude that the world is essentially friendly, since it is directed and governed by that amiable and strong being.

c.2) Personal Structure

The child also forges in the first years the bases of his personality and, here as well, the parents' attitude (and the siblings' as well, although to a lesser degree) is determinant, since the child is a being intrinsically in need of orientation and help, and the quality, adequacy and constancy with which these needs are

---

[17] Cf. R. Vera, *La relación paterno-filial. Análisis desde el personalismo*, "Quién" 4 (2016), 89-113.

fulfilled will be fundamental in his evolution.[18] The final objective is that, at the end of adolescence, he may possess a stable personality, that is, a personality which is secure, with its own criteria for action, understanding, and with an adequate level of self-esteem. And this is only possible, in the first place, with the constant and adequate attention of the parents who orient and form the child in such a way that he may gradually correct his defects, overcome problems and difficulties, and strengthen his positive qualities.

This task is not simple and together with solid criteria for action, it requires a daily dedication, constant over time, since we persons only modify our personality little by little and with difficulty.[19] In addition, it also requires *a specific dedication both from the father and from the mother*, since each one plays a different role in the education of the children. The mother is the *principal of security*. She is, above all, the one who protects us physically and affectively, gives us what we need and especially makes us see that the world is friendly. She is also the representative *par excellence of unconditional love*, love that is always there and in any circumstance is available for our needs. Independently of what we do or of how we behave, we know that in our mother we will always find refuge and affection. Thus, we may say that she also constitutes the greatest existential point of reference of the person, who roots us in being, not only because she is the one who in the most direct way has given us being, but also because her affective permanence roots us in the world and gives emotional meaning to our existence.

The father's mission is, in part, different and consists of making present the *principle of reality*. The father must teach the child that the world has laws and that others have their rights and their subjectivity, that is, that not everything is available; that the world is not a mere extension of the desires that mother grants us. Therefore, "a man without a father," Buttiglione says, "tends to think that the world can be transformed according to his desires, without any effort being needed on his part. In addition, he will tend to appropriate to himself the good things of life without keeping in mind the analogous right of the rest of humanity. He will be unable to receive any gift,

---

[18] Different studies have been done, attempting to establish the most important phases in the evolution of the subject's identity. Some of the most well-known are those of Freud and Erikson. A summary of the positions of these authors and a general systematic and developed treatment of the topic can be found in K. Stassen, R. A. Thompson, *Psicología del desarrollo: infancia y adolescencia* (Madrid: Editorial Médica Panamericana, 1998).

[19] Although it is not a topic to be treated in this work, it is convenient to note that the effort of parents and family to forge persons should not only be protected and facilitated by society, but adequately compensated because of the benefits which it reaps for society.

because he will not ask anything of anyone, but rather will act as if everything belonged to him from the beginning. In such case, he could commit the greatest injustices without even realizing that he commits them."[20] That hardness and consistency of the world should not be understood necessarily as a limit that the father imposes on the child; many times it will be, on the contrary, an indispensable stimulus for development. The world, indeed, offers endless possibilities which would never be reached if one remained on the protecting maternal lap and it is the mission of the father to introduce the child into that world and its richness, even if this means taking risks.[21]

It is important to emphasize, in any case, that *these roles of the father and the mother are not exclusive or excluding,* but rather the focal point or point of convergence of the fatherly or motherly attitudes. In fact, both the father and the mother can develop the functions of the other: the father, for example, also has an important protecting capacity and the mother can prompt the child to face the world. Moreover, this distribution does not imply that the mother loves the children more than the father does (or vice versa), but simply that she gives a different orientation to an equally radical love. When a child gets on a toboggan in a park, the mother may start to yell, "get off of that this instant," because her sensitivity to danger leads her to activate her protective instinct. The father, on the contrary, may encourage the child to slide on the toboggan, even teaching him (to the mother's scandal) more risky ways than normal, but also with a loving objective, although different: to develop the child's muscles and personality and to become strong and agile. It is the same love which manifests itself in two different and complementary ways.

Finally, Buttiglione has incisively indicated that the *religious sentiment* of the parents can be especially important when the child reaches the phase of his evolution in which he vindicates his independence. The realization that the parents do not constitute the final center of existence at the moment, but rather that there is a Being above them that governs all, can help the child to assimilate the difficult process which implies *discovering the parents' limits*

---

[20] Cfr. R. Buttiglione, *La persona y la familia,* 129. Buttiglione has delved specifically into this topic, taking as a starting point the elements of Freud's psychoanalysis, but adapting them to his own personalist categories.

[21] The persistent (and just) criticisms on the part of feminism of the old patriarchy and the profound changes which have occurred in the family structure are leading lately to the opposite extreme: a crisis of the father figure which causes the father not to know exactly what his role in the family is. One of the negative consequences of this situation is that the education of the children can become unbalanced and incomplete. A valuable analysis of this entire problem is offered by P. J. Cordes, *El eclipse del padre* (Madrid: Palabra, 2003), 57-79.

and determining the attitude which one should adopt in that new situation. If all meaning was proportioned by the parents, when the adolescent discovers that they are limited and fragile he may reach the conclusion that, in reality, no ultimate meaning exists, but just a happy childhood experience that disappears when one reaches maturity and lucidity regarding existence. But if, on the contrary, the adolescent knows that his parents are also subjected to a higher meaning, the discovery of their limits does not have to imply any irreparable trauma in the adolescent's life itinerary, even if it does not free him from the difficulties of adolescence.[22]

12.4 The Place of Existence

The great importance of the family in the adult life of people becomes manifest in at least the following areas.

a) The Place of Roots

The family is the place of personal roots. Thanks to them, we know who we are, where we come from and what our connection is with the rest of humanity, to which we evidently feel solidarity. Family roots are clearly reflected in our name, which is our social identity. Our first name indicates our radical identity, our self, which is unique in the world, but our last name indicates our origin and provenance: the roots of our self. In previous times, one's lineage was very important, that is, the ancestors who preceded us during many generations. Today, in modern societies, that has changed, and closer generations are the fundamentally important ones: parents and grandparents.

We can discover the importance of origins, by contrast, in the compassion produced by the orphan characterized by his lack of something essential. Evidently, the orphan can fully develop his existence, but always with a limit and a lacking with respect to the ideal situation: the presence of the parents and of one's own origin. And the efforts made by some people who do not know their father or mother to find and localize them – although in the end they can only say "I know who my father is" – also speaks to us of the importance of roots.

The family generally gives us roots, not just on the personal level, but also on the territorial and cultural levels. Through it, we settle in a territory and in

---

[22] Cordes has emphasized, on the contrary, how the father figure influences the conception of God (the Father) to the point that it can come to block the religious sentiment if the father figure does not respond to the child's expectations (*El eclipse del padre*, especially,113ff.). Regarding this question, Kierkegaard's reflections on Abraham in *Fear and Trembling* are especially interesting.

a determined culture which will always be our land or our country. Thus, the family is also, in some way, the place to which we belong and to which we can always return.

b) Affective Center

As songs and movies often remind us, what is most important in life is to love and be loved. But where that occurs in a radical way is in the family. That is why it is doubtless the person's most important affective center.

First of all, it is the place where *we are loved* in a radical and *unconditional* way. We are loved for being who we are, independently of our age, condition, health or qualities, and that is something that is of an inappreciable value for every person. In fact, although the human being is certainly a unique and unrepeatable being, this only becomes manifest existentially in the family environment; especially in such transcendental occurrences as life and death. "The birth of a human being is extraordinary and unrepeatable and, at the same time, new, personal and communitarian. But beyond this dimension, beyond the limits of the family, this reality loses that character and becomes a statistic, the topic of objectifications of a different type, to the point of the mere *registration*, which statistics uses. *The family is the place in which every human being is revealed in his unicity and unrepeatability.*"[23]

Simultaneously, the family is the place where *we love* in the most decisive way, where we develop to the maximum our capacity for love and self-giving, and where those who give meaning to our life are.

c) Family and Work

The relationship between family and work is also very deep, although in this aspect a major evolution has occurred. In the so-called traditional European family, which was in existence when a rural culture predominated, family and professional work came to coincide. Artisans, small merchants, farmers, etc., worked in the same place they lived, and they taught their own children their trade. With the social process which urbanization and industrialization brought with them, this relationship became fractured and weakened.[24] That being said, an important relation still exists between family and work.

---

[23] K. Wojtyła, *La familia como «communio personarum»*, in *El don del amor. Escritos sobre la familia* (Madrid: Palabra, 2000), 228.

[24] The evolution of this relation between family and work is particularly well described in C. Hall, *Dolce casa*, in P. Ariès, G. Duby (eds.), *La vita privata. IV. L'ottocento* (Rome-Bari: Laterza, 1988), 55-61.

Above all, what we could call "the work of home-making" still exists, including all the tasks necessary so that the family system may function adequately. This work implies, on the one hand, the set of more instrumental tasks: the ordering and decoration of the house, food, clothing, etc., and on the other hand, a series of more personal tasks, related to the care and education of the children and the adequate maintenance of the couple's relationship. This set of activities is an important type of work and should be much more valued by society than it currently is.

On the other hand, leaving aside the fact of the number and importance of family businesses which still exist, one must not forget the importance that the family has as the motor of professional work. In many people – independently of whether they have a genuine appreciation for their profession – the need to find sufficient economic means so the family-system can function adequately is at times the strongest impetus toward reaching determined work goals or quotas.

d) The Place of Death

Finally, the family is also in a certain sense the "place" of death; that is, the adequate affective space in which every human being should die.[25] If the family is so important and if in the family the people most important to the subject are found, it is logical that those people accompany him in the most decisive moment of existence, that in which one leaves for an afterlife, perhaps known by faith, but dark from an existential point of view (cf. Ch. 14.2-3). In that definitive moment, which the human being in any case goes through alone, it is very important that the person be surrounded by his loved ones, so that they may help him to pass that always bitter stage and may attend to him in those especially difficult moments. But, in addition, a human being should be surrounded by his family because what surrounds him in death is a sign of what his life has been. If he finds solitude, he may take to "the other side" a sensation of failure and desolation, while, on the contrary, if he finds love, he will be surrounded by a sensation of fullness. It is not always possible for the human being to die physically in the family home, but affectively, he should always die in family, that is, surrounded and loved by his own.

---

[25] Cf. R. Buttiglione, *La persona y la familia*, 133-165.

Chapter 13

The Person in Society

Persons relate with other persons (Ch. 11) and form families (Ch. 12), but they do all this in the context and in the framework of a diffuse reality, enveloping but always present and necessary: society. Now it is time to investigate this question: the relationship and the influence that society has on the person. We will do this from two perspectives. In the first place, we will set forth the overall features of person-society relations; then, in the following sections, we will see three concrete modes in which society influences the person: the process of socialization, social structures and tradition.

13.1 Models of Social Relations

That human beings are naturally social is something evident and something that has been highlighted from antiquity, beginning with Plato and Aristotle. The life of human beings outside of society makes no sense and is unthinkable except as an exceptional or extreme case. It is not, therefore, a matter which it is worth the effort to insist on. What interests us here is to determine *the adequate relationship* between person and society; that is to say, the correct anthropological and social mode through which the human being gives to and receives from society. It is easy to see that this is a very complex question to which it is not possible to give a response totally independent of history and cultural context. So, we are going to place ourselves in a specific context, Western society of the twentieth and twenty-first century. And in this context, we will describe three particularly important models of relation between human beings and society: collectivism, individualism and personalism.[1]

---

[1] The position of the personalists on this point is practically unanimous and presents the same formulation, with slight differences of nuance, in Mounier, Maritain, Buber, Stefanini, Lacroix, Wojtyła, etc. And analysis of Maritain, Mounier and Ricoeur in Dries Deweer, *Ricoeur's Personalist Republicanism: Personhood and Citizenship* (Lanham: Lexington Books, 2017).

a) Collectivism

Collectivism is one of the major models that has recently impacted European history, with dire results. Its major thesis is the primacy of society over the individual. Starting from different theoretical bases (organicism, Hegelianism, etc.) the different types of collectivism (Marxism, Nazism, Fascism) maintain the basic and principal thesis that the individual must be at the service of society because society is the real, important and transcendent entity in the face of the precariousness of the individual.

Within this global framework, collectivism also shows the following characteristics:

1) collectivism proposes values and ideals to the individuals that make up the society: the primacy of race, proletarian revolution, the conquest of an empire etc.

2) collectivism appeals to altruism and sacrifice for the realization of these values, that is to say, it has a moral, and even religious dimension: the conquest of a specific objective is the means of salvation for the country or for society.[2]

3) collectivism proposes that the person substitute their individual smallness through identification with the collective project. "You, as an individual, are no more than an anonymous entity just like many others, but ideally you can make yourself as great as the project to which you contribute."

On the basis of these proposals, collectivism achieved the mobilization of enormous masses of people, but the very important anthropological errors that characterized them, eventually transformed those energies into a shapeless mass of tragedy and sorrow: the Second World War and the Marxist dictatorships, some of which still survive today.

One of the basic problems that collectivism poses is that the person's radical self-giving to the collective value that is proposed to him or her implies that, if the collective value is immoral, the person is perverted and degraded automatically, wasting his or her vital energies on an unjust objective. But, moreover and above all, however correct the values that are proposed by the collectivity might be, a person cannot be placed completely in the service of

---

[2] For the "religious" characteristics of Marxism, see Jacques Maritain, *Integral Humanism.*

the collectivity because the person is the supreme value (cf. Ch. 13). These aspects of collectivism resulted in a conversion of the subject into a mere instrument that can be utilized according to the interests of the collective.[3]

b) Individualism

The second major Western model of person-society relationship is individualism, which proposes a thesis opposed to collectivism. For individualism, persons must be fundamentally at the service of themselves, and of their interests, and not at the service of society. Society is, at best, an instrument to be exploited to the individual's advantage. An *extreme* example of individualism can be seen in the early phase of the Industrial Revolution, which took place in England at the end of the nineteenth century and the beginning of the twentieth century, which was also the era of unbridled capitalism whose economic laws had as their fundamental objective enrichment independent of the social consequences from which it derived.

In a very schematic development of the basic characteristics of individualism one can indicate the following:

1) individualism is based on the autonomy, independence, ability, and value of the individual subject.

2) individualism encourages the person to act with diligence and initiative, to overcome difficulties in an autonomous manner and to develop to the fullest one's capacities for achieving maximum well-being.

3) individualism tends to sharply separate the private and public spheres, avoiding as far as possible any interference that may restrict freedom and individual autonomy.[4]

Confronting collectivism, individualism has a positive aspect that values the individual above society and urges the individuals to develop their qualities

---

[3] This is what happens with a certain frequency in nationalism, which, being a legitimate value, tends to become the ultimate social rule which governs all the other values, including the rights and the life of persons. Cf. E. Gellner, *Nations and Nationalism* (New York: Cornell University Press, 2008).

[4] "The individual need not give account of his or her acts to society, as long as these acts only affect his or her personal interests." J. Stuart Mill, *On liberty* (World's Classics Edition), 115.

and initiatives for their own benefit. For individualism, the human being is not an unformed part of the collective, but rather, on the contrary, an independent and autonomous being. Where individualism falls short is in its tendency toward *lack of solidarity and toward egotism.* "If by egotism we understand the attitude of not giving what one can give, individualism is a behavior that does not share, that does not engage in dialogue, that does not accept help, that does not engage in communal tasks, but rather considers *the human being as self-sufficient and having no need for the rest of humanity.* The two things are not exactly the same, but in both cases the result is that each one has to fend for himself, alone. An individualist mentality can easily devolve into egotism without feeling any remorse."[5] For this reason, individualism also produces a certain social disarticulation because it understands society primarily as a means of acquiring benefits, which is of interest only and exclusively to the extent that it provides those benefits, not as an environment in which to dwell and cohabit with others.[6]

Contemporary Western societies have some features of individualism without lacking attitudes of solidarity. Along with the intensive search for personal benefit there are both personal and social controls that counteract these tendencies. There are also persons in both public and private institutions that seek the dissemination of social well-being: Social Security, Non-Governmental Organizations, etc.

---

[5] R. Yepes, *Fundamentos de antropología*, 261. See also A. de Tocqueville, *Democracy in America* (New York: Penguin 2008), Ch. 22-24.

[6] This is one of the problems that communitarianists correctly caution about the liberal position (which cannot be identified point blank with individualism). Rawls, for example, considers that society should be based fundamentally on justice and freedom, which implies that it should occupy itself above all with basically preserving the subjects' autonomous ability to choose, independently of what his or her concept of the good may be and, in any case, to establish rules to harmonize divergent goods. But for communitarianists, this position is unsatisfactory and poses important problems. On one hand, this position has the pretention that subjects detach themselves from their concept of the good, if necessary, but above all it considers society as something secondary in which subjects participate only when they are already completely individualized and only in order to be able to reach agreement about is convenient for them. It does not take into account the fact that society forms part of the identity of the individual, nor that the individual seeks in society more elevated values than those of his or her own convenience. Rawls has expressed his position basically in *Theory of Justice* and the communitarianist critique is found, among others, in M. Sandel, *Liberalism and the Limits of Justice* (Cambridge: Cambridge University Press, 1982); A. MacIntyre, *Three Rival Versions of Moral Enquiry*, and Ch. Taylor, *Sources of Self.* For an overall view of the problem, see S. Mulhall and A. Swift, *Liberals and Communitarians* (Wiley, 1996).

c) Personalism

Communitarian personalism is the third possible model of person-society relation, which arose as an alternative to collectivism and individualism, most noticeably during the interwar period.[7] Personalism (in its political version) sought to offer a practical alternative that could avoid the errors of the other positions while retaining some of their positive elements. The political influence of communitarian personalism has been important and has been incorporated into the constitutions of numerous European states.

The basic premises of communitarian personalism are the following:

1) *Social primacy of the person.* This is a matter of basic principal in regard to the person-society relation. If the person is a being with dignity and value or excellence, this means that above all, society is at the service of the person and not the reverse, that is to say that the state with all its structures, enterprises and social institutions achieve their meaning in so far as they serve in one way or another the good of the person, the person having the highest ontological status. This also means that the person has some inviolable rights that the state may never transgress because it would violate the dignity of the person and alter the appropriate order of things between the individual and society.

2) *The duty of solidarity on the part of the person.* The social primacy of the person is balanced by another anthropological principle: the need to give oneself to others in order to attain personal plenitude. We have already analyzed this question from the point of view of interpersonal relations (cf. Ch. 11.3). In its social aspect, this principle imposes a moral obligation on each man and woman to strive to contribute to society to achieve some aspect of the common good. This duty can, on occasions, become very serious, even to the point of imposing onerous personal sacrifices in exceptional situations of

---

[7] By communitarian personalism we mean here the way personalism understands the relationship between person and society. The name comes from Maritain and the first formulations from Mounier. Here, our own, very elemental, personal synthesis is exposed upon. See also Herman Van Rompuy, *Du personalisme a l'action politique*, "Notes et Documents", 2009 36-40, J. N. Mortensen, *The Common Good: An Introduction to Personalism* and L. Stefanini, *Personalismo sociale.*

emergency or of social crisis, but this requirement can never
be imposed at the cost of the fundamental rights of the person
and especially of the person's dignity. If this were to happen, it
would mean that society would be imposing itself over the
person, destroying the proper order which always gives pride
of place to the subject.

Let us now briefly conclude by considering how this development can
overcome the problems of collectivism and individualism while taking up
some of their positive elements.

With regard to collectivism, one can reject the reductive vision of the person
and affirm that the *person always prevails over the abstract idea* (nation, race,
revolution of the proletariat, etc.) but at the same time embracing the
altruistic element and collective ideas that serve to unite and bring a society
together. The duty of social solidarity, in effect, imposes the *duty to construct
society* and to dedicate to it one's vision, resources and efforts.

With respect to individualism something similar occurs. Some of its positive
elements are embraced: *the primacy of the individual over society* and the
intuition that social structures ought to serve concrete persons, while
rejecting the lack of solidarity that borders on egotism. A person cannot pull
their wagons in a circle, as it were, reserving their skills and independence
only for themselves, forgetting the weak, those in need, those who are
unhappy, or simply the persons around us with whom we live.

Now that the general framework of person-society relationships has been
established, we are going to analyze in a little more detail how these are
established, distinguishing, to facilitate this, between the process of
socialization of the person and the institutions that mediate or enable this
process[8].

13.2 The Process of Socialization

a) Definitions and Characteristics

When someone who has never used the subway needs to use it for the first
time, that person must learn a body of knowledge and practices: what a

---

[8] Pier Paolo Donati has developed a contemporary sociology that can easily be
integrated into the framework of personalist political philosophy. See P. Paolo Donati,
Relational Sociology: A New Paradigm for the Social Sciences (New York: Routledge,
2010) and many other works.

subway station is, where tickets may be bought, how to move through the turnstile, what is a subway line and how to pass to a different line if needed, how often the trains run, etc. At first it will take the person some effort to execute the intended behaviors, but little by little they will be assimilated and integrated until, with the passage of time, they will be internalized and the person will move through these actions automatically. Well, this same process that we carry out to know how to manage ourselves in new situations we also have to carry out with the *whole of society* and it is called *socialization*. Socialization, writes Guy Rocher, is "the process by which the human person learns and internalizes, in the course of their life, the sociocultural elements in their environment, integrates them into the structure of their personality under the influence of experience and of significant social agents, and thus adapts to the social environment in which one must live."[9]

We can distinguish three main moments in socialization: primary, secondary and adult socialization. *Primary socialization* is the process that allows a child to integrate in an elementary way in society, for which he needs to be able to develop basic functions: walking, talking, eating, orienting himself, knowing the basic rules of behavior, the most elementary social customs, etc. Primary socialization is carried out, fundamentally, by the family (Ch. 12.3).

Secondary socialization continues the socialization process through a more complex and sophisticated formation or modulation process that includes education (secondary and perhaps higher), detailed knowledge of the customs of a city or of the country, learning and putting into practice of the modes of social relationship, the first rudiments about one's personal position in the social context, etc. When secondary socialization ends it can be considered that the person is already adult and mature, and she is able to interact autonomously, rationally and appropriately in the society to which she belongs.

The socialization process, however, does not end at this time since every society is in continuous movement and evolution, so the individual must continually adapt to these changes so as not to be left out of the social stream. Technologies provide an ideal example in this regard. Any adult who, in our time, cannot assimilate technological changes, is separated from the central flow of society and relegated to secondary positions that will generate continuous difficulties for him. We call this third moment *adult socialization*.

---

[9] G. Rocher, *A General Introduction to Sociology. A Theoretical Perspective* (Calcutta: Academic Publishers, 2008).

Logically, the main socialization process is the one that takes place in the formative phase and includes the primary and secondary levels, because in them the personal and social identity of the subject is largely decided. But the socialization process never stops as person and society continually interact in a dynamic and changing way.

Posed in this way, one might think that socialization consists in submitting ourselves to an enormous number of social rules that could oppress the subject, but this would be a very superficial view. The person is born with some potentialities (knowledge, skills, etc.) that can only be developed in society and, therefore, it is natural and desirable for them to relate to the social group to acquire and deploy them. Therefore, assuming social norms and customs is, generally, a process that is not traumatic but, on the contrary, attractive and stimulating because those norms and customs allow the subject to interact in an increasingly effective and intense way with the society in which they live, becoming one of its components. Therefore usually these norms and customs are internalized, that is, they are internally integrated, becoming part of the identity of the subject who, from that moment on, will not be, so to speak, an undifferentiated person, but a Spaniard, an American, a university professor, a singer, etc. Socialization, therefore, is a natural and spontaneous process, though, as with any reality, it can be subjected to excesses or developed inadequately.

b) Mechanisms of Socialization

We will now present the main mechanisms of socialization, insisting, in accordance with what we have just pointed out, on primary and secondary socialization, but without neglecting that, in different ways, these mechanisms are also active in adulthood.

1) *Imitation.* Children have an innate tendency toward imitation, to do what others do. In this way children develop skills and acquire knowledge. One might think that this is an instinctive phenomenon, but we have seen that human beings never act without putting into play their intelligence in one way or another. Children, for example, do not imitate everything, nor do they do the things they imitate in the same way that their model does, and they can in fact at times opt for an opposite attitude, one of rejection. An extreme case of imitation happens when a child not only seeks to copy specific actions or behaviors, but also to identify in a very deep way with a figure (father, mother, brother) and seeks to resemble those persons as closely as possible. Imitation, moreover, is not only

limited to childhood. It is of enormous importance in adolescence (fashion being an obvious example) and also occurs in adulthood.

2) *Motivated learning* is another of the central mechanisms of socialization. It consists of directly influencing the child through rewards and punishments and contributes little by little to assimilating knowledge of social rules. This process (with different variations: rules, responses, etc.) remains present and operative during the educational process in adulthood as well, for example, in the mechanisms of progress in one's profession.

3) *The response of the "other" to our behavior* is a third mechanism of socialization. The reactions of others to our behavior can cause us to modify our behavior, and it also influences the orientation of our personality. If in a social setting I behave in a specific way and I notice that people look at me strangely or are surprised by what I have done, I will try to determine what I did wrong and modify my behavior so that it does not happen again.

c) Principal Agents of Socialization

1) *The family*, as we have seen, is one of the principal agents of socialization, above all in what is referred to as *primary socialization*, that is to say, in the acquisition of the most fundamental and basic social content: orientation, essential knowledge, primary skills, basic social relations, language, etc. (cf. Ch. 12.3b). The importance of family, moreover, resides not only in the transcendence of the contents that the family transfers to the subject but in the great efficacy with which they are transferred, due to the affective relevance the family has for the person. Everything that happens in the family is particularly important and, therefore, the customs and knowledge that proceed from the family environment are also impressed with a special force.

2) The second factor in socialization is the person's *group of friends*, generally known as one's peer group. Its importance is rooted in the fact that it is the first contact the person has with the social environment outside of the protective bubble of the

family. In a group of friends, the person is no longer someone "special," who is valued for who he is independently of his qualities, but as an *equal* among others whose position in the group will depend on the capacities and skills the person demonstrates. The peer group represents, then, a first confrontation with reality, the first encounter with the world which must be managed without the protection of the family which, if it were always present, would pose a hindrance to personal development.

3)   The *school* is another essential factor in socialization. In the first place, from a cognitive perspective, because it is only in school that one can soundly acquire the amount of knowledge needed in order to integrate successfully into society. In addition, in school we also learn *values and attitudes*: order, a sense of discipline, how to do rigorous scientific work, the degree of importance assigned to professional success, companionship, etc. These values will later be key in the shaping of the social attitude of the person.

4)   *The media,* lastly, have an increasing weight in the modeling of customs and mentalities. Different media *explicitly* influence us through cultural programs, informational programs, documentaries, etc., but their most decisive influence is achieved in a more indirect way through the proposal (or rejection) of customs or ways of life mediated through advertising, movies, television programs, talk shows and other types of programming. The media thus coincide with one's peer group in that they do not expressly seek the socialization of the individual, that is, the media do not have as their explicit mission the formation of the person but this is in fact what they do. In contrast, the family and the school are explicit social agents that expressly seek to form the subject to act in specific ways.

5)   *Social networks* can be considered part of the media, since, generally, they are integrated into it; but they can also be considered independently since their main objective is *communicative,* not informative. Their influence is enormous in our time due to their peculiar characteristics: ease of access, globality, immediacy of communication, possible direct and continuous impact on people, etc. Due to their social power

and ability to model behavior, they are currently one of the main fields in the battle for political and social power.

13.3 Social Structures

Socialization is a process, but it also depends on structural and stable elements that mark its fundamental lines defining the common path that the socialization process will follow in a given social context. We will now examine three singularly relevant social structures. [10]

a) Status and Functions

Subjects act in society in many ways but some ways are more important than others. It is not the same thing to buy trinkets in a shop as it is to practice a profession or to be a student. In the first case we have socially irrelevant actions; the others are significant behaviors, so society regulates and shapes them. This is where the notion of *status* arises and it can be described in a first approximation as a *relevant mode of being a member of a society*: police officer, worker, student, politician, etc.

Why do these social categorizations arise? The reasons are multiple but we can indicate, fundamentally, two. On one hand, society needs the fulfillment of certain tasks, and in order to achieve this it develops specific social positions: baker, farmer, merchant, etc. It is also necessary for the members of such groups to be identifiable, in order for society to know what it can and cannot expect of such persons. This double necessity is what ends up configuring what sociologists refer to as *status*, that is to say, *stable, specific and known* social positions. Status is defined in practice by associated functions (or roles), in other words, by the *set of characteristic behaviors that the person who possesses the status must comply with and the society expects that they will comply with.*[11] It is expected that a police officer defends public order, that he chases thieves, that he be honest and disciplined, etc. A soccer

---

[10] The concept of social structure was introduced by H. Spencer, who gave it an organicistic approach. The most important subsequent lines of investigation have been those of H. Radcliffe-Brown, *Structure and Function in Primitive Society* (Free Press, 1965); the structuralism of Lévy-Strauss, *Structural Anthropology* (Basic Books, 1963); and the functionalism of Parsons, *The structure of Social Action* (Free Press, 1968). See an evaluation of these theories in A. Lucas, *Sociología* (Pamplona: Eunsa, 2011), part II: "Las teorías sociales".

[11] Linton was the first to use the term role (or function) to refer to tasks associated with a status. Cf. R. Linton, *The cultural Background of Personality* (New York: Routledge 1998).

player is expected to entertain the public, score goals and make money. The student is expected to attend class and to study, etc.

The *personal importance* of *status* is very great.[12] In the first place it is socially necessary to have a defined status since, without it, an imbalance can be created which "expels" the subject from their environment. If, for example, a 35-year-old person does not have a definite profession he automatically becomes an atypical subject situated on the margins of habitual social channels and will have difficulty integrating into society. Furthermore, status also notably determines the life of persons because it *configures a person's behavior in clear cut ways.* If I am an office worker I have to get up at 7 o'clock in the morning, go to my company, work following a series of norms, etc. If I am a homemaker I have to follow a different series of behaviors also very clearly defined. And, since these patterns of behavior occur over many years, they become rooted and so strong that they have an impact on my personality and general attitude toward life. It is very different to be an office worker, a member of the military, a merchant or an artist - each one faces life with very different social parameters, objectives and attitudes. Status, moreover, also affects *the degree of fulfilment of persons and, therefore, their happiness.* If the person performs functions in accord with what he or she considers to be his or her personal skills, the person will have a sense of satisfaction, while in the opposite case, that person may feel frustrated and unhappy.[13]

b) Groups

Alongside status, the person influences society and is influenced by it through his or her participation in *specific social structures.* The two most important are groups and institutions.

A *social group is an association of persons with the following characteristics:* there are reciprocal interactions between the members of the group (all the doctors in a city or country do not form a group); members of a group have a group consciousness (ourselves and others); groups have objectives, values and activities that are shared (people in a train car, for example, do not form a

---

[12] We are not going to consider its relevance for the articulation of *society*, since that is more a topic for sociology or social philosophy. And, in the same way, we will not enter into historical considerations or related concepts such as the Marxist class.

[13] The majority of the examples of status that we have given refer to *professions* because it is the *dominant* status in our society (see Ch. 10), but this is not always necessarily the case and it varies with cultures. Profession, in addition, is an *acquired* status, but there are others, like age, sex, and race, that are *independent of personal choices* and which also configure in a relevant way our social identity.

group); groups have stability and duration depending on the objectives that they pursue; and, finally, they are socially identified. At the same time it is possible to distinguish two classes of groups. *Primary groups* (in the main, family, friends and neighborhood) are characterized by relations between people that are personal, direct, informal and have a strong affective character. *Secondary groups* are characterized, in contrast, by relationships between members that are anonymous and interpersonal, that have a strong formal organization, a large number of members, and the members participate in the group not for the sake of the members who make it up, but rather to obtain a series of objectives. Examples of formal groups include professional associations, working groups and companies, etc.

The influence of groups on the person is notable from many points of view. Primary groups (and especially the family) create the essential affective framework for the person to feel loved, welcomed and valued. Secondary groups establish part of the tables of values that the person wishes to reject or achieve, which is why they constitute essential vital reference points. A person can resolve to enter a certain club or association or to be an elite athlete as an important objective, so the result of their efforts will configure their degree of personal and social fulfillment. If she achieves her goals, she will feel satisfied and fulfilled, while if she does not achieve them, she may run the risk of falling into frustration. Furthermore, it is important to keep in mind that every person needs to belong to some group because, being the primary elements of the social fabric, they constitute the primary ways of integration into society. If a person does not belong to any group he becomes hopelessly isolated and uprooted.

c) Institutions

Every society has a series of basic needs that cannot be satisfied by individual people acting in isolation. Not even statuses with their associated functions can solve these problems. To feed a city, for example, it is not enough for there to be merchants; farmers, transporters, distributors, and traders are needed, and all must be properly coordinated with each other.[14] Only then is it possible for a person who lives in that city to acquire what is necessary for them to live each day. The complex networks of relationships that society creates in order to satisfy these needs, are, precisely, the institutions which, therefore, can be defined *as organized and stable systems of social behavior that have as their objective the addressing of specific social necessities.*

---

[14] What happens in fact is that *status* are not possible without institutions.

Institutions arise around each basic need of a society and, according to the Polish sociologist Malinowski, these can be grouped into four fundamental areas: economics, social control (that is to say, technical and moral regulation of human behavior), education, and political organization, which determines who holds power and how that power is executed.

What impact does the existence of institutions have on the individual person? First of all, *they facilitate life in society* because through them the individual receives what is necessary in order to satisfy basic needs: education, food, justice, etc. On the other hand, as social institutions are stable and permanent, they provide individuals with security and stability and the tranquility of knowing which are the socially accepted modes of behavior. This last fact might seem to come from a submissive or routinized attitude, but we need only think for a moment about what would happen if the rules of social behavior changed suddenly, unexpectedly and in an uncontrolled fashion. The resulting social chaos and the harm to each one of us would be immense.

What can be said with certainty is that the existence of institutions implies and involves an adaptation on the part of the individual. The person does not establish social institutions but rather encounters them as already given and therefore there is a need to *adapt to them and assimilate them.* As this process occurs within the process of socialization, citizens have a tendency to see these institutions as something of their own culture and not as an imposed structure. But, what happens if a society comes to be governed by institutions that are obsolete or unjust? Obviously, it is possible or even probable that the citizens of a given country will find inadequate or unjust institutions because institutions are no more than a product of human activity, a complex mode of articulation of interpersonal relationships which inevitably is fallible and can be improved. In these cases one can (and must) work and struggle to modify them. However, the energy and effort that one must dedicate to achieving such changes can only be determined in each specific context, because the situations in which these things occur are extremely varied. What should be kept in mind in any event is that this obligation must be reconciled with the fact that each individual human being is very weak and limited in the face of institutions and, therefore, should take measure of their strength before launching into an uneven struggle that could gravely harm him or herself.

13.4 Tradition

Tradition can be defined as *the array of knowledge, customs, ways of life, beliefs, facts, etc., that are transmitted from previous generations.* The modern era has generally been hard on tradition, perhaps out of ignorance, out of pride, and undoubtedly, influenced by the long shadow of rationalism. In point of fact, today there is a certain tendency to underestimate the past and to think that we can do without it, starting from scratch. In any case, this attitude is changing somewhat as we are becoming more conscious that the person can only live and develop fully in the context of a tradition.[15]

a) Elements of Tradition

What is it that tradition contributes or, in other words, what are the elements that make it up and that connect us with the past? Tradition offers us, first of all, *the living and useful contact with our origins*, with what came before us, but continues to live in some way. Tradition arises from life that has already passed on, though it has not passed on completely because it has been relevant for those who have preceded us and, therefore, it has been deposited in the marrow of society and has been transmitted from generation to generation, either in a mysterious way through collective consciousness, or explicitly, in customs, oral traditions, writings, monuments. From the point of view of the origins, tradition tells us who we are and where we come from, who our ancestors were and what their place was in history and in the life of nations. This knowledge permits us to engage with our past and in this way creates a solid basis for constructing the future.

Tradition also offers us an immense trove of accumulated knowledge both in writings and in other cultural expressions. Books are, evidently, a privileged place of transmission of culture but knowledge is transmitted in many other ways as well. It is also transmitted to us through customs and practices, that is to say, concrete ways of doing specific tasks, and also through technical devices. It is enough to consider the knowledge and information physically accumulated in a computer or in a television set and to understand that if it could be passed over to people of earlier ages, it would enable them to advance in spectacular ways. Knowledge is also transmitted through the organized systems of a society. Our current democratic system, for example, presupposes the effort of countless people over many centuries to achieve an effective and just system of government.

It is possible to dance in many ways, to cook in many ways, to have many types of interpersonal relationships and there are very different ways of having fun, but in our city, in our country, there is a specific and concrete way

---

[15] Hermeneutics, especially Gadamer, has insisted on this point with regard to knowledge, emphasizing the impossibility of starting from scratch in any cognitive act. There is always previous pre-comprehension that is influenced by the tradition in which one lives. MacIntyre has developed this idea, analyzing how different traditions influence the comprehension of moral problems and even the very conception of what ethical reason is. Cf. A. MacIntyre, *Three Rival Versions of Moral Enquiry*.

that has been forged over generations, and that makes it our way of drinking, living, dancing or relating, a unique way that separates us from the rest of the world, makes us different and gives us our personality.

b) Possible Attitudes toward Tradition

As we have indicated, the modern era has adopted a generally negative attitude toward tradition which can be called *progressivism*.[16] Perhaps because of the strong influence of the spectacular technological and scientific advances of our era, we have tended to trivialize or devalue the past and to naïvely think that only recent advances are truly important. This is, obviously, an unjust, impoverishing and incorrect attitude that arises from an inability to value what is foreign to us, and an inability to enter into other modes of thought that are distinct from our own. The opposite attitude – also incorrect, but more common in previous eras – is *traditionalism*, which can be defined as a systematic distrust of anything that is new. Just as progressivism distrusts what is old, traditionalism distrusts what is new and tries obsessively to cling to the values of the past, based on the fact that they have already been put to the test by innumerable generations and therefore should not be changed.

Neither of these two postures – progressivism and traditionalism – do adequate justice to tradition because both are excessively radical. Traditionalism is correct in valuing the past but the attempt to cling to it in an obsessive manner loses sight of reason, because human history is unstoppable and what was valid one day or in one era may not be so in a subsequent era. Human beings are forever in a struggle with contingence and with time and must continually adapt to the changes that occur or that they create. This is a point on which progressivism is correct, but it is erroneous in believing that human beings change radically, that we have very little to gain from those who preceded us or that we are infinitely superior to them. It is true that we can be different from our predecessors, especially when time seems to accelerate, but we always owe a lot to those who preceded us and we can learn a lot from them. For these reasons, an adequate attitude toward tradition must combine a love for the past with a love for the future, respect for the old along with an attraction to the new. "The essential movement of history," Jaspers explains, "requires remembering the incomparable value of the past, creatively realizing the present, and living the truth of the present based on the points of reference of the criteria of what was great in times past."[17]

---

[16] We use the term from a social point of view rather than a political one.
[17] K. Jaspers, *Lo trágico. El lenguaje*, 184.

We ought to love and respect our own origins and at the same time love and respect our forebears. First of all, because we come from them. We owe them our being as a people or as a nation and this is already a debt impossible to repay. But tradition, moreover, offers us knowledge and distinguishes us from the rest of humanity. To reject or despise this knowledge would be absurd and immature; it would mean that we would have to start building from scratch instead of building on what has already been created, something that would be unpardonable. And to reject the specific customs of our tradition is, in a certain sense, to reject our own identity, something that can only be achieved with rupture and pain.

However, tradition cannot be taken on as a burden that inevitably conditions the future. Both personal liberty and social liberty transcend any specific tradition, and tradition itself must be confronted by these liberties in a way that is just and appropriate. The reason for this is obviously that *the fact that something proceeds from the past does not necessarily mean that it is good or valid*. There may be ignominious traditions that justify a radical rupture, or simply antiquated or rustic traditions that can (or perhaps must) die in the face of stronger, more energetic or sophisticated ways of performing similar tasks. The relationship with tradition, then, is always a difficult balance between respect and novelty, between veneration of the past and passion for the new. This balance, on the other hand, cannot be defined precisely, since it depends on the social actors, their attitudes and their decisions regarding the old and the new, which will always be bathed in unpredictable freedom.

Part V.
The Destiny of the Person

We have already studied the person from many perspectives: being and internal structure (Parts I and II), action (Part III) and the way in which the person relates with others (Part IV). It remains for us to confront the most decisive and ultimate question which we have called the destiny of the person. What is truly the ultimate meaning of human life? What happens when we die: do we disappear or remain? Where does the person who dies go? Is there a hereafter? What place does God have in human life? These are questions which every human being poses because they decide the general and ultimate orientation of existence. We can live from day to day setting partial, concrete goals which work for short periods of time, but the radical questions are there and at some point they appear, with their devastating force, demanding answers.

The objective of this fifth and final part is to explore what philosophy can (and cannot) say about the definitive destiny of the person. And we are going to enter into this question through the study of temporality, because it is precisely time or, better still, the end of human time which makes the better part of the questions about the radical meaning of life arise.

Chapter 14

Time, Death and Immortality

14.1 Time

a) The Temporal Character of Human Life

The first consideration which should be made about time is its essential character in human life. The human being is constitutively a *temporal being*: he inhabits time and moves within the framework and horizon of temporality. Our existence, without a temporal reference, would be completely different.[1] Philosophy has gradually become more conscious of this fact[2], but it has not always been that way and two errors have appeared with some frequency. The first has consisted in thinking of the human being as a fundamentally static being and introducing time from outside, as something that exists but whose importance is accidental. The human being would be, in a certain sense, like a mechanical toy, which moves if you wind it up, but whose structure does not change essentially by being stopped or in movement. The second error is to limit the influence of time to corporeality, that is, understanding temporality as a fundamentally biological and bodily process: the change and modification of our organism which leads to aging and, finally, to death. But, while this is obviously true, time, or better, the temporality of the human being, is much more than that, it is a *mode of being*, the human being's specific mode of being in the world, and it thus affects all of his dimensions: being, psyche and spirit.

What does this mean more concretely?

It means, in the first place, that *the person is a successive being*. We are not definitively given in one moment and forever, but rather we are beings in movement, who live from a past that we no longer are, while we think and act in view of a future which we will be later on. "Birth," Julián Marías explains, "is the absolute past; what I mean to say is that, while all the content of my past life has been present at some time, birth never was: it was never present *to me*, I did not attend it. The past is remembered in the memory and the future is

---

[1] Which does not mean, as we will later see, that our existence is exhausted in temporality.
[2] In particular, the 20th century has insisted a lot on temporality as an essential feature of the person. See, for example, M. Heidegger, *Being and Time* (Harper Collins, 2008).

anticipated in the imaginary project; but in a more immediate way, life is retention and protention."[3] The human being is, thus, a dialog of past and future which occurs in the present. What I am and what I do depend on what I have been and what I want to be.[4]

The temporality of human life, furthermore, is not made of instants, of disconnected temporal points, but of moments that are meaningfully linked. "The 'instant' is not a point without duration, but rather a temporal *environment* when one is speaking of human life and not cosmic time. Past and future are present in a *decision*, in a human acting; what is done, is done 'because of something and in order for something' and that presence – as 'abbreviated' as it may be – of motivation and finality introduces temporal extension, duration, into each instant of my life; which means that, speaking with rigor, life is not made up of instants, but of *moments.* This is the form of the temporality intrinsic to human life."[5]

The time of human life, in addition, is *structured* or, in other words, it is not homogenous. Time as a physical quality, as a measure of the movement of bodies and especially the objectified time of clocks, is homogenous and flows constantly. But the time of human life, the temporal development of personal life is not.[6] There are, in the first place, *external* structures: days and nights, seasons and years. The succession of my life does not articulate itself automatically around the second hand of the clock, but around periods and events that have a determined extension and depth. If I have reached the end

---

[3] J. Marías, *Antropología metafísica*, 180.
[4] The ontological entity of the future and of the past is not a futile question. St. Augustine indicates in this sense: "There is a clear and manifest fact: neither the future nor the past exist. Nor is it exact to affirm that there are three times: past, present, and future. Perhaps it would be more exact to say that there are these three times: the present of the past, the present of the present, and the present of the future. These three classes of times exist in a certain way in the spirit, and I do not see that they exist in another place; the present of the past is the memory, the present of the present is vision, and the present of the future is expectation." (St. Augustine, *Confessions* XI, 20, 26). And Pareyson, commenting on him, adds: "Augustinian spiritualism has definitively demonstrated that one may not affirm that memory and expectance subsist inasmuch as past and future subsist; rather, one should affirm, on the contrary, that past and future subsist inasmuch as memory and expectance subsist, that is, it is not time which makes the history of the soul possible; rather, the history of the soul makes time possible." L. Pareyson, *Esistenza e persona*, 162-163.
[5] J. Marías, *Antropología metafísica*, 180.
[6] Here we are not talking about physical time as a mere measure of movement, but about the temporal character of human life, although they are obviously related.

of the day, I do not continue acting in a way similar to how I have been acting during the day; my world stops and reposes, recollecting itself until a new day begins. And, in a similar way, at the beginning of a new school year, my temporal structuring is very different from when I finish a school year. At the beginning, I am full of projects, ideas, I am turned toward the future, toward what I am thinking about and hoping to do; at the end, I aspire for repose and tranquility, enjoyment of the present without concerning myself with the future or the past.

There is also a *cultural* structuring which depends on our way of understanding time and of relating to it, and which changes with societies and eras. In the medieval West, time was considered something fundamentally given which filled human life with meaning; in modernity, it is the human being who should give meaning to time which, otherwise, is empty and unbearable. But even within modernity, there are different ways of confronting time. Currently, Alacevich affirms, "our temporal model of reference (the 'normal' model) is still fundamentally that which was imposed starting with the industrial revolution: a time that flows collectively (the most explicit symbol of which were the factories' sirens which regulated the life of citizens), rigid (the work schedules were not just fixed and generalized, but work times were clearly separated), obligatory (determined by the rhythms of production which, different from what occurred in the business of artisans, are now imposed on individuals) and, above all, reconstructed from the starting point of work."[7] This structuring, however, is in the process of being modified and is becoming ever more flexible and less rigid and synchronized.

Finally, time is *finite and limited*. I do not have at my disposal all the time I want and when I want it, but rather it is given to me; it is a stream which I cannot increase or decrease. There is, on one hand, a *daily and domesticable finitude*: to have or not to have time in a specific context. I want to do this, and I do not have time, but I can try to go faster in order to "buy" time, or I can leave it for tomorrow. And the contrary may also occur, I may have too much time, to the point of having to dedicate myself to "killing time". But there is a much more profound and radical finitude which comes because my overall time is limited. I have a finite life span, although I do not know how much it is, and that fact is so decisive that it structures temporality *internally*, forging what tend to be called the stages of life: childhood, adolescence, maturity, old age. If I am young, my past is scarce and the future, infinite. Therefore, it is only a question of living because I have all the time in the

---

[7] F. Alacevich, S. Zamagni, A. Grillo, *Tempo del lavoro e senso della festa*, 17. See also R. Sennett, *The Corrosion of Character*.

world. If I have reached maturity, the situation changes because my past is within me and I am no longer entirely free (and empty), as I was in my youth. In addition, I begin to perceive the end and I know that my time is limited, although I still have a lot of time ahead. If I am old, on the contrary, the past spans almost everything, in such a way that the horizon of my life is limited and narrow and is centered on the impending end.[8]

b) The Fight against Time

The finitude of time has always driven the human being to struggle to dominate and control time, to hold it back. We desire to do things and we do not have enough time, or we want certain moments or works to remain, that they not be mined by the passage of time, which forgets everything and undoes everything. Haste, technology, works that endure have always been the barriers which the human being has tried to put up in order to detain the flow of the hours. And, in our era, thanks to the prodigious advances of technology, that struggle seems to have tended partially toward the human being's side of the battle, although with a paradoxical result. The incredible means we possess seem to eliminate temporal boundaries: everything is done more quickly and in less time. But that velocity ends up accelerating the course of life in such a way that, paradoxically, it ends up enslaving the human being and keeping him from enjoying what he has. We continually do more things because existentially we have more time at our disposal, but we have continually more things to do and thus we fall into haste, anxiety, or stress.

Because – and here we run into the most radical dimension of temporality – time always ends up escaping, *time always wins*. We would like to detain it, to control it, but we cannot, and that incapacity causes us anguish and wounds us internally because time is not something foreign and exterior: it is we, it is our life which escapes us, which weakens and disappears.

The singer-songwriter Manolo García has reflected very well the mix of feelings which are produced by the recognition of the fugacity of life and the human being's incapacity to detain it.

---

[8] The temporality of human life also allows for history. Cf. H.U. von Balthasar, *Il tutto nel fragmento. Aspetti di teología della storia* (Milano: Jaca Book, 1970); J. Pieper, *The end of time. A Meditation on the Philosophy of History* (San Francisco: Ignatius Press, 1999).

I held the fleur-de-lis in your hair.

I held the fleur-de-lis, feeling
that time escaped me.
In your kisses, serious, fierce,
I held the flower, and in my fingers
I felt that everything withers
and everything escapes us
Like the slow wheat fields,
slowly toward forgetfulness.
Slowly, without remedy.

We find in this song in the first place a feeling of *sadness* because life appears as something immensely valuable, but subject to a fleeting and uncontrollable succession. It slowly withers and escapes without remedy because that precariousness is not something superficial that can be dispensed with. I cannot and I do not want to do without time, but regardless of my wishes, it ends and concludes. Thus another typical element in the experience of temporality arises: *perplexity*, the person's astonishment before his incapacity to stop that flow, because in the end he thinks that he should be able to do it, that his destiny cannot be death or disappearance, since in the person something infinite is hidden, something that should last forever. Time thus inevitably leads to the final and ultimate question: that of death and immortality.

14.2 What is Dying?

a) The Fact of Death

Death is, above all, an inevitable fact which we run into. No one doubts that he will die. All the human beings that have preceded us have died and all the human beings that currently live on Earth will die. In any case, one may pose the question from a theoretical point of view – and some have done so – as to whether we can be so sure of that certainty of death. After all, there are many human beings who have not died – all those who are now living – and some event could occur in the future which might modify human life in such a way that death would no longer have a place. That possibility, however, is not able to penetrate our intelligence, because the certainty of death does not only proceed from what we observe in the world, that is, exterior realities, but also from our interior. We know that we are going to die because we realize that *our structure as persons is headed toward death.*

First of all, *our body grows old* and finally becomes incapable of fulfilling the organic functions and causes death. This growing old is something we all observe, and it indicates to us with full sureness that, at some point, the end will arrive. But, in addition, it is *our own psychological structure that produces in us the consciousness of death.* Scheler has expressed it by saying that all people possess a flow of life whose horizon becomes gradually reduced with age.[9] A young person's horizon – we have already noted it – is almost infinite and he feels that he has all the time in the world to do whatever he wants. But this does not happen in the mature person, and much less in the elderly person, who feels that his time is ending. Death, therefore, is presented as a fact not just because of an external observation, but because of a personal and interior experience. And this leads us to the question about the meaning. What is dying? What does it consist in?

Here one may distinguish basically two positions.

The *classical* position has insisted on death as the separation of the soul from the body and, on this basis, it has centered on proofs of immortality and the condition of the soul after death. This posture is obviously correct, but not exempt from difficulties. The first is that *it seems to limit death to the body;* the body would be the one that principally suffers in death, while the soul would be free. Cicero summarizes it accurately: "You are not mortal, your body is."[10] Death would exclusively affect the body understood, in addition, in a fundamentally biological way, as a mere material support for the soul. Another problem that this position poses, which is sometimes linked to an insufficient consideration of temporality, is that death tends to appear only at the end of life, it is not common to ask what role it plays during the life of the human being.

Faced with this position, some *more recent* philosophies – personalism among them – have attempted to orient this question in a new way. In the first place, by emphasizing that death is not something that happens only at the end of life, but rather *it is present in life,* and what that presence consists of must be studied. Secondly, by insisting that "in death, strictly speaking, neither the body of the human being nor the soul die, but the human being in himself, that is, the person dies."[11] Let us now analyze these two aspects.

b) Death as an Essential Dimension of Life

How is death present in the life of the human being? Before this question we may perhaps be tempted to answer spontaneously that its presence is scarce

---

[9] Cf. M. Scheler, *Muerte y supervivencia* (Madrid: Encuentro, 2001), 20-29.

[10] Cicero, *El sueño de Escipión* (Madrid: Instituto A. Nebrija, 1950), n. 26, 666. English version: *Somnium Scipionis, the Dream of Scipio Africanus Minor* (BiblioBazaar, 2009).

[11] J. A. García Cuadrado, *Antropología filosófica* (Pamplona: Eunsa, 2001), 230.

and not very relevant. But this is not the reality, but exactly the contrary. Death plays an essential role in our life, to the point that life would be radically different if the certainty of death did not exist. Let us look into it with a little more detail.

Death becomes present in life first as a *possibility*. We know that in theory we could die at any moment. Human life is fragile. An accident, a sudden illness, could end anyone's life, even that of the strongest. But this mere possibility, the fact that we could die now or in a week influences our life in a more anecdotal way. It is possible, but it is highly improbable and, furthermore, it is something that does not depend on us at all. Thus, we live, setting aside that possibility which, however, is real.

Very different is the *certainty* of death, that is, the fact that we know that we are going to die, although we do not know when. This knowledge, on the contrary, "accompanies the whole of life as an element of *all* its moments."[12] The fact that I am going to die, that I have a limited time, structures my entire existence because it imposes a unique and irreversible character on each one of my acts. If I were not going to die, if I did not have a limited amount of time, perhaps, for example, I would leave writing these pages for another moment which would require less effort of me. Or maybe I would never write them, precisely because I would always have a later time to write them.

And this leads to a perhaps paradoxical but true consideration: *the need for death as an essential element of a humanly serious and valuable life*. Death, curiously, is what gives value to life. Borges said this in a magnificent way in the story *El inmortal*. The immortals were human beings who had drunk from a river that granted them immortality, but that gift became, with the passage of time, a curse. They had stopped being active, brilliant, and powerful human beings, becoming practically immobile and almost primal, since they completely lacked motivation. Everything that they could do they had already done or they had an infinite amount of time to do it.[13]

"Death (or the allusion to it)," says the protagonist, "makes human beings precious and pathetic. They cause compassion because of their ghostly condition; each act that they execute could be the last one; there is no face that is not about to be blurred like a dream. *Everything, among mortals, has the value of the irrecuperable and haphazard.* Among the Immortals, by contrast, each act

---

[12] M. Scheler, *Muerte y supervivencia*, 33.

[13] Something similar happens with the doctrine of reincarnation. The possibility of an infinite chain of lives leads to a fatalistic and static behavior in relation to real life, which is singular.

(and each thought) is the echo of others that in the past preceded it, without a visible beginning, or the faithful omen of others that in the future will repeat it incessantly. There is nothing that is not as if lost among indefatigable mirrors. *Nothing can occur once, nothing is preciously precarious.*"[14]

Death, therefore, is part of life in the sense that the human being knows that he is going to die and lives according to that knowledge. Thus, at times, human beings are simply called mortals. "Mortals," Heidegger says, "are human beings. They are called mortals because they can die. To die means to be capable of death *qua* death. Only the human being dies. The animal simply perishes."[15] And from this perspective the old thesis which hides from death denying its existence seems banal. "Only what is felt exists," Epicurus says, "and since death is not felt, death does not exist."[16] Or in Schelling's version: "O death, I should not fear you because when you are, I am not; and when I am, you are not." But, as we just saw, death is not just at the end, but in every act of life.

That death is not just at the end does not mean, however, that it is something natural; it is natural inasmuch as it is a reality with which we cohabit, but at the same time it is profoundly antinatural; more still, it is what is most contrary to human nature, because it means its destruction. Thomas Aquinas has summarized it in one short sentence: "Death is in some sense natural, but also in some sense antinatural."[17] Therefore, although we cohabit with the idea of death and although that idea determines our way of acting, our normal attitude is of rejection and expulsion of it from our life horizon. "There is a repression of the idea of death which in a certain way represents a *general and normal* phenomenon of human nature. And this phenomenon is, without any doubt, of great utility in life. Only thanks to this repression of the idea of death, leaving it out of the zone of clear consciousness, does there arise in each one of the useful actions of the human being that 'seriousness,' that importance and significance

---

[14] J. L. Borges, *El inmortal* in *El Aleph* (Madrid: Alianza, 1997), 25-26 (the emphasis is ours). Thus, the Immortals decided to lose their gift. "*There is a river whose waters give immortality; in some region there must be another river whose waters erase it.* The number of rivers is not infinite; an immortal traveler who goes throughout the world will end up, someday, having drunk from them all. We proposed to discover that river." (ibid.)

[15] M. Heidegger, *Vorträge und Aufsätze* (Günther, 1954), quoted in R. Lucas, *El hombre, espíritu encarnado. Compendio de filosofía del hombre* (Salamanca: Sígueme 1999). As is known, Heidegger understands the human being, in addition, as a being-for-death. But this posture goes beyond what we want to express here, because in the human being there is a nucleus of immortality.

[16] Epicurus, *Letter to Menoeceus* (CreateSpace Independent Publishing Platform, 2016).

[17] Thomas Aquinas, *Quaestiones disputata de malo*, 5, 5, ad 17. Cf. J. Pieper, *Death and Inmortality* (St. Augustine's Press, 2000).

that they would lack if the thought of death were always clearly and distinctly present in consciousness."[18] Or, said in a droll way:

> Each time that I consider
> that I have to die
> I spread my cape on the ground
> and I sleep a long while.[19]

In other words, we know that we are going to die, and that knowledge influences our life, but we cannot root ourselves in an excessively deep way in that thought, because it would remove us from life. Everything would seem banal and excessively passing. We can attend a funeral with sorrow and conviction, especially if it is a loved one's funeral, but in the end we feel obligated to return to life, to our life, because we have not died and our loved one has entered a world into which we cannot follow him.

c) Death as Destruction of the Person

The previous reflections lead us now to the essential question: What does death consist of? Because, if death has an important part in life, it is due to that in which it consists, it is due to what it is. And, what happens in death?

This is an essential question, but one that, in addition, poses for us, for the first time, a difficulty which up until now had not been presented in our now wide overview of the human world: *we do not have direct experience of death*, because those who die are always others. "My relationship with death," Levinas affirms, "consists in not knowing about the fact of dying."[20]

This lack of experience, in addition to being an insurmountable obstacle – we will only have direct experience when we die and then it will no longer be of any use – indicates to us that we begin to enter into the *limits of philosophy*, that is, in those zones in which the human intellect begins to lose its footing and confront problems that radically exceed it. Because, there are questions that we do not know today, but which, with effort and perhaps luck, we will be able to unravel tomorrow; but there are other problems which human intelligence will never be able to resolve because they are situated in an area that essentially exceeds its ability. Death is one of those problems.

---

[18] M. Scheler, *Muerte y supervivencia*, 34.

[19] Quoted in C. López Pardo, *Sobre la vida y la muerte* (Madrid: Rialp, 1973), 52.

[20] E. Levinas, *Dios, la muerte y el tiempo* (Madrid: Cátedra, 1994), 30. English versión: *God, Death and Time* (Stanford: Stanford University Press, 2000).

In any case, and despite the fact that we may be conscious of those limits, philosophy cannot (and should not) cease in its questions. It should attempt, within the measure of its possibilities, to answer the question about the essence of death. And, regarding this fact, *external experience* which we possess shows us fundamentally three things. First, death is *a fading away and a disappearance from the world*.[21] The person disappears, and the cadaver is there to show it. Its physical presence is dramatic precisely because it shows a non-presence, a disappearance, that of the person who was there, but no longer is, and we do not know what has been of him.

Death implies, in addition, the *loss of corporeality*. The human being dies due to the deterioration of his body which interrupts its vital functions and impedes the person from continuing to live. The body then becomes a cadaver, a strange and painful reality because it was human, but it no longer is, at least in a complete way. But it is important to realize, as Scheler has noted with acuity, that loss of corporeality is not to be identified with the cessation of biological activities, because these, in reality, never cease: the cadaver is subject to a considerable biological activity. The loss of corporeality certainly depends on the cessation of some human biological functions, but it means much more than that because, as we previously have seen, the body is not a mere appendix of the person, but, so to speak, the person's physical mediation (cf. Ch. 2.1).

Therefore, the loss of the body means the *destruction of the person*. It is not the body alone that dies, the entire subject dies, the man or the woman. "It is not a question of abandoning corporeality like the skin of a reptile and escaping intact to other worlds. On the contrary, the condition of the existence of death is that death occurs, that is, that death happens to *someone*, and this someone – *me, you* – actually dies."[22]

Therein lies the drama and the horror of death, because it is opposed to everything that the human being is, and thus the force of the instinct of survival. To live is to be and to die is to disappear, to abandon all that is known and loved, to suddenly interrupt our temporal structure, thus impeding any new project, any new experience. And to die is to pass into the dark and unknown regions of the non-being, from which no one has returned to explain to us how life is there, if there is life there. Death is, therefore, horrible,

---

[21] Cf. J. Marías, *Antropología metafísica*, 220ff.

[22] J. Marías, *Antropología metafísica*, 216. If the body is an essential part of the person, death implies the destruction of that person. But that does not mean that nothing of the person remains after death, even a "personal" dimension. Cf. J. Marías, *Mapa del mundo personal* (Madrid: Alianza, 2006).

and its harshness demands a response. The human being needs to know what happens after death so that his life and death may have meaning.

d) The Death of the Contemporary Person

Death always has the characteristics that we have just noted, but the way they are lived out concretely is modulated by the culture of each era. The death of the contemporary human being is principally characterized by *the attempt to conceal death*, due to the radical rejection of death and its expulsion from the terrain in which the contemporary person lives.

We have said that a certain repression of the idea of death is normal and even useful, because only in that way is it possible to live with serenity. But the contemporary person has radicalized that repression to the point of turning it into a concealment and a disappearance.[23] The yearning to live, to exhaust all the possibilities that an ever more accelerated world offers, and also the blocking out of transcendence, present death to the contemporary person as a fact that is especially contrary to everything that constitutes his way of life and aspirations. Previously, the situation was different: the slower and more paused rhythm of life, more monotonous and linked to the seasons and the forces of nature, allowed people to understand experientially that they too would one day be subjected to those natural forces and would die. Today, by contrast, technology permits the human being to dominate nature and the possibilities of living and enjoyment constantly multiply. Thus, death seems particularly repulsive and surprising and there is an attempt to expel it from one's existence[24].

The word death is substituted by softer and sweeter expressions, the technical and commercial organization around death facilitates and simplifies the process and eludes the confrontation with the harshness of that moment, the time dedicated to mourning is reduced and its external manifestations are suppressed, etc. In summary, death is privatized, it becomes a personal and private reality which society hides with apprehension.[25]

---

[23] For Ariès, we are in a period of "denial of death" with the result that, in the 20th century, "death has become savage," since it has progressively lost the containment of the walls of family, community and religion. Cf. P. Ariès, *Western Attitudes Toward Death. From the Middle Ages to the Present* (Baltimore: John Hopkins University Press).

[24] Contemporary transhumanism drinks from this source.

[25] "An education about death proportions a meaning and a series of attitudes toward death and ways of confronting it. But these teachings, which are an essential part of education in different cultures and were previously so in our culture, have been lost and in their place there is no more than a denial and concealment of death." M. I. Rodríguez, *Génesis y evolución de actitudes ante la muerte en la infancia*, Cuadernos de Bioética, XI.41 (2000), 114.

And thus, when it appears, it looks surprising and especially incomprehensible. It is not a reality with which one has cohabited and, thus, to which one has been able to give a meaning, but rather a wall which appears suddenly, unexpected and inevitable, and against which it is only possible to crash into absurdly. Of the two dimensions which death includes anthropologically, the contemporary person tends to keep only the second one, the destruction of life.

14.3 The Mystery of Immortality

The human rejection of death manifests itself in the longing for immortality, in the desire to remain, to last forever, to not sink into the swamp that seems to lead to nothingness and darkness, and in the desire to know if beyond death something exists which might guarantee survival.

a) Longing and Conviction

a.1) "Non omnis moriar": The Remembrance of Humans

A first manifestation of immortality is the desire to remain in some way among humans after death.[26] We desire that our presence not be extinguished immediately or shortly after death. We want to be remembered when time passes because, otherwise, we would have the impression that, in reality, we have not existed, that our terrestrial pilgrimage has been like the passage of water between rocks, leaving no mark or trace.

That desire of every human being is manifested in many ways but all of them have a common denominator: leaving something behind that will remain after our passing. Children, people whom we have formed according to our ideals, works or actions. Some of the greatest architectural enterprises of the kings and emperors of the past – pyramids, basilicas, mausolea – had in part this objective: to construct a kind of detention wall against the flow of time in such a way that, with the passage of the centuries, its presence would challenge the past and would bring to mind – and in some way resuscitate – those who made it possible. Perhaps no one has ever said this better than the Roman poet Horace:

---

[26] Hannah Arendt distinguishes between immanent or earthly immortality, which the ancients sought avidly, and transcendent eternity, understood as an immortal destiny of the human being, linked especially to the appearance of Christianity. (cf. H. Arendt, *La condición humana*, 30-33; English version: *The human condition*).

I have crafted a monument more lasting than bronze,
and loftier than the royal pile of the pyramids,
a thing which neither biting rain nor the obstreperous
North Wind can destroy, nor the countless run of years,
The flight of time.
I will not totally perish and much of me will survive
Oblivion; I will go on living in the praise of those who
Postdate me, as long as the demure Vestal accompany
The priest who climbs the Capitol.[27]

a.2) Personal Immortality

The desire to remain in the memory of humans is good and legitimate, but it is not sufficient. It is not, above all, because it is only within the reach of a few people. No one will remember the immense majority of us after a relatively brief lapse of time. And the memory of the majority of humans who are famous today will only resist a very brief period of time in comparison to the whole of human history. But, in reality, even if everyone remembered me, that memory would be anecdotal in the face of the central and decisive question: *personal and real survival.* One thing is the fact that my influence may survive in the world in some way, and another, very different, is that *I* will survive after death. What is it possible to say about this central fact for the meaning of human life?

Above all, it is a *generalized conviction of humanity.* The belief in the existence of some type of life after death appears in practically every era and culture and is manifested in multiple ways. The veneration of the dead is one of them. "All authors consider that ritual practices (of burial) imply a belief in some type of immortality. This belief is as old as the consciousness of death, since at the very moment that the human being discovers that he is mortal, he thinks of himself as immortal, in such a way that the first knowledge of death already implies the denial that in death the human being perishes absolutely. This link between burials and belief in some type of survival after death is proven archeologically *ad nauseam.*"[28]

What is this belief in survival based on? On one hand, it is based on the religious doctrines that affirm it and propose a specific content about what occurs in the hereafter, in the world of the dead. But that affirmation of the religions could not have such a generalized acceptance if it were not supported in turn by something which, in one way or another, human beings

---

[27] Horace, Book III, *Ode* 30, trans. Terry Walsh.
[28] J. Vicente, *El horror de morir* (Barcelona: Tibidabo 1992), 323.

could experience. If, to use a trivial example, a religious doctrine said that the human being could fly, it might be able to find some fanatics who might believe it, but the majority of humans would realize that it was a false and impossible doctrine. But this does not occur with immortality. The majority of religions affirm it and the human being accepts it without problem, which means that humans intuit that it is something coherent and true.

What does that intuition consist of? It is obviously a difficult question, but it seems to us that it may be affirmed that it is rooted in the realization that in the person, in each one of us, there seems to be something that should not and cannot die, there is a nucleus of immortality. Goethe has expressed it clearly: "This thought (of death) leaves me absolutely tranquil, because I have the firm persuasion that our spirit is an essence of an absolutely indestructible nature, it is something that continues acting for an eternity of eternities, like the Sun, which seems to set only before our terrestrial eyes, but which, in reality, never sets, but continues to shine incessantly."[29] And, along the same lines, an infinity of other testimonies could be offered.

b) Philosophical Proofs of Immortality

This inner intuition that there is in us something indestructible, an ultimate ability to conquer death despite the fact that we are apparently conquered by it, together with the message of immortality of the different religions, has been sufficient for the majority of humans, who have died thinking that, in one way or another (that is another question), they would survive. But here we must pose the question *from a philosophical point of view*. Are there philosophical proofs of immortality?

The topic is obviously very complex and here we cannot study it with the necessary depth, but we can indicate what, in our opinion, constitute the essential keys for confronting the question.

Above all, there are several *classical proofs* to provide a foundation for immortality which do not seem completely convincing. One of them, along Augustinian lines, is the ability of the human being to know the truth. Since truth is immortal and does not change with time, its seat, which is the human being, also has to be immortal.[30] However, this demonstration does not seem sufficiently conclusive. "It is true," Scheler indicates, "that in these acts I *transcend* everything that is still relative to life, and I can say that in such acts my spirit touches a dominion, a *sphere of intemporal and eternal units of*

---

[29] P. Eckermann, *Conversaciones con Goethe*.
[30] See, for example St. Augustine, *Soliloquies*, II, XIX, 33.

meaning. But I can say no more. That the acts I perform, or that my person who performs them, also *survive* when I cease to live, does not follow at all from the essential connection between the idea of an act and object."[31]

Another proof, in this case proposed by Thomas Aquinas, is the impossibility that what nature desires not be fulfilled. "Everyone who has an intellect naturally desires to be always. The natural desire cannot be in vain. Thus, the entire intellectual substance is incorruptible."[32] It is undoubtedly a powerful argument but, in our opinion, it has a weak point, namely, the key to this proof, the impossibility that natural desire is in vain, is something that needs to be demonstrated, it cannot be accepted point-blank. Why does a natural desire have to be fulfilled? In life, we desire many things that we do not obtain, and we can become very frustrated by not achieving them. Why could not the same occur with the yearning for immortality? In the end, the human being could be defective and desire something that he cannot achieve. And recourse to God the Creator to resolve this difficulty is not something evident because the fact that there is a God who watches over us, who is concerned for us and who loves us is not something that can be easily deduced philosophically; we know it through Christian Revelation.

These two proofs, in any case, point to a nucleus that does constitute, in our opinion, the key to a foundation for continued existence after death: *the existence in the human being of a spiritual nucleus, which is classically called the soul, which transcends corporeality and time.* We have seen that the human being has a bodily dimension, a psychological one and a spiritual one plus the Self, and we have also seen that that spiritual dimension plus the Self, although it depends for its exercise on the bodily basis, transcends it and is above it. So here is the key to the question. If what is spiritual transcends what is bodily and does not *depend entirely* on it, then when the body disappears, the spiritual dimension of the person need not disappear; it possesses the ability to continue existing in one way or another with its own entity.[33]

This transcendence of the human spirit beyond the body is the basic intuition which every human being has about himself and which, even if he does not know how to formulate it technically, allows him to feel or experience that he will not disappear completely after death. And that basic intuition developed philosophically is what constitutes the radical and

---

[31] M. Scheler, *Muerte y supervivencia*, 55.

[32] Thomas Aquinas, *S. Th.*, I, q. 75, a. 6.

[33] Death, on this concrete point, does not imply, according to Scheler, an essential change: "just as during life his acts 'transcended' his bodily states, so also do they now transcend the destruction of his body." M. Scheler, *Muerte y supervivencia*, 66.

resounding proof of the *immortality of the soul*. St. Thomas has developed this thesis from a metaphysical perspective through his description of the soul as the substantial form of the body. When the body disappears and corrupts, the soul remains as a separated substance. Personalism and phenomenology have posed this question, as we have done, from a more anthropological perspective: the existence of a spiritual nucleus in the human being which transcends corporeality. But the basis of the demonstration is the same.

c) The Hereafter

Philosophy, we have just seen, is able to affirm the continuing existence of the human being after death, but it is *only* capable of affirming this, which poses two problems that are difficult to solve.

c.1) The Status of the Person after Death

The first problem is the status of the person after death. The human being continues to exist, but how does he continue to exist? Moreover, how is that continual existence possible, if we have said that the body is an essential part of the person? It is not an easy problem to resolve, not even theologically, and it poses the known problems of intermediate eschatology. We can reduce the questions to two. What is it that continues to exist? And, what is the type of activity of that which continues to exist? Lucas has indicated that the greater or lesser difficulty in answering these questions depends on the starting anthropology and, more concretely, on whether one insists on the unitary or the dual character of the human being. "In an anthropology with dualistic features, *unity* is the secondary moment of a process of *composition*. Strictly speaking, what one tends to see in the human being, more than unity, is the fact of *being united*. On the contrary, a realist and unitary anthropology will see the human being above all as a psychosomatic unity, as *incarnate* freedom and consciousness, as *incarnate spirit*; only in second place will one see, through analysis, in this unity, a duality."[34]

So, in a more dualistic anthropology, the problem is minimized because one may say that the one who continues to exist after death is the soul, which is separated from the body and which has, all in all, its own entity, although that does not mean that it ceases to pose problems, in particular, how could the soul act without the body. If one insists, however, on the unitary character of the person, the disappearance of the body is more problematic. In reality, one could not even speak of a person, since we have seen that the body is one of

---

[34] R. Lucas, *El hombre, espíritu encarnado*, 337.

the person's essential dimensions and the body no longer exists. In addition, the question remains completely open as to how a spirit could operate which, even though it transcends corporeality, needs the latter to act. These are questions that are difficult, not to say impossible, to resolve, since they escape and will always escape the area of our experience.[35]

c.2) What is There Afterwards?

The fact that we may not be able to elucidate the status of the person after death is not, in any case, something excessively concerning. In a certain sense, it is more of a technical question, of specific interest to philosophers and theologians. The existential question, the one whose answer really interests us, is the following: What is there afterwards? What happens after death? And the problem posed before such a question is that philosophy, that is, the human being, does not only have nothing to say, but never will, since it is an area which completely escapes his control. That information, however, is completely necessary because the meaning and value of this life depends to a great measure on what happens in the next life. Thus is prepared the topic that we will face in the last chapter: the ultimate meaning of life and the role that religion plays in the life of the human being.

---

[35] The problems which it poses are so serious that Thomas Aquinas postulated philosophically the need for a resurrection of bodies as the only means of returning to the person his unity and lost completion.

Chapter 15

The Ultimate Questions and Religion

15.1 The Ultimate Questions

Death has raised questions for us that are very difficult to resolve strictly through philosophical reflection, but death is not the only deep and decisive question that arises for human beings, nor is it the only question that is difficult to answer. There are other questions that are difficult to answer. In this chapter, we are going to study these questions, grouped into two categories: the question about the meaning of life, and the question of God.

a) The Question about the Meaning of Life

Pain and suffering are ultimate questions that arise in human beings of all times. The world is filled with pain that, moreover, on some occasions, seems especially absurd and cruel: the death of the innocent, torture, deaths rendered absurd by accident or by chance, wars, failures of different types, etc. This may present itself to us as an enigma because we are not made in order to suffer, but rather on the contrary, to be happy. Human reflection, and within this, philosophy, can perhaps understand some kinds of pain in particular, but of the great dramas that afflict individuals and peoples it is very difficult, not to say impossible, to find a rational justification. What meaning is it possible to give, for example, to the immense and boundless tragedies of the Second World War, or the frustrated destinies of generations in countries governed by dictators like Cuba, Iraq or North Korea?[1]

In contrast to pain, but not only in this context, happiness also becomes an ultimate issue. It is an ultimate question because of its radicality. What we seek definitively is *happiness*. And it is also ultimate because of the difficulty in reaching it - pain always lurks - and because of the difficulty in determining exactly what it is or where it is. That is why Marías has called happiness the necessary impossibility.[2]

---

[1] Eugenio Corti has portrayed human pain throughout the Second World War with mastery and depth in *Il Cavallo Rosso*.

[2] Julián Marías, *La felicidad humana* (Madrid: Alianza, 1991).

We have already spoken of *death* and the afterlife and of the unresolvable problems that arise from them. Now we can add problems relative to *origins*. On the one hand is the mystery of the beginning of the human race, which anthropologists have struggled to unravel with much difficulty. On the other hand, there is the *mystery of our own origin*. From where have we arisen? Where do we come from? And, consequently, who are we? We are undoubtedly aware that we have not placed ourselves in existence and, since we have an incorruptible spiritual core, we can intuit that Someone had to create us as we are. But to what extent can we be sure of this? And who is this Someone? What is this Someone like?

The limits of human beings, which can be grouped around the term *finitude*, open up another field of difficult questions. We have great aspirations, we have an insatiable desire for knowledge and our desire for power is immense. But our limits are also immense. A small illness and we can fall prostrate and helpless. And the inevitable passage of time prevents us from going back and changing lost time.

These questions and others that could be added, taken together, lead to the essential question: why and for what do we live? What is *the ultimate meaning of our existence?* It is important here to stress the word "ultimate." What man asks himself with this question is not about his existence at this or that moment, but about the overall and radical meaning, about the reason for life as such. What am I seeking with my life, with my whole life? Does it make sense and to what extent?

b) The Question of God

The other radical question that every human being asks himself is the question about God. And, in this question, we can clearly distinguish two levels. The first is the question about God's *existence*; the famous *an Deus sit* with which Thomas Aquinas begins the Summa. Does God exist? In reality, although, due to the cultural milieu that surrounds us, we may be inclined to think otherwise, the answer to this question is not very problematic. The overwhelming majority of human beings from all ages – including many of the most eminent intellectuals – have responded affirmatively. And the same happens in our age, though with some peculiar features related to the existence of an important process of secularization.[3] But, in spite of this, the percentage of persons who declare

---

[3] Cf. Jurgen Habermas and Josef Ratzinger, *Dialéctica de la secularización* (Madrid: Encuentro, 2006); H. McLeod and W. Ustorf, eds., *The Decline of Christendom in Western Europe (1750-2000)* (Cambridge: Cambridge University Press, 2003).

themselves atheists remains low because there are many things in the world, beginning with human beings themselves, that cannot be explained or justified in terms of themselves, so that the existence of a supreme being to account for human beings is imposed upon our intelligence.[4] St. Augustine has expressed it through the aesthetic way, although it can be formulated in many other ways: "To all the things that stand around the doors of my flesh I said, 'Tell me of my God! Although you are not he, tell me something of him!' With a mighty voice they cried out, 'He made us!' My question was the gaze I turned on them; the answer was their beauty."[5]

Therefore, although the existence of God may not be evident and may open the interesting and complex chapter on the demonstrations of God's existence, the question that is frequently more important from a personal point of view is: *What is God like?* What is fundamental, what is decisive, is not to know if some type of higher being exists, since this seems relatively clear, but rather to know what God is like, who God is. Is God one or many? Kind or cruel? Is God interested in human beings or disinterested in their destiny? Does God have some plan for human beings now or when they die? And the problem that we find, as in the rest of the questions that we are dealing with now, is that the human being, by himself, can hardly outline an answer. If intelligence can come more or less clearly to affirm the existence of God, what is completely forbidden to our forces is the concrete knowledge of the characteristics of divinity.[6]

c) Attitudes and Responses

The two groups of questions we have just considered have a double characteristic. The first is their *centrality*. That we respond to them in one way or another affects the overall orientation that each person may give to their existence. For example, that there exists an afterlife governed by a loving God leads to a vital stance that is very different from someone who thinks that there is no afterlife or that it is governed by a God who is anarchic or indifferent. If God loves me, I can feel the inclination, impulse or obligation to

---

[4] We are not giving here, obviously, a "demonstration" of the existence of God, but rather showing in an elemental manner the path that leads the majority of people to God in different ways.

[5] Augustine, *Confessions* X, 6, 9.

[6] From this arises the religious concept of *revelation or illumination*: a special knowledge that someone receives, generally gratuitously and undeservedly, and that allows them to guide other humans in these dark questions. What is specific about Christianity is that it is *God himself* who has become incarnate and has made that revelation.

love others. In contrast, if God does not care about me, I may think that I have no need to care for others and adopt arrogance as my logic for life.

The second characteristic that these questions possess and that, in a certain sense, is opposed to the first one (*centrality*), is the *difficulty* of giving an adequate response to them. All these questions raise issues that are placed on the limit or rather outside the possibilities of human intelligence to respond, generating a powerful feeling of uncertainty, existential indigence and fragility.

Karl Jaspers recalled a medieval saying that synthesizes the difficulty with lucid irony:

> "I come, but I do not know from where.
> I am, but I do not know who.
> I will die, but I do not know when.
> I journey, but I do not know to where.
> I am surprised that I am content."[7]

The medieval dating of this saying also informs us about *the limited influence of time* on the human capacity to respond to these questions. While practical advances of the human race in other fields such as technology are both incredible and spectacular, in the terrain of essential questions we find ourselves in practically the same place as our predecessors.

We thus come to a very peculiar and paradoxical situation. The person knows that there are a number of key issues to guide his life, however he is unable to resolve them. And this not only in a conjunctural way but, so to speak, in a structural way; that is to say, it is not that I, now, at this moment, do not know how to answer them but that, probably, no one will ever be able to answer them. What, then, would be a reasonable attitude toward this situation?

We will analyze four possible responses.[8]

Scientistic materialism has responded to this problem by *denying its existence*. The dilemma simply does not exist. Human beings are no more than a conjunction of matter, so it makes no sense to try to develop answers to these types of questions. It makes no sense to ask "metaphysical" questions that go beyond the purely factual empirical data that we encounter. Specific questions that can increase our knowledge make sense, but questions about meaning are irrational because man is a mere product of nature.

---

[7] Karl Jaspers, *Cifras de la trascendencia* (Madrid: Alianza, 1993), 18.
[8] Cf. R. Yepes, *Fundamentos de antropología*, 465ff.

Relatively close to this attitude, but from a much more hedonistic perspective, is the position that chooses to enjoy the moment (*carpe diem*), what one has. Ultimate questions, say those who take this perspective, are too complex, distant and unsolvable. Confronting them leads nowhere but to a futile and sterile endeavor. Therefore, the sensible and reasonable thing is to enjoy what you have and live from day to day.[9]

A third posture, especially widespread in the twentieth century, of which Heidegger was a paradigmatic representative, is to consider the human being as *a being for death*.[10] For this position, and unlike scientism, the human being is not pure materiality and, therefore, can neither deny the fundamental questions nor avoid them superficially with a frivolous reference to momentary enjoyment. But this greater seriousness is finally turned into frustration and failure because, from this perspective, it is argued that the human being's own peculiar destiny is death. And it is not just that it is proper for man to die - this, as we have seen, can also be affirmed from other anthropologies - but that death ends everything, the human being and his problems and his existential anguish. There is the end beyond which you cannot go.

These are three possible responses, but they are minority responses and weak ones. That the human being is a mere grouping of matter is something radically untenable in the face of a minimally attentive analysis of personal reality (cf. all of Part II) and death as an absolute end is opposed to the existence of a spiritual nucleus. Finally, *carpe diem* only has an existential value for certain times of life in which everything can smile at us: youth, a certain maturity. But it is clearly insufficient in the face of its dramatic aspects and, in particular, in the face of death. Can we enjoy the moment when we suffer, when a loved one has died, or when we are approaching death?

There is a fourth and final position that has been adopted by the vast majority of people across many cultures: *the religious position*. We might formulate this in the following way. If there are a series of mysteries in my life that I am not able to answer due to my finitude or my limitations, but there exists, at the same time, a higher being who is responsible in one way or another for my existence and for the existence of the world, it is logically to this being that we must turn

---

[9] *Do what you must,*
be wise, cut your vines
and forget about hope.
Time goes running, even as we talk.
Take the present, (carpe diem); the future's no one's affair.
(Horace, *Odes, Book I.* source: https://www.poetryfoundation.org/poems/48703/ode-i-11).
[10] Cf. Martin Heidegger, *Being and Time*, 253-291.

to in order to find the answers that we need. Religion thus appears as the most convincing response to the fundamental questions about human existence. This is the response that we will now explore.

15.2 What is Religion?

a) Religion as the Question of Ultimate Meaning

Religion is normally understood as the relationship with God, the orientation to God.[11] This, evidently, is its basic meaning. But the reflections that we have made remit us to a *previous and original understanding* that gives this definition an anthropological connection, a connection with the vital fabric of the person. Religion, understood in this way, is the place where human existence is decided in its radicality, or, in other words, the area in which the human being wonders about and receives the answer to the overall meaning of his life and existence. "The religious factor," affirms Giussani, "represents the nature of the self expressed in certain questions: What is the ultimate meaning of existence? Why do pain and death exist? Is life really worth living? Or, from another perspective, from what and for what is reality made? It coincides with the radical commitment of our self to life that is manifested in these questions."[12] Frankl, in the same sense, affirms that "it is justifiable to define religion as man's search for ultimate meaning."[13] And a similar development can be found in Guardini when he speaks of "religious depth,"[14] in Buber,[15] and in many other authors' work.[16]

---

[11] "Religio propie importat ordinem ad Deum," (Thomas Aquinas, *S. Th. II-II*, q. 81, a. 5).

[12] L. Giussani, *El sentido religioso*, 4th ed. (Madrid: Encuentro, 1993), 61. English version: *The religious sense* (Montreal: MacGill-Quenn's University Press, 1997), and subsequently, he defines the religious sense as "the place of nature where one affirms the meaning of everything" (ibid., 64).

[13] Viktor Frankl, *Man's search for meaning*, 24.

[14] Cf. R. Guardini, *Introducción a la vida de oración* (Madrid: Palabra, 2002), 46; english version *The Art of Praying: The Principles and Methods of Christian Prayer* (Sophia Institute Press, 1995).

[15] "In all religion, the religious essence can be discovered in its most elevated assurances. This is the assurance that the meaning of existence is something open and accessible in our living situation, concrete and real, not above the struggle with reality, but within it." (M. Buber, *Eclipse de Dios. Estudio sobre las relaciones entre religión y filosofía* [México: FCE, 1995], 63; English version: *Eclipse of God: Studies in the Relation Between Religion and Philosophy* [UK: Prometheus Books, 1988]).

[16] Ll. Duch, *Antropología de la religión* (Barcelona: Herder, 2001) contributes, in this same sense, the opinions of Malinowski, W. James, Lenski and others.

From this understanding of religion there arises a basic perspective: the relationship with God. We must always remember that this perspective acquires its value in this anthropological anchor and, for this reason, it is not possible to do without it. Otherwise, God appears as an entity that hovers uncomfortably around me intending to break into my life although I do not need him, when, in reality, the situation is precisely the opposite: God and religion constitute the response to the crucial questions of my life, questions that clamor for a solution. So, *in a certain sense, one can affirm that every human being is necessarily religious, since inevitably, he or she has to stand before the ultimate questions and give an answer.* To pass over or to leave out religion means, in reality, giving to these questions a specific response: the frivolous and insufficient vital attitude of *carpe diem* or the frivolous and insufficient intellectual response of scientism.

This perspective, on the other hand, also allows us to explain why some religions exist without God, such as Shinto or Confucianism. These doctrines are religious because they respond to the ultimate questions but have the peculiarity of not making an explicit reference to divinity. They are sets of moral practices to achieve perfection (Confucius) or ways of participating in ritual ceremonies that establish a connection with ancestors (Shinto) but there is no doctrine of God (although neither is there a rejection). This approach, in any case, is exceptional because religious practice is overwhelmingly identified with a specific conception of God or of divinity.

b) Religion as Relationship with God

The second fundamental sense of religion is that of the relationship of the person with God and all that this implies: prayer and praise, supplications and rites, joys and sorrows, light and mystery, attitudes toward life, death and human beings. It is an immense and decisive world, mysterious and difficult to circumscribe but essential in the life of human beings and in the history of the world which cannot be understood without religion. Given how vast and unfathomable this topic is, we will limit ourselves to noting briefly the two aspects that seem most basic to us and that we will detail in the next section: the subjective or personal and the objective or institutional dimensions of religion.[17]

Appendix. On Religion and the Sacred

To conclude this section, we will make reference to the concept of the *sacred* since it is a notion that, at times, is confused with that of religion and thus it

---

[17] A more elaborate treatment corresponds to the philosophy and sociology of religion.

should be delimited. The *sacred* refers to something *distinct, separate, different* from the normal world and placed in a different order of things. We encounter this category in a wide range of religious realities: the temple as a space reserved for worship and prayer, the priest as a distinct person specially dedicated to religion, etc. Some authors, however, have seen in the sacred the *essential category* of the religious realm, to the point of identifying the two. Martín Velasco, for example, affirms that "something is religious to the extent that it has a relationship with the sacred," and also along this line of thinking indicates that "the first feature that characterizes any religious manifestation is the rupture that it establishes with ordinary life."[18]

This position, however, in light of our considerations, appears to be incorrect. While it is true that in some areas of religion there is a separation from the ordinary, this separation is something accidental and does not constitute the essence of religion. Religion, in reality, not only does not constitute a break with ordinary life, but rather arises precisely out of this daily life; it is the question that each of us asks ourselves about our destiny, and the relationship with God that arises from the answer. In fact, all of human life is, to a certain extent, religious, since, as we have said, it is influenced in one way or another by the response to the ultimate questions and by the concept of the divine and, therefore, it does not make sense to identify the sacred, understood as separate, with the religious. The sacred, as Pieper affirms, "means more than specific empirical realities - places, times, actions that possess particular characteristics - that order themselves to the sphere of the divine in a way that falls outside of the field of the everyday."[19] The sacred *is a special field within the religious realm* that has its own importance, but that does not constitute the central category because the ultimate element of the religious realm is radicality and ultimacy, not separation. Therefore, the sacred has a value for human beings not in itself, by virtue of being something separate, but because it places us in contact with God and with religious experience. I am interested in going to church or to a priest not because this is a way of leaving my ordinary world, but because this separation could facilitate my contact with God. In the words of Zubiri:

---

[18] J. Gómez Caffarena and J. Martín Velasco, *Filosofía de la religión* (Madrid: Rialp, 1973), 77. Martín Velasco, on the other hand, offers in this text a good synthesis of the principle theses of the phenomenology of religion.

[19] J. Pieper, *¿Qué significa sagrado? Un intento de clarificación* (Madrid: Rialp, 1990), 21; English version, *In Search of the Sacred: Contributions to an Answer* (San Francisco: Ignatius Press, 2000).

"certainly religion can be sacred. But it is sacred because it is religious, not religious because it is sacred."[20]

15.3 Dimensions of the Phenomenon of Religion

Let us now turn to the principal ways in which religion is embodied through a conceptual instrument that we have utilized already on several occasions: the distinction between the subjective dimension and the objective dimension which, in this case, basically coincides with the distinction between the personal and the institutional relationship with God.

a) The Subjective Dimension: Religious Experience

a.1) Characteristics of Religious Experience

By the subjective dimension we understand the lived personal and individual experience of religion that coincides fundamentally with the concept of religious experience that has been brilliantly developed during the previous century by phenomenology of religion. Given that there are many religions, evidently, religious experience is necessarily diverse, but, nevertheless, it is possible to bring them together, especially if we focus on what is most central in religions, the principal characteristics. Ferrer has indicated the following characteristics[21]:

- real: a human being lives out the religious phenomenon as something real, not as an invention of his or her intelligence; religion, and all its dimensions, is a reality that humans experience[22];

---

[20] X. Zubiri, *El problema filosófico de la historia de las religiones* (Madrid: Alianza, 1987), 26 and 57. The logical consequence is the "the sacred and the profane are two slopes of the same reality that is precisely the religious life, religious reality." (ibid., 93).

[21] Cf. J. Ferrer, *Filosofía de la religión* (Madrid: Palabra, 2002), 281ff. Furthermore, one can find a good summary of the principal philosophical postures about religious experience on pages 175-203.

[22] In *Eclipse de Dios*, Buber has strongly insisted on the reality of God and on the understanding of religion as a relationship with this reality in the face of all modern attempts to eliminate religion (Heidegger, Sartre) or the reduction of religion to different categories (Jung). Marina, on the contrary, is clearly situated in this reductionist line, since he fundamentally considers religion as "an invention" (*Dictamen sobre Dios*, 22) and that is why he ends up emptying religious experience of all valid and original content.

- transcendent: the world of religion transcends human beings, is superior to them and is situated in a different plane characteristic of divinity;

- mysterious: the religious world does not present itself with the clarity of other human realities, but rather is wrapped in a halo of mystery by its transcendence and depth and the difficulty of the truths that it transmits;

- personal: although it is not possible to say this of all religions, in the majority of them religious experience is lived out as a relationship with a personal being to whom we can address ourselves individually;

- holy will: religious experience also tends, in general, to show a will of God for human beings which we must carry out if we want to achieve salvation;

- salvific character: persons, finally, live religion as a way of salvation, that is to say, as a means to live a full and adequate human life, to resolve the puzzles that one cannot answer, and to enjoy a happy life now and in the life after death.

a.2) Religious Acts

Religious experience also translates into a series of religious actions and behaviors that respond in diverse ways to the needs that arise. These acts are many and very diverse, and we will not treat them in detail here. We refer only to three especially important ones.[23] *Prayer* is the dialogue and personal relationship with the Supreme Being in which persons make known their desires and needs. "In personal prayer I stand, as a person, before God. God created me and called me to the life of grace. He is my truth. He is my true 'Thou,' and, in relating to him, I acquire my authentic 'I,' I become myself. All of this is expressed in personal prayer which is the dialogue of each individual person with God."[24] In *adoration*, persons express in a specific manner their veneration or respect for the transcendent Being. "Before the greatness of God, man kneels. But this is not just an outward submitting, but also an

---

[23] Saint Thomas adds, moreover, devotion, oblations, votive acts, oaths, incantation and invocation of the holy name of God. Cf. *S.Th.* II-II, qq. 81ff.

[24] R. Guardini, *Introducción a la vida de oración*, 203.

interior one with an attitude of piety and devotion. And it is not only to a certain degree, or with great depth and availability, but totally and definitively, as a creature before the Creator. That is to say, the person worships God."[25] And in *sacrifice* he offers something to God either as an offering or to make it suitable in a certain circumstance.

b) The objective dimension

The objective aspect of religion is found in its structural manifestations, which are above the position of each individual. It is what religion offers to the individual as such, as well as social and cultural ways in which these contents are expressed and manifested.[26]

b.1) A Vision of God and a Vision of the World

The first thing that religion provides is a vision of God and of the world. Human beings, as we have seen, seek in religion the answer to their fundamental questions and this is, therefore, what religion must offer to them: who God is and what God is like, where we come from, what our destiny is, why the world exists, etc. Concrete ways in which each religion gives us responses vary greatly but one can indicate, fundamentally, two. A characteristic of the most primitive religions is *myth*. Rationalism initiated a campaign to discredit myth and to identify it with an irrational and nonreflective mode of knowledge, but phenomenology of religion and anthropological studies have returned myth to the place that corresponds to it: the place of *a narration about the origins*. This narrative is necessarily obscure and difficult due to the subject to which it refers but this does not mean that it is irrational. Myths, writes Ferrer, "are attempts to respond to the mystery of the origins and destiny of the cosmos and of human beings, of life in the hereafter and of death", [27] and the famous scholar of religions Mircea Eliade affirms the same idea, although in a more developed way. "Myth narrates a sacred history; it recounts an event which took place in primordial time, the fabled time of the 'beginnings.' To put it another way, myth narrates

---

[25] Ibid., 82.

[26] Cf. J. Ferrer, *Filosofía de la religión*, 28ff.

[27] J. Ferrer, *Filosofía de la religión*, 30. In the same sense, see E. Trías, *Pensar la religión*, 22: "All mythology is already, in itself, revelation." For Trías, in any case, each revelation is always partial and for this reason he advocates for a syncretistic religion that reunites the essential elements of each of the religions.

how, thanks to the feasts of the Supernatural Beings, a reality came into existence, be it the entire reality, the cosmos, or only a fragment."[28]

The second way in which religion provides a vision of the world is through *systems of doctrine*. This mode is typical of evolved religions and, in particular, the great monotheistic religions. By systems of doctrine, however, we do not mean an axiomatic and perfectly structured doctrine in a rationalist mode, but rather a system of elaborated beliefs, sophisticated and sufficiently coherent to respond to criticism or to intelligent questions.

b.2) A Mode of Living a Worship Relationship

Religion also contributes *a concrete way of entering into contact with the divinity*, usually effected through a system of specific practices that can be called *cult* or *worship*. The justification for this dimension lies in the fact that the human being is interested in religion not only for its doctrine but also for the possibility of *effective and efficient contact with God*, something that he cannot achieve alone, or at least not in a sufficiently satisfactory way. And worship and worship practices precisely offer a door that allows the human being to enter effectively into the realm of the divine.

The cultic practices of religions are many and varied, but the fundamental ones are rite and sacrifice.

The *rite* is characterized as being a religious practice with *stable and defined characteristics set by God or his representatives*. Rite is not a merely human invention and from this fact it obtains its value. Therefore, one can only enter into contact with God and obtain what one seeks if the ritual action is performed in the prescribed moment and mode. Human intervention can only have a secondary importance and can never become the protagonist, for example, through substantial modifications of the rite, because then the rite is distorted. It becomes something merely human with human effects, something that any person can do on their own, not through participating in a channel or flow of assistance established by God.[29]

Sacrifices are the other widespread cultic practice. It is not easy to define their exact meaning but, in general, we can say that they are a way of relating with the divinity mediated by *the renunciation of a personal good*. Sometimes sacrifices are divided into three fundamental types according to what the person is seeking: the sacrifice of offering intends to recognize the majesty of

---

[28] M. Eliade, *Mito y realidad* (Madrid: Guadarrama, 1973), 18; English version: *Myth and reality* (Allen and Unwin, 1964).

[29] This general way of approaching rituals is present in the Christian sacraments.

God, the sacrifice of expiation seeks reparation for wrongs that have been done, and the sacrifice of communion seeks union with the divine.

Worship also extends to other areas such as sacred space and sacred time, and to the characteristics of persons who are especially dedicated to relating to divinity (priests), etc.

b.3) Moral Knowledge

The third point in the objective aspect of religion is a knowledge of salvation. The vision of God and of the world provides a theoretical response to human disquiet because it allows humans to know. But human beings, in addition, *need to know what they have to do and how they must act* in relation to what arises in their nature and to what God asks of them. Most religions respond to this question with a fairly specific code of moral behavior. Religion thus enters the realm of ethics.

A secondary but important effect of the entrance of religion into the world of ethics is that it allows for an *anthropological evaluation of religions.* Religions always present themselves as ultimate answers, radical answers, and in some cases indisputable ones because they appeal to God as the foundation of their doctrine. But this appeal does not release human beings from an intellectual evaluation. The person must analyze the responses of religion in order to see if they correspond to one's desires, hopes and convictions, and also in order to assess *consistency and reasonableness.* This evaluation, however, is not easy to do in topics relating to the afterlife or to the characteristics of God, since human beings lack points of reference, while this is much easier to do with regard to anthropology and morality. So, the moral proposals of each religion are an important point in establishing their validity. If, for example, a religion proposes suicide as a means to resolve some types of problems or if it permits or even encourages human sacrifice then we have a clear indication that this is a false and inhuman religion.

15.4 Religion and religions

These reflections naturally lead us to the final topic that we are going to consider: the diversity of religions and their impact on the person. What does it mean for human beings that different religions exist and what is the attitude toward them that we can adopt? We began with a brief survey of the principal religions.

a) The Diverse Types of Beliefs

There are now, and there have been throughout history, many types of religions, and many attempts have been made, including recently, to systematize and catalogue them. Let us briefly present two of them.

The first is by Manuel Guerra, who has grouped religions around four constants: the telluric, the celestial, the ethnic-political, and the mystery-based.[30] The *telluric* constant is characterized by the divinization of mother Earth as a carrier of the mystery of life and divinity, and is basically linked to animism. The *celestial* constant is typical of more developed peoples and takes its name from the belief that the divinity comes from the sky where it lives. The *ethnic-political* constant places in relief the social dimension of religion and its intimate relationship with the identity of the people and of the nation. Typical examples are the religions of Greece and Rome. Finally, the *mystery* religions are the opposite of the ethnic-political religions and place the accent on the interior and deeper dimension of human beings, rejecting an excess of ritualism and of external practices.

The second classification is proposed by Ferrer following Zubiri[31] and Danielou.[32] It is less descriptive and cultural, focuses on the conception of God proper to each religion and consists of four elements: polytheism, pantheism, dualism, and transcendent monotheism.[33]

Polytheism is characterized by the belief in many gods which, moreover, are typically associated with specific entities that are either material or abstract: the goddess Earth, household gods, gods of war or of love, etc. A point of truth in polytheism is that it notes the presence of the sacred in all of reality. Its principal weakness is that it personalizes this presence, dispersing the Absolute into the multiplicity of beings without realizing that, if God exists, God can only be one. The existence of an infinite number of small gods is an absurdity[34].

Pantheism corresponds to a much more reflective mentality and is characterized by erasing the borders that separate creatures from God by not taking into account their absolute transcendence. God is present in reality but in pantheism this happens with such depth and intensity that in the end creatures disappear, absorbed by God. Pantheism has only an anecdotal existence in the West, while many of the more disseminated Eastern religions, like Buddhism or Hinduism, have pantheistic features, since they do not insist on the perfection of the individual but rather on the individual's absorption by

---

[30] Cf. M. Guerra, *Historia de las religiones*, 3 vol. (Pamplona: Eunsa, 1980).

[31] Cf. X. Zubiri, *El problema filosófico de la historia de las religiones*.

[32] Cf. J. Danielou, *God and us* (Mowbray 1957, 2008).

[33] Cf. J. Ferrer, *Filosofía de la religión*, 235-280, where the reader may find a detailed description of these types of religiosity and of the specific religions to which they conform.

[34] Although we are far from a polytheism or the divinization of the Earth, the increasing relevance of mother earth, in different versions such as the Pachamama or others, points in this direction.

or identification with the principle or with the One, bringing about the loss of one's own identity.

Dualism is a minority current that has been significant in the East, where it arose, fundamentally as a response to the presence of evil in the world. While most religions posit the Good as the supreme principal, dualism, in the face of the abundance of evil, responds by considering that, in reality, there are two principles, that of good and that of evil, which battle each other.[35]

Finally, there is *transcendent monotheism*, which is comprised of three great religions: Judaism, Islam, and Christianity. All three of them are characterized by affirming the oneness of God and God's transcendence over the world. God is one, all-powerful and omnipresent, but not identified with creatures. Islam has especially insisted on the unity of God while Christianity through the mystery of the Trinity has maintained the existence of God both as unity and as diversity. God is One and Three simultaneously, one nature and three distinct persons, three "I's". "God, whose essence and whose life exceeds everything human, is also a person in a distinct and prodigious way. Each human being is a singular person: he says 'I' in an individual and unique way. In God there are Three who say 'I.' Three are the faces that stand out in God's life. Three are the modes of God's self-possession of his life... Human beings can only say 'you' when they direct themselves to another person. In contrast, God encounters in his own life one to whom he can say 'You.'"[36]

b) The Anthropological Problem of the Diversity of Religions

The diversity of religions raises, as one can easily see, a set of problems. The first and most important is *the search for the true religion*. Of all the religions that exist, which one is the one that really responds to the truth of things, to what God and human beings are? But, however important this question may be, it is not the only one that can be raised. Religious diversity can raise a previous problem: *the questioning of the very validity of religion*. There are two possible positions regarding this: atheism and agnosticism.

For the *agnostic*, the existence of multiple religions serves to demonstrate that almost nothing about God can be known with certainty and, therefore, the most serious and coherent attitude is the acceptance of ignorance before

---

[35] A characteristic example of dualism is Manicheism. Cf. A. Alessi, *Filosofia della religione* (Rome: LAS, 1991), 47-81.

[36] R. Guardini, *Introducción a la vida de oración*, 113-114. These considerations permit us to point out, moreover, how, through this perspective, it is possible to enter into a theology of a personalist orientation.

the divine: a kind of intellectual shrug of the shoulders, in principle not out of spite or disinterest but out of impotence in the face of the mystery of transcendence. The *atheist*, however, arrives at a different conclusion: what the multiplicity of religions demonstrates is the nonexistence of God. Divinity and gods are, actually, a human invention by which human beings attempt to fill a gap in their existence which, in reality, cannot be filled. The diversity of religions in different cultures and epochs shows precisely the invented character of religion. As the human being is, so are the gods he invents to compensate for his shortcomings, limitations and fears[37].

Atheism and agnosticism are positions, to a certain extent, that are reasonable, especially agnosticism, since the ultimate questions are not within the direct reach of our intelligence, so it would make sense to answer certain questions with "I don't know". But, at the same time, they are both minoritarian and weak. On the one hand, they leave the deepest questions of the human being unanswered, which, obviously, is a problem. But above all, they are not justified, especially atheism, because the manifestations of the existence of a Higher Being are as reasonable as they are overwhelming. And so has it been considered by the majority of humanity, including the most brilliant philosophers and thinkers. Thus, the adequate anthropological attitude is the *search for the true religion*, which necessarily must be a central goal in the life of each person and which one must not renounce even when the efforts that one makes have not born fruit.

Furthermore, the difficulty posed by the multiplicity of religions should not be exaggerated either. In practice, each person is faced with a limited number of religions which are the ones that the person must evaluate and to which the person must grant or withhold his or her assent. Error is certainly possible, but this also occurs in other areas of life, such as the moral sphere. The person faced with different moral options has to make a decision. In these cases, what is important is to act with honesty without giving in to the comfort of not getting involved. And the same must be said, perhaps in an even more radical way, of the search for God. That longing arises from the deepest interior of the human being and, therefore, it must be prolonged until one possesses the interior conviction that one has found the truth.

---

[37] Cfr. L. Feuerbach, *The essence of Christianity* (Dover Publications, 2008).

Bibliography

Abbà, G. *Lex et virtus. Studi sull'evoluzione della dottrina morale di san Tommaso d'Aquino*. Rome: LAS, 1983.

——. *Felicità, vita buona e virtù. Saggi di filosofia morale*. Rome: LAS, 1989.

Acero, J. *Filosofía del Lenguaje I. Semántica*. Madrid: Trotta-CSIC, 2007.

Alacevich, F., Zamagni, S., Grillo, A. *Tempo del lavoro e senso della festa*. Milano: San Paolo, 1999.

Alessi, A. *Filosofia della religione*. Rome: LAS, 1991.

Allport, G. *The nature of prejudice*. Anchor, 1958.

Altolaguirre, M. *El egoísta*, in *Antología de los poetas del 27*, Madrid: Espasa-Calpe, 1983.

Amscombe, G. E. M., *Intention*. Cambridge: Harvard University Press, 2009.

Appel, K. O. *Die idee der Sprache in der Tradition des Humanismus von Dante bis Vico*. Bonn: Boubier, 1975.

Arendt, H. *The human condition*. Chicago, University of Chicago Press, 2018.

Ariès, P. *Western Attitudes Toward Death. From the Middle Ages to the Present*. Baltimore: John Hopkins University Press.

Ariès, P., G. Duby, G., (eds.). *La vita privata. IV. L'ottocento*. Rome-Bari: Laterza, 1988.

Aristotle. *Politics*.

——. *De Anima*.

——. *Metaphysics*.

——. *Nicomachean Ethics*.

——. *Economy*.

Artigas, A. *Knowing things for sure. Science and truth*. University Press of America 2006.

Augustine, *The Confessions*. trans. John K Ryan. New York: Image Books.

——. *The City of God*.

——. *De Trinitate*.

——. *Soliloquies*.

Austin, J. L. *How to do things with words*. Cambridge, Harvard University Press, 1975.

Atkinson, R. C. and R. M. Shiffrin, R. M. *Human memory: a proposed system and its control processes*, in K. W. Spence, *The psychology of learning and motivation*, vol. 2. New York: Academic Press, 1968.

Beauregard, J. *Philosophical Neuroethics: A Personalist Approach*. Volume 1 - Foundations. Wilmington: Vernon Press, 2019.

Beltrán, J. *Para comprender la psicología* (6th ed.). Estella: Verbo Divino, 2000.

Bengtsson, J. O. *The worldview of personalism*. Oxford: Oxford University Press, 2006.

Berlin, I. *Four essays of Liberty*. Gryffon Editions, 1996.

Beuchot, M. *Tratado de hermenéutica analógica. Hacia un nuevo modelo de interpretación,* (5ª ed.). México UNAM, 2015.

Blondel, M. *L'action.* Paris, 1893.

Boethius. *Liber de persona et duabus naturis contra Eutychen et Nestorium,* PL 64.

Bombaci, N., *Una vita, una testimonianza: Emmanuel Mounier.* Armando siciliano Editore 1999.

Borges, L. *El Aleph.* Madrid: Alianza, 1997.

Borne, E. *El trabajo y el hombre.* Buenos Aires 1945.

Bowne, B. P. *Personalism.* Cambridge: The Riverside Press, 1908.

Buber, M. "What Is Man?" in *Between Man and Man.* New York: Routledge, 2002.

———. *Eclipse of God: Studies in the Relation Between Religion and Philosophy.* UK: Prometheus Books 1988.

———. *I and Thou,* Translated by Walter Kaufmann. New York: Scribner's Sons, 1970.

Burgos, J. M. *Diagnóstico sobre la familia.* Madrid: Palabra, 2004.

———. *Reconstruir la persona. Ensayos personalistas.* Madrid: Palabra, 2009.

———. *La experiencia integral. Un método para el personalismo.* Madrid: Palabra, 2015.

———. *Integral experience: a new proposal on the beginning of knowledge,* in J. Beauregard, S. Smith (eds.), *In the Sphere of the personal. New perspectives in the philosophy of person.* Wilmington USA Vernon Press, 2016, 41-58.

———. *Repensar la naturaleza humana* (2ª ed.). Ciudad de México: Siglo XXI, 2017.

———. *Historia de la psicología.* Madrid: Palabra, 2017.

———. *El yo como raíz ontológica de la persona. Reflexiones a partir de John F. Crosby,* "Quién, Revista de filosofía personalista" 6 (2017), 33-54.

———. *La vía de la experiencia o la salida del laberinto.* Madrid: Rialp 2018.

———. *An Introduction to Personalism.* Washington, DC: CUA Press, 2018.

———. *De la sustancia al yo como fundamento de la persona. Respuesta a John F. Crosby,* "Quién, Revista de filosofía personalista" 10 (2019), 27-44.

———. *Wojtyła's Personalism as Integral Personalism. The future of an Intellectual Project,* Questionaes Disputatae, vol 9. N. 2 (2019) 91-111

———. *¿Qué es el personalismo integral?,* "Quién. Revista de filosofía personalista" 10 (2020), 9-37.

———. *Personalismo y metafísica. ¿Es el personalismo una filosofía primera?.* Madrid: Ediciones Universidad San Dámaso 2021.

———. *Person in personalism,* Conference "From *Logos* to Person", Instituto Polis of Jerusalem, John Hopkins University, Israel, 2021 (to be published).

Burgos, J. M. (ed.), *El giro personalista; del qué al quién.* Salamanca: Mounier, 2011.

Buttiglione, R. *La persona y la familia.* Madrid: Palabra, 1999.

Cajetan. *Commentaria in Summam Theologiae, S. Thoma Aq.* Rome: Leonina, 1891.

Campanini, G. *Realtà e problemi della famiglia contemporánea. Compendio di sociologia della familia.* Milano: Paoline, 1989.

Carro, A. J. *Historia social del trabajo* (8ª ed.). Barcelona: Bosch, 1992.

Castilla, B. *Persona masculina, persona femenina,* Rialp, Madrid, 1996.

Castilla de Pino, C. *Teoría de los sentimientos.* Barcelona: Tusquets 2000.

Catechism of the Catholic Church.

Cervantes, Miguel de, *Don Quixote.*

Chul-Han, B. *Psychopolitics: Neoliberalism and New Technologies of Power.* Verso Books, 2017.

Cicero. *On Friendship.*

——. *Somnium Scipionis, the Dream of Scipio Africanus Minor.* BiblioBazaar, 2009.

Cook, V. J., & Newson. M., *Chomsky's Universal Grammar.* Oxford: Blackwell, 1996.

Cordes, P. J. *El eclipse del padre.* Madrid: Palabra, 2003.

Crosby, J. *The Selfhood of the Human Person.* Washington, DC: The Catholic University of America Press, 1996.

——. *On solitude, subjectivity and substantiality. Response to Juan Manuel Burgos,* "Quién, Revista de filosofía personalista" 8 (2018), 7-19.

Danielou, J. *God and us.* Mowbray 1957, 2008.

Dahl, R. A. *On Democracy.* Yale: Yale University Press, 2015.

Deweer, D. *Ricoeur's Personalist Republicanism: Personhood and Citizenship.* Lexington Books, 2017.

De Finance, J. *Essai sur l'agir humaine.* Rome: Presse de l'Universitè grégorienne, 1962.

De Rojas, F. *La Celestina.* Madrid: Edaf, 1991.

Descartes, R. *Principia philosophiae,* AT, VIII.

——. *Discourse on the Method of Rightly Conducting One's Reason and of Seeking Truth.*

Díez, F. *Utilidad, deseo y virtud. La formación de la idea moderna del trabajo.* Barcelona: Península, 2001.

Di Nicola, G. P. *Uguaglianza e differenza. La reciprocità uomo donna.* Rome: Città Nuova, 1989.

Domínguez Prieto, X. M. *Antropología de la familia. Persona, matrimonio y familia.* Madrid: BAC, 2007.

Donati, P. P. *Manuale di Sociologia della Famiglia.* Bari: Laterza 2006.

——. *La familia il genoma che fa vivere la società.* Rubettino, 2013.

——. *Relational Sociology: A New Paradigm for the Social Sciences.* Routledge, 2010.

Duch, Ll. *Antropología de la religión.* Barcelona: Herder, 2001.

Ebner, F. *La palabra y las realidades espirituales.* Madrid: Caparrós, 1995.

Eliade, M. *Myth and reality.* Allen and Unwin, 1964.

Epicurus. *Letter to Menoeceus.* CreateSpace Independent Publishing Platform, 2016.

Erikson, E. *Childhood and Society.* New York: Norton, 1950.

Escrivá, J. *Furrow.* New York: Scepter, 2002.

———. *Christ is passing by.* New York: Scepter Publishers, 2010.

Ferrater Mora, J. *Diccionario de Filosofía.* Barcelona: Ariel, 2004.

Ferrer, J. *Filosofía de la religión.* Madrid: Palabra, 2002.

Ferrer, U. *¿Qué significa ser persona?* Madrid: Palabra, 2002.

Feuerbach, L. *The essence of Christianity.* Dover Publications, 2008.

Forment, E. *El personalismo medieval.* Valencia: Edicep, 2002.

Frankl, V. *Psicoanálisis y existencialismo.* Mexico: FCE, 1987.

———. *Man's Search for Meaning.* Beacon Press, 2006.

Gadamer, H. G. *Truth and method.* London, Sheed and Ward, 1989.

García Cuadrado, J. A. *Antropología filosófica.* Pamplona: Eunsa, 2001.

Gardner, H. *Multiples Intelligences.* Basic Books, 2006.

Gellner, E. *Nations and Nationalism.* New York: Cornell University Press, 2008.

Gilson, É. *Methodical Realism.* Front Royal, Va.: Christendom Press, 1990.

———. *The spirit of mediaeval philosophy.* Notre Dame, Ind.: University of Notre Dame Press, 1991.

———. *Linguistics and Philosophy: An Essay on the Philosophical Constants of Language.* Notre Dame, Ind.: University of Notre Dame Press, 2017.

Giussani, L. *The religious sense.* Montreal: MacGill-Quenn's University Press, 1997.

Gómez, J., and Martín, J. *Filosofía de la religión.* Madrid: Rialp, 1973.

Gregory of Nyssa. *Vita Moysis,* PG XLIV.

Grice, H. P. *Studies in the Way of Words.* Cambridge: Harvard Univ. Press, 1989.

Guardini, R. *The World and the Person.* Translated by Stella Lange. Chicago: Henry Regnery, 1965.

———. *Persona e libertà. Saggi di Fondazione sulla teoria pedagogica.* Brescia: Scuola, 1987.

———. *The Art of Praying: The Principles and Methods of Christian Prayer.* Sophia Institute Press 1995.

———. *Las etapas de la vida* (3rd ed.). Madrid: Palabra, 2000.

Guerra, M. *Historia de las religiones,* 3 vol. Pamplona: Eunsa, 1980.

Habermas, J., Ratzinger, J. *Dialéctica de la secularización.* Madrid: Encuentro, 2006.

Heidegger, M. *Letter on humanism.*

———. *Being and Time.* Harper Collins, 2008.

Herlihy, D. *La famiglia nel medioevo.* Bari: Laterza, 1994.

Hernández, M. "*Obra poética completa.* Madrid: Alianza, 1990.

Horace. *Odes,* transl. Terry Walsh.

Hume, D. *Enquires concerning the human understanding and concerning the principles of moral.* Oxford: Clarendon Press, 1927.

Husserl, E. *Ideas pertaining to a Pure Phenomenology.* Springer 1983.

Innerarity, D. *Hegel y el romanticismo.* Madrid: Tecnos, 1993.

James, W. *Principles of Psychology.* Dover Publications, 1950.

Jaspers, K. *Filosofía,* vol. I. Puerto Rico: Revista de Occidente, 1958.

——. *Cifras de la trascendencia.* Madrid: Alianza, 1993.

——. *Lo trágico. El lenguaje.* Málaga: Librería Agora, 1995.

——. *General Psychopatology, vol. I.* John Hopkins University Press, 1997.

Jung, C. G. *Los complejos y el inconsciente.* Madrid: Alianza, 1969.

Kant, I. *Critique of pure reason.*

——. *Foundations of the Metaphysics of* Morals.

Kaplan, H. I., Sadock, B. I. *Synopsys of Psychiatry.* Lippincott Williams and Wilkins, 2014.

Kierkegaard, S. *Diario,* 1854, XI. Madrid: Planeta, 1993.

Kuhn, T. S. *The structure of scientific revolutions.* Chicago, The University of Chicago Press, 2012.

Lacroix, J. *Le personnalisme.* Lyon, 1982.

Laín Entralgo, P. *Teoría y realidad del otro.* Madrid: Alianza, 1983.

——. *Sobre la amistad.* Madrid: Espasa-Calpe, 1986.

Levinas, E. *Totality and Infinity: An Essay on Exteriority.* Pittsburgh, Pa.: Duquesne University Press, 1969.

——. *Ethics and Infinity: Conversations with Philippe Nemo.* Pittsburgh, Pa.: Duquesne University Press.

——. *God, Death and Time.* Stanford: Stanford University Press 2000.

Levinson, D. J. and Gooden, W. E. *The life cycle* in H. I. Kaplan, B. I. Sadock, *Synopsis of Psychiatry* I, 1-13.

Lévy-Strauss, C. *Structural Anthropology.* Basic Books, 1963.

Linton, R. *The cultural Background of Personality.* New York: Routledge, 1998.

Lipovetsky, G. *La tercera mujer.* Madrid: Anagrama, 1999.

Locke, J. *A letter concerning toleration.* Merchant Books, 2011.

López Pardo, C. *Sobre la vida y la muerte.* Madrid: Rialp, 1973.

López Quintás, A. *Inteligencia creativa, El descubrimiento personal de los valores.* Madrid: BAC, 2002.

——. *El amor humano.* Valencia: Edibesa, 2017.

Lorda, J. L. *Antropología. Del Concilio Vaticano II a Juan Pablo II.* Madrid: Palabra, 1996.

Lozano, S. *La interpersonalidad en K. Wojtyła.* Valencia: Edicep, 2016.

Lucas, A., *Sociología.* Pamplona: Eunsa, 2011.

Lucas, R. *El hombre, espíritu encarnado. Compendio de filosofía del hombre.* Salamanca: Sígueme, 1999.

Lyons, W. *Emoción.* Barcelona: Anthropos, 1993.

Lyotard, J.-F. *The postmodern condition. A report on knowledge.* Manchester: Manchester University Press, 1984.

Machado, A. *Poesías completas.* Madrid: Espasa-Calpe, 1963.

MacIntyre, A. *Whose justice? Which rationality?* London: Duckworth, 1988.

——. *Three Rival Versions of Moral Enquiry.* London: Duckworth, 1990.

——. *After virtue. A study in moral theory.* Notre Dame, Ind.: University of Notre Dame Press, 2007.

Malo, A., *Antropologia dell' affettività.* Rome: Armando, 1999.

Marañón, G. *Vocación y ética y otros ensayos.* Madrid: Espasa-Calpe, 1981.

Marías, J. *Metaphysical Anthropology: The Empirical Structure of Human Life.* University Park, Pa.: Pennsylvania State University Press, 1971.

——. *La mujer y su sombra.* Madrid: Alianza, 1987.

——. *La felicidad humana.* Madrid: Alianza, 1991.

——. *La educación sentimental.* Madrid: Alianza, 1993.

——. *Persona.* Madrid: Alianza, 1997.

——. *Mapa del mundo personal.* Madrid: Alianza, 2006.

Marina, J. A. *Dictamen sobre Dios* (4th ed.). Madrid: Anagrama, 2002.

Maritain, J. *Art et scolastique,* Oeuvres Complètes, vol. I.

——. *The degrees of knowledge.* Notre Dame, Ind.: University of Notre Dame Press, 1995.

——. *Integral Humanism: Temporal and Spiritual Problems of a New Christendom,* in *The Collected Works of Jacques Maritain,* vol. 11. Notre Dame, Ind.: University of Notre Dame Press, 1996.

——. *Man and the State.* Washington: Catholic University of America Press, 1998.

——. *Principes d'une politique humaniste,* Oeuvres Complètes, vol. VIII.

——. *La loi naturelle ou loi non écrite.* Fribourg, Switzerland: Édition Universitaires, 1986.

——. *Creative intuition in art and poetry.* Cluny Media. 2018.

——. *Christianity and democracy.* San Francisco: Ignatius Press, 2012.

McCool, G. A. *From Unity to pluralism. The internal Evolution of Thomism.* New York: Fordham University Press, 1992.

McLeod, H., and Ustorf, W. eds., *The Decline of Christendom in Western Europe (1750-2000).* Cambridge: Cambridge University Press, 2003.

Mèda, D. *El trabajo. Un valor en peligro de extinción.* Barcelona: Gedisa, 1998.

Merton, R. K. *The Sociology of Science: Theoretical and Empirical Investigations.* Chicago: University of Chicago Press, 1979.

Millán-Puelles, A. *La estructura de la* subjetividad. Madrid: Rialp, 1967.

——. *La libre afirmación de nuestro ser.* Madrid: Rialp, 1993.

Mondin, B. *L'uomo: chi è? Elementi di antropología filosofica.* Milan: Massimo, 1989.

——. *Storia dell'Antropologia Filosofica,* vol. 2. Bologna: ESD, 2002.

Moreno, B. *Psicología de la personalidad. Procesos.* Madrid: Thomson-Paranfino, 2007.

Mortensen, J. N. *The Common Good. An introduction to personalism.* Wilmington: Vernon Press, 2017.

Mouroux, J. *The Meaning of Man.* London: Sheed & Ward, 1948.

Mounier, E. *Personalism.* London: Routledge and Kegan Paul,1952.

——. *A Personalist Manifesto,* edited by Joseph T. Delos et al. New York: Longman, Green, 1938.

Mulhall, S. and Swift, A. *Liberals and Communitarians.* Wiley, 1996.

Myers, D. G., *Psychology.* Worth Public Inc, 2011.

Nédoncelle, M. "Prosopon et persona dans l'antiquité classique. Essai de bilan linguistic." *Revue des Sciences Religieuses* 22, no. 3-4 (1948): 277-99.

Nubiola, J. *La revolución pragmatista de la filosofía analítica.* Pamplona: Eunsa, 1996.

Ortega y Gasset, J. *Meditación sobre la técnica.* Madrid: Santillana, 1997.

Pareyson, L. *Esistenza e persona.* Genoa: Il Melangolo, 1985.

Parsons, T. *The structure of Social Action.* Free Press, 1968.

Pérez-Soba, J. J. *La pregunta por la persona. La respuesta de la interpersonalidad.* Madrid: Facultad de Teología San Dámaso, 2004.

——. *El amor: introducción a un misterio.* Madrid: BAC, 2011.

Piaget, J. *The psychogenesis of knowledge and its epistemological significance,* in M. Piatelli-Palmarini (ed.), *Language and learning.* Cambridge, MA: Harvard University Press, 1980.

Pieper, J. *The four Cardinal Virtues.* Notre Dame, Ind.: University of Notre Dame Press, 1990.

——. *The end of time. A Meditation on the Philosophy of History.* San Francisco: Ignatius Press 1999.

——. *In Search of the Sacred: Contributions to an Answer.* San Francisco: Ignatius Press, 2000.

——. *Death and Inmortality.* St. Augustine's Press, 2000.

——. *Leisure. The basis of culture.* San Francisco: Ignatius Press, 2014.

——. *Faith, Hope, Love.* San Francisco: Ignatius Press, 2015.

Pinillos, J. L. *Principios de psicología* (18th ed.). Madrid: Alianza, 1994.

Plato. *Gorgias.*

Polo, L. *Antropología trascendental. I. La persona humana.* Pamplona: Eunsa, 1999.

——. *Tener y dar,* in *Estudios sobre la Laborem excercens.* Madrid: BAC, 1987.

Radcliffe-Brown, H. *Structure and Function in Primitive Society.* Free Press 1965.

Rawls, J. *A Theory of Justice.* Segment Book, 2019.

Requena, F. *Amigos y redes sociales. Elementos para una sociología de la amistad.* Madrid: CIS, 1994.

Rocher, G. *A General Introduction to Sociology. A Theoretical Perspective.* Calcutta: Academic Publishers, 2008.

Rodríguez, M. I. *Génesis y evolución de actitudes ante la muerte en la infancia,* Cuadernos de Bioética, XI.41 (2000).

Rosanvallon, P. *The Populist Century: History, Theory, Critique.* Polity Press, 2021.

Rourke, Th. R. y Chazarreta, R. A. *A Theory of personalism.* Lanham: Lexington Books, 2007.

Sandel, M. *Liberalism and the Limits of Justice.* Cambridge: Cambridge University Press, 1982.

Sanguineti, J. J. *Filosofía de la mente.* Madrid: Palabra, 2007.

Scheler, M. *Zur Phänomenologie und Metaphysik der Freiheit,* Obras, I. Bern: Francke, 1957.

——. *Man's Place in Nature.* New York: Noonday, 1961.

——. *Formalism in Ethics and Non-Formal Ethics of Values.* Evanston, IL: Northwestern University Press, 1973.

——. *Muerte y supervivencia.* Madrid: Encuentro, 2001.

Searle, J. R. *Speech Acts: An Essay in the Philosophy of Language.* Cambridge: Cambridge University Press, 1989.

Second Vatican Council. Pastoral Constitution *Gaudium et spes.*

Sennett, R. *The Corrosion of Character: Personal Consequences of Work in the New Capitalism.* WW Norton and Co, 1998.

Singer, P. *Practical Ethics.* Cambridge: Cambridge University Press, 1973.

Spaemann, R. *Persons. The difference between "someone" and "something".* Oxford: Oxford University Press, 2006.

Stassen, K. Thompson, R.A. *Psicología del desarrollo: infancia y adolescencia.* Madrid: Editorial Médica Panamericana, 1998.

Steiner, G. *Real presences. Is there anything in what we say?.* London: Faber and Faber 1989.

Stefanini, L. *Personalismo sociale* (2nd ed.). Rome: Studium, 1979.

Stuart Mill, J. *On liberty.* World's Classics Edition.

Taylor, Ch. *Sources of the Self.* Cambridge: Cambridge University Press, 1990.

Théry, I. *Le démariage. Justice et vie privée.* Paris, Odile Jacob, 1993.

Thomas Aquinas, *Summa Theologiae.*

——. *De Veritate.*

——. *Quaestiones disputata de malo.*

——. *Sententia super libri Ethicorum.*

Tocqueville, A. de. *Democracy in America.* New York: Penguin, 2008.

Trías, E. *Pensar la religion.* Barcelona: Destino, 1997.

Unzueta, I. *La crisis de la «sociedad del trabajo» (De Marx a la escuela de Francfort).* Bilbao: Servicio editorial de la Universidad del País Vasco, 2002.

Vera, R. *La relación paterno-filial. Análisis desde el personalismo,* "Quién" 4 (2016), 89-113.

Vicente, J. *El horror de morir.* Barcelona: Tibidabo 1992.

Vicente J., Choza, J. *Filosofía del hombre. Una antropología de la intimidad,* 4th ed. Madrid: Rialp, 1995.

Von Balthasar, H. U. *Il tutto nel fragmento. Aspetti di teología della storia.* Milan: Jaca Book, 1970.

Von Hildebrand, D. *The Heart.* South Bend, IN: St. Augustine's Press, 2007.

——. *Ethics.* The Hildebrand Project, 2020.

Weber, M. *The Protestant Ethic and the Spirit of Capitalism.* New York: Routledge 2013.

Whorf, B. L. *Language, thought and reality.* Martino Fine Books 2011.

Wittgenstein, L. *Philosophical Investigations,* trans. G.E.M. Anscombe. New York: The Macmillan Company, 1953.

Wojtyła, K. *El don del amor. Escritos sobre la familia.* Madrid: Palabra, 2000.

——. *The Acting Person*. Translated by Anna-Teresa Tymieniecka. Annalecta Husserliana 10. Dordrecht: D. Reidel Pub. Co, 1979.

——. *Opere letterarie. Poesie e drammi*. Roma: Libreria Editrice Vaticana, 1993.

——. *El hombre y su destino*. Madrid: Palabra, 1998.

——. *Mi visión del hombre. Hacia una nueva ética*, 2nd ed. Madrid: Palabra, 1998.

——. *Love and Responsability*. Pauline Books & Media, 2013.

Wojtyła, Karol-John Paul II. *Man and Woman He Created Them: A Theology of the Body*. Trans. by Michael Waldstein. Boston: Pauline Books & Media, 2006.

——. Encyclical *Fides et ratio*.

——. Encyclical *Veritatis Splendor*.

——. Encyclical *Laborem Exercens*.

Yepes, R. *Fundamentos de antropología. Un ideal de la excelencia humana*. Pamplona: Eunsa, 1996.

Zambrano, M. *Persona y democracia. La historia sacrificial*. Anthropos, Barcelona 1988.

Zizioulas. Jh. D. *Communion and otherness. Further studies in Personhood ant the* Church. T&T Clark International, 2009.

Zubiri, X. *Man and God*. University Press of America, 2009.

——. *El problema filosófico de la historia de las religiones*. Madrid: Alianza, 1987.

——. *Inteligencia y razón*. Madrid: Alianza Editorial, 2008.

Zuboff, S. *The Age Of Surveillance Capitalism: The Fight for a Human Future at the New Frontier of Power*. New York: Public Affairs, 2020.

Index